UNCHARTED TERRAINS

Uncharted Terrains

New Directions in Border Research Methodology, Ethics, and Practice

EDITED BY

ANNA OCHOA O'LEARY, COLIN M. DEEDS,

AND SCOTT WHITEFORD

THE UNIVERSITY OF
ARIZONA PRESS
Tucson

The University of Arizona Press
© 2013 The Arizona Board of Regents
All rights reserved

www.uapress.arizona.edu

Library of Congress Cataloging-in-Publication Data
Uncharted terrains : new directions in border research methodology, ethics, and practice /
edited by Anna Ochoa O'Leary, Colin M. Deeds, and Scott Whiteford.
    pages cm.
  Includes bibliographical references and index.
  ISBN 978-0-8165-3055-7 (pbk. : alk. paper)
  1. United States—Emigration and immigration. 2. Emigration and immigration—
Government policy—United States. 3. Border security—United States—Research.
4. United States—Boundaries—Mexico—Research. I. O'Leary, Anna Ochoa.
  JV6465.U43 2013
  325.73—dc23
                                        2013009922

This research was supported by the United States Department of Homeland Security
through the National Center for Border Security and Immigration under grant
number 2008-ST-061-BS0002. However, any opinions, findings, and conclusions or
recommendations in this document are those of the authors and do not necessarily reflect
the views of the United States Department of Homeland Security.

18   17   16   15   14   13   6   5   4   3   2   1

This book is dedicated to Raquel Rubio Goldsmith, whose lifelong struggle for social justice has been an inspiration to all who know her, and whose love of science and methodology provided us with the illuminating vision for this book.

The editors thank the following research assistants for their invaluable efforts in organizing the Border Research Ethics and Methodologies workshops, conference, and manuscript: Lisa Gardinier, Adrian Mendoza, and Azucena Sánchez.

Contents

Preface

This volume is a collective effort to grapple with some of the methodological and ethical dilemmas that have emerged from conducting border research. In 2009–2010, the *Border Research Ethics and Methodologies (BREM) Project* helped bring together interdisciplinary groups of scholars to address the complications emerging from the gathering, use, and management of data, and their engagement with various constituents (e.g., academic, institutional, funding sources, immigrant communities, and border crossers) while conducting research — all of which we felt were entitled to the benefits of research.[1] An important goal of BREM was to promote a binational dialogue between researchers from Mexico and the United States. Initially two workshops in 2009 helped organizers identify themes that would stimulate interdisciplinary and binational discussions of methodologies and ethical issues in borderland research. Together, BREM participants engaged in questions about research ethics and developed a personal code of ethical conduct for border research. We consider this to be a working document and we include it at the end of the volume. The themes that emerged from the workshops were also expanded into a framework for organizing a national conference along the same lines. The conference, "Between the Lines: Border Research Ethics and Methodologies," was held in Tucson, Arizona, on April 24, 2010, the day that Arizona's infamous SB1070 was signed into law by Governor Jan Brewer.

This conference yielded a collection of papers that were thematically organized for this volume. The collection illustrates how researchers increasingly struggle to balance constraints formulated by the conventions of science and the academy with the need for interdisciplinary and binational collaboration and emerging social instability "in the field" due to the unpredictability of clandestine border crossing of people and contraband, often resulting in violent outbreaks. In each chapter, contributing authors reflect on their methods for examining border phenomena where people are engaged and enmeshed in precarious conditions from which creative survival processes emerge. Our collective concern was to make explicit those moments of negotiation and improvisation that are increasingly an inevitable part of the research process. In this way, contributors made their preoccupations with the process known.

It should not come as a surprise that the idea for engaging scholars in this manner came from a border region setting. Geopolitically, Tucson and the University of Arizona are in a state where law and politics have vividly transformed social life and economic livelihood in recent years. Policy changes—especially since the mid-1980s—have inspired scholars to consider frameworks of analysis as they outwardly reach for new ways of understanding the proliferation of mechanisms of state control of immigration and border-crossing processes, while contending with individual agency. Arizona's policies intended to control immigration stem in part from the state's growing awareness of its role as a major migration corridor, and while the growing number of undocumented immigrants in the state is historically related to its proximity to Mexico, negative attention to the state has been fomented by sensationalized media reports and images depicting the border region as lawless and violent and saturated by migrants seeking welfare benefits. It was perhaps a fitting moment when on April 24, 2010, soon after the afternoon sessions of the BREM conference had begun, conference participants learned with dismay that Arizona's controversial anti-immigration measure, Arizona Senate Bill 1070 (SB1070), had been signed into law by Governor Jan Brewer. This law proposed that local police be required to investigate the immigration status of those detained for other violations. This state-level incursion into what many legal experts believe to be the federal government's exclusive authority to determine immigration policy was challenged later, in July 2010.[2] While the impact of this law on immigrant communities is yet unclear, in the broadest of terms, SB1070 reveals a growing animus towards immigrants, and more specifically, towards those with ties to Latin America who do not possess official authorization to work or reside in the United States. The moment underscored the timeliness of border-related inquiry, reflection, and regeneration needed to crystallize the importance of investigative practices while history is in the making.

Notes

1. Funding for the two workshops and national conference that made this volume possible came from the Department of Homeland Security Center for Excellence grant to the Binational Migration Institute of the Department of Mexican American Studies and the Center for Latin American Studies, all at the University of Arizona in Tucson.

2. Included in the list of plaintiffs that argued for an injunction to prevent the law from being implemented were the U.S. Government, the Mexican American Legal Defense Fund (MALDEF), and the League of United Latin American Citizens (LULAC).

UNCHARTED TERRAINS

Introduction

Anna Ochoa O'Leary, Colin M. Deeds, and Scott Whiteford

Foundations

With rapidly changing patterns of migration, violence, and boundary enforcement, border regions are quickly becoming transformed. In the process, a range of actors are also transformed, among them researchers who
then contribute to the reformulation of ideas and practices. This dynamic
process reveals new prospects, missed opportunities, and new methodological and ethical challenges. However, while the foregoing is true of
most all research, some very unique concerns arise along tension-laden
international borders and because of them, researchers find themselves
increasingly navigating uncharted terrains. The chapters in this book offer
a sampling of the issues contemplated by and experienced by scholars
from different fields, who, in the course of designing and completing their
projects, contribute to our understanding of the dynamics of research. It
is a way of looking under the hood, so to speak, of knowledge production. Moreover, beyond the mechanics of research, many who work on
transborder themes routinely navigate significant ethical considerations.
Intricately woven into their efforts is the conspicuous relationship between
the knowledge and understanding that research provides and the design of
policies that impact communities and families. In the balance, we argue,
are researchers' ethical responsibilities to funders and other stakeholders,
the academic institutions under whose auspices they work, and affected
populations. Also conspicuous is that in spite of the fact that publishing

is such an important part of the academic process, researchers are rarely encouraged or required to reflect critically on their methodologies and those processes by which often contradictory priorities and values are reconciled. Indeed, as Bilger and Van Liempt (2009a: 1–2) note, the relative lack of publications on the topic points to serious dilemmas associated with very personal methodological and ethical questions. Herein lies this volume's contribution. With both public and private universities becoming increasingly dependent on support from nonpublic funding sources, researchers' ethical responses to public concerns may be compromised (Garofalo and Geuras 2006). In fact, stakeholders may reflect competing priorities and interests that contradict each other, resulting in ethical dilemmas. For example, the Border Research Ethics and Methodology (BREM) workshops and conference—through which the papers for this volume were collected—were supported by a Center for Excellence Grant from the U.S. Department of Homeland Security, a powerful governmental agency whose mission includes securing the nation's air, land, and sea borders and enforcing U.S. immigration laws. In this case, as investigators for the project, we had to consider how our research agendas might continue to attend to the concerns of the communities we worked with and the ways in which these did not quite align with funding objectives centered on achieving greater enforcement.

As in our case, the quest for methodological ethical clarity begins with how contemporary globalization has cast doubt on older approaches to scientific inquiry. These more conventional approaches often assume the enforceability of political boundaries; they often assume that processes taking place within national boundaries can be easily separated from those outside (Wimmer and Schiller 2003). Referred to as methodological nationalism, these scholarly conventions rely on the idea of the nation-state as a "container" of social phenomenon. This tendency has traditionally shaped social science thinking about governance and institutions (Wimmer and Schiller 2003: 579). Paralleling significant historical events (such as conquests or war), methodological nationalism has served to validate popular ideas about nationhood, national identity, and sovereignty. Up until World War II, social science research in the United States also reflected a nation-building paradigm premised on the idea that borders were fixed, and where movement across borders was an exception to the rule rather than the norm. The essays in this volume refute this notion in various ways.

Beginning with invigorated globalization in the 1980s, the older perspectives have been demonstratively negligent in addressing the history and dynamics of how modern nations evolve out of their interconnectedness to other nations. Moreover, this framework for analysis has been further weakened by contemporary realities, by the incremental and sustained social, political, and economic exchange relationships that link local communities within the nation-state to those outside its boundaries (Levitt 1998). This dynamic has contributed to the reordering of ordinary lives and familial relations; in the process, those who are displaced become entangled and altered by the state (Greenhouse 2002). This dialectic explains the robust scholarly focus on the topics of migration, mobility, diasporas, transnational communities, and immigration as topics of scholarly inquiry. Ultimately, these foci belie the model of national boundedness, and researching them is a stark reminder that borders are fragile and that movement across them is a common if not inevitable force of history and human development. It follows then that border and immigration researchers contribute to the reformulation of theory, practice, and intellectual enterprise that might be perceived as not conforming to the nationalism paradigm. Moreover, by unsettling the conventional nation-building paradigm promoted by political and nationalistic discourse, these scholars increasingly direct the public's gaze toward the nation's extant diversity that has largely come about through cross-border movement (Wimmer and Schiller 2003). These are just a few ways that ethical and methodological considerations distinguish those whose research is carried out with feet planted on both sides of the border.

Another phenomenon—the militaristic approach to boundary enforcement (Dunn 1996)—has had an immense impact on the communities with whom these researchers are engaged. Policies related to boundary enforcement have historically emanated from the nation's interior (in Washington and not the border) and these have largely focused on regulating the movement of goods and people (Heyman, Morales, and Nuñez 2009). However, intertwined within these developing policies are residents of the border with long but varied connections to it and the region, resulting in variances in immigration status (O'Leary and Sánchez 2011). History notwithstanding, since the 1980s, the United States has initiated greater efforts to develop systems for control of migration from Mexico (Heyman and Ackleson 2009; Shirk 2003). Heyman and Ackleson (2009) point out that even before the 9/11 terrorist attacks in 2001, almost all of the resources targeted for border enforcement went toward increasing the number of U.S. Border Patrol agents and upgrading operational equipment in sectors along the U.S.–Mexico border. These measures, beginning with the Southwest Border Strategy in 1993, included the building of walls between the two countries in urban areas. The system of border wall constructions became better known as *Operation Hold the Line* in El Paso, Texas (in 1993 and 1997), *Operation Gatekeeper* in San Diego, California (in 1994), *Operation Safeguard* in Nogales, Arizona (in 1995), and *Operation Rio Grande* in Brownsville, Texas (1996). It is also important to point out, as Heyman and Ackleson do, that the purpose of the enforcement efforts of the pre-9/11 period that realized massive concentrations of energy and material resources on the border was not to identify specific potential terrorist activity but rather to slow the movement of millions of unauthorized immigrants from Mexico.

At the same time, political discourse dehumanizing Mexican migrants has supported the state's gradual seizure of greater power to enforce boundaries. This discourse has been amplified by media reports depicting the U.S.–Mexico border region as lawless and unrestrained, and Mexican immigrants as criminals (Santa Ana 1999). Santa Ana (1999) has examined how print media texts helped frame the 1994 political debate and the campaign in California over an anti-immigrant referendum, Proposition 187. He makes clear the relationship between the less-than-human representations of immigrants and the support mustered for a policy measure aimed at restricting immigrants' access to social welfare programs (Inda 2006). This tendency to dehumanize and criminalize foreigners became especially contentious after the 2001 attacks on the World Trade Center when a highly charged debate over national security and the nation's flawed immigration system heated political clamor to secure the nation's borders once and for all.

The ensuing outcome of this acrimony was the growing perception that immigrants were the natural enemies of the state (Wimmer and Schiller 2003). Consequently, in the post-9/11 environment, enforcement policy initiatives that had not received much traction gained political momentum and became viable (Heyman and Ackleson 2009). In this post-9/11 context, a host of legislative measures followed, such as the Uniting and Strengthening America by Providing Appropriate Tools Required to Intercept and Obstruct Terrorism Act of 2001 (better known as the U.S. Patriot Act). These in turn subjected a larger number of populations to policing and gave new meaning to the word "vulnerable." Furthermore, even though these measures were created to apply specifically to noncitizens whose mere presence potentially represented a crime and an affront to the territorial boundedness of the state (Barsky 2009), with greater frequency their application also engulfed citizens, including the U.S.-born children of immigrants (O'Leary and Sanchez 2011). The legislative measures have been countered by innovative ways of circumventing them in an endless cycle, aggravating existent social divisions based on ethnicity, race, and language (Romero 2008; Goldsmith, Romero, Goldsmith, Escobedo, and Khoury 2009). These developments complicated the research process in ways not imagined by university institutional review boards (IRB) for the protection of human subjects, the oversight mechanism that obligates researchers to observe established ethical standards for the conduct of human research. At the same time, in the wake of 9/11, research dollars have shifted away from economic security and quality of life issues toward military preparedness and defense (Garofalo and Geuras 2006). These changes have normalized armed responses as immigration enforcement tactics, in turn producing reformulations of migrant agency vis-à-vis state power. The new policies have created a troublesome tension between researcher compliance with the objectives dictated by the state, along with defense-related industry and technology, and the expectations and inherent values of the academy as a public institution that privileges the nurturance of democracy, global awareness, and moral agency (Garofalo and Geuras 2006). Accordingly, the U.S.–Mexico border engages many scholars who must navigate the new terrain wrought by displacement and turmoil, more than ever fraught with growing clandestine activity (Erfani 2009; Heyman 1999), violence (Slack and Whiteford 2011), and political wrangling. Perhaps Magaña (this volume), in alluding to this as a metaphoric "shifting ground," says it best:

> As researchers try to comprehend border phenomena, the challenge at hand is to study the practices that give rise to the border as a social field—which may include border crossing and policing, migrant smuggling and rescue, injuring and healing, exposing and protecting—without exposing practitioners to undue risk and danger.

For research projects in which the primary mode of data gathering involves personal interaction with the subjects within social fields that are in disarray—such as those produced by displacement, clandestine and illicit activity, and turmoil—specific ethical dilemmas warrant special methodological attention (Greenhouse 2002). The chapters in this volume demonstrate how researchers are often preoccupied by their responsibilities toward participants who are in the midst of turbulent, transnational displacement (Hannerz 1998; Wimmer and Schiller 2003). While codes of professional conduct provide researchers with a template of appropriate action, once out in the field, operating precepts are frequently tested, and often invite renegotiation (Manderson and Wilson 1998: 215). For this reason it is incumbent upon researchers to be aware of ethical principles and assure that these are honored.

In the pages that follow, we highlight the ways in which research might be subjected to a wide range of border-related contingencies. Relatively few works provide discussions about the difficulty of experiences, and how these impact results, inherent biases, and ethical and methodological issues of researchers' positioning (Bilger and Van Liempt 2009a: 2). To address this gap, two workshops and a conference on Border Research Ethics and Methods (BREM), organized in 2009 and 2010, brought together researchers whose primary focus was the border and immigration. They were asked to use a case study approach to analyze their particular experiences and in so doing highlight important ethical and methodological moments, negotiations, and lessons learned. From these two workshops, a broader call for conference papers on the topic, the BREM conference, was developed. After the BREM conference in April 2010, conference and workshop participants were asked to submit their papers to be considered for publication. Of those that were submitted, the editors accepted a selection of papers that provided intimate reflections on issues posed by the choice of methods or on the ethical dilemmas contemplated during the course of their research. While some of the illustrations overlap, researchers weigh in on different factors in varied ways. They all offer fragments of larger success stories and point to the broader implications of the intellectual exercise for the modern research process and for the gathering of policy-relevant data about how transnational activity and state power increasingly collide (Greenhouse, Mertz, and Warren 2002). In the sections that follow, we draw attention to some of the central methodological issues and ethical themes found in the book, before highlighting the individual contributions to timely and ongoing discussions.

The Methodological Issues and Ethical Themes

Research Methods

With increased interest in border enforcement policies and violence, researchers are contributing to a rich body of empirical evidence that captures social realities of the border and immigration. However, positioning themselves to depict emerging conditions is a complex undertaking. This book presents a sampling of different methodological approaches from various fields. Anthropological methods and techniques are represented, as are case study, quantitative, and mixed-method approaches. The chapters illustrate the challenges of collecting and extrapolating data. It is important to point out that useful methodological trends include multidisciplinary research not just within the social sciences but also linking to law, public health, and other fields. Interdisciplinary approaches have a rich tradition in border research, especially in the arena of environmental research (López Hoffman, McGovern, Varady, and Fiessa 2009).

The chapters in this book offer crucial insights into how the aforementioned political and policy developments have affected local communities, and thus the researchers' engagement with them (Heyman, Morales, and Nuñez 2009). In contexts where research participants are displaced persons and in particular those labeled as "illegal" or "undocumented," appropriate methodologies consider the buildup of enforcement that makes data gathering increasingly sensitive. Following Heyman (in press), the essays in this book help make a case for the argument that research and its methodological considerations are not distant intellectual exercises but rather a part of an ongoing stream of reflexive, moral thinking in which researchers with extensive social science expertise engage with local, underserved communities and local problems.

Conventionally, a project might be conceived by delimiting a social field, or population. However, where populations are in transit and therefore no longer defined by their social boundaries, this approach poses a dilemma (O'Leary 2008). For researchers doing quantitative research, it also raises issues of sampling. Those engaged in qualitative research face another problem: how to gain the trust of potential research participants where the time to develop relationships is limited. In addition, the same rapidly emerging policy changes that have contributed to a research participant's vulnerable status can further complicate research once it has begun. For one example, in her contribution to this volume, Erika Montoya reflects on the methods employed for obtaining information about undocumented Mexican women who owned or worked in hair styling businesses in a metropolitan area of Arizona just at the time when greater scrutiny over the employment of undocumented immigrants began. She shows how combinations of both qualitative and quantitative methods allowed researchers to adjust to the greater anxiety generated by the enforcement climate in the state. In this case researchers were forced to broaden the population frame that was the focus of the study to include all female stylists who were willing to participate. This slight change from the original research design resulted from trends toward harsher measures aimed at detecting undocumented or unlicensed employees. The book contains other examples in the chapters by Goldsmith, Corbett and Cruz Martínez, and O'Leary and colleagues that describe how researchers must be increasingly sensitive to emerging punitive social and political climates. Such conditions may add to respondents' reluctance to divulge information that might reveal the identity of someone who resides and works in the United States without official authorization.

How fear influences research has been little studied. In an early article, Cornelius (1982) addressed some of the methodological compromises involved in designing projects for populations that may be fearful of reporting self-incriminating information regarding immigration status. This conundrum is no less true today (see Corbett and Cruz Martínez, this volume) where vulnerable populations may require "more stringent proof of good faith" that researchers will maintain high standards to minimize the possible adverse impact of their studies on the respondents (Manderson and Wilson 1998: 215).

In terms of both theory and practice, contributors to this volume reflect responsibilities and commitments to contending cross-sectors of society. In addition to the conventional list of stakeholders (business, government, and civic groups with constituencies that are likely to be impacted by policies), a growing number of projects include immigrant-serving organizations that advocate for powerless and marginalized (and therefore underserved) communities (Heyman, Morales, and Nuñez 2009; see also the Goldsmith and Staudt chapters in this volume). For academics, the implications of collaborating with stakeholders are complex, as the chapter by Goldsmith demonstrates. They must weigh the possible consequences of sharing information across competing sectors against the opportunities for civic engagement that might enhance the ability of decision makers to resolve rival solutions (Heyman, Morales, and Nuñez 2009). Similarly, many contributors to this book reflect the difficulties of taking a social justice stance in their research while also perceiving their findings to be necessary for formulating policy.

Research and its dissemination thus serve as mechanisms that operate under the assumption that an informed public will ultimately press for problem-solving policies, and by doing so, advance democracy (Hayes 2009). Indeed, researchers consistently respond to important and controversial topics like Arizona law SB1070, which supports local law enforcement officials' efforts to enforce immigration law and codifies racial profiling (Chin, Byrne, and Miller 2012). Simultaneously, heightened anti-immigrant discourse and current profiling practices pose new methodological challenges for researchers driven by ethical imperatives to uncover facts that threaten social harmony and peaceful coexistence. Predicatively, as greater concentrations of economic and commercial wealth continue their upward spiral (Reich 2010), those outside the political system will be even less taken into account. This prospect calls out to researchers who, as committed intellectuals with a concentration of cultural capital (Bourdieu 1998), are well positioned to analyze social phenomena, including the impact of discursive attacks (O'Leary and Romero 2011), and offer alternative explanatory narratives and solutions (Heyman, Morales, and Nuñez 2009).

Ethical Themes

Our review of the BREM conference papers revealed a rich body of work that can be used to illustrate and discuss some of the ethical considerations that buoy border research practices. According to Andre and Velasquez (1987), ethical behavior operates at two levels. At the most fundamental level, it revolves around a reasonable expectation of what constitutes right and wrong, which, in turn, prescribes what humans ought to do. At this level, the idea of what rights people have help determine what is just and virtuous. Beyond this are standards of ethical behavior established collectively and, in some way, codified by a group. For example, the American Anthropological Association has a code of ethics that is routinely revised by members of the organization. At this group level, BREM workshop participants engaged cooperatively to develop a personal code of ethical conduct for border research, a working document that we include at the end of the volume. Our discussion of general ethical issues thus includes examples of research that necessarily consider dealing with intersecting clandestine activities such as human smuggling, smuggling contraband across borders, or entering the United States as "illegal" or "undocumented" immigrants.[1] According to Bilger and Van Liempt (2009a: 11), ethical standards in social science research are based on three principles: respect for human dignity, justice, and beneficence. These concepts are commonly found in the guidelines provided by U.S. research institutions through their review boards or committees that oversee research design and researcher conduct. In this regard, the papers in this collection reflect these ethical concerns and, in addition, capture the context where potent immigration enforcement programs are premised on the supremacy of national sovereignty and a discredited subject—a process that increasingly relies on promoting differences and distrust of people based on immigration status, gender, ethnicity, and race. With each intersecting division, insecurity and vulnerability grow, leaving researchers increasingly contending with confidentiality issues and a heightened awareness of how, by obtaining sensitive information, they automatically become "bearers of secrets" (Bilger and Van Liempt 2009a). Several authors raise the importance of protecting the hard-earned trust given to them by the researched, who may be understandably suspicious and fearful of those asking questions. These examples help generate questions and discussions about choices researchers need to consider in weighing the potential benefits of research against actions that may harm.

An ethical commitment to social justice and human rights runs throughout the book, reflecting rights-based or justice-based approaches to research practice (Velásquez et al. 1996). According to Velásquez and colleagues (1996), a rights-based approach to research resides in the acknowledgment of the fundamental human right to be free from injury by the research or its products. The justice-based approach rests on questions about the fairness of an action and whether the impact of the research is disparately distributed. In much the same way, border scholars grapple with harmful conditions and suffering that are already unequally distributed along the social divisions present in society. Discriminatory and unequal social structures, known as "structural violence" (Galtung 1969), have been blamed for the hardships that drive migration (Farmer 2003), and ultimately explicate how the poor are disproportionately subjected to violence at the hands of bandits (O'Leary 2009a), their often unscrupulous guides (O'Leary 2009b), and narco violence (Slack and Whiteford 2012) as they make their way to the United States in search of not only economic improvement, but also survival. Not surprisingly, such ethical concerns for the systematic abuse, extortion, privation, and death that hundreds of migrants face each year have been raised by many scholars researching borderland phenomena (Cornelius 2001; Goldsmith et al. 2006; Eschbach et al. 1999; O'Leary 2008; Hinkes 2008).

Many of the contributors to this volume demonstrate the ethical obligation to share information with community members with whom they have worked in their research. They argue for a common good approach to ethics. Velásquez and colleagues (1996) write that this approach to ethics assumes that society is comprised of individuals linked inextricably by what is good for the whole community. The common good approach thus encourages researchers and communities outside the academy to recognize and further those goals they have in common. Accordingly, some of the chapters illustrate a range of ethical preoccupations about collaborative activity between researchers, community groups, and border crossers. We invite readers to examine all of the chapters with an eye to the variety of ethical issues addressed by the contributors, including sociocultural variations in the principles that guide them through the research process (Corbett and Cruz Martínez, this volume; Whiteford and Trotter 2008: 9).

Organization of the Volume

The book is organized into four parts: part 1, "The Big Picture"; part 2, "The Border as an Unstable Place"; part 3, "Fieldwork among Entrapped Communities"; and part 4, "A Fence on Its Side Is a Bridge." The chapters in part 1 introduce some of the broader questions and issues posed by research in the border region. For example, immigrant vulnerability is a recurrent theme found in many of these chapters. So it follows that in "Vulnerable Immigrant 'Subjects': Definitions, Disparate Power, Dilemmas, and Desired Benefits," Finch and Fernández expand on the discussion of the power dynamics that contribute to vulnerability as "any person or group who can be easily taken advantage of due to the disparate power relations present in the context of the specific research project." The authors raise concerns about how researchers can appropriately document the many ways in which populations are made vulnerable as well as how research might ultimately benefit subject communities. Another recurrent theme is the importance of collaborative relationships. Whether it is with community immigrant rights organizations or other academic institutions, researchers consistently seek out and cultivate these vital relationships. For example, in "The Good, the Bad, and the Ugly: Border Research Collaboration," Staudt examines the creation of research opportunities shaped by cross-border community organizations and other collaborative activities and explores what good collaboration is. As Staudt notes, "good collaboration" is difficult to measure and, perhaps because of this, is under evaluated. Institutions offer no clear way for measuring the input of time and energy when community participation is a central feature of the research process. A series of vignettes, "the good, the bad, and the ugly," registers both benefits and challenges of community collaboration (e.g., navigating bureaucracies, differing regulatory procedures, and expectations), providing us with illustrations drawn from invaluable experience. Here, the ethical and methodological concerns center on operational transparency, and are exalted as key for building trust and for finding common ground shared by binational partners.

Many of the contributors reflected on the research process, one of the most salient of the BREM conference themes. In this regard, Gans's chapter critically discusses how research issues are framed, alerting us to the importance of safeguarding the integrity of the research process from agendas that are politically motivated. Her sensitivity to this issue is sure to resonate with borderland researchers who work in an environment where heated immigration policy debates are constant. For this reason, she argues, researchers should routinely reflect critically on how framing might problematize both reported facts and policy issues. She begins her essay with important questions, encouraging researchers to resist buckling to political pressures and ideologies in the interest of introducing moral and ethical concerns into the political debate.

Part 2, "The Border as an Unstable Place," highlights the issues arising from research in environments that are fragmented and unstable. In such environments, there is a dire lack of "effective mediating institutions or established routines . . . even within state agencies" (Greenhouse 2002: 2). The improvised nature of such places exposes tensions in the social fabric, as well as the systemic gaps in legitimized mechanisms for maintaining order and authority, for example when legal protection is systematically denied to those populations confronting conditions of extreme physical and psychological duress. Magaña's experience zooms in on such an environment where research can often be disrupted. In her chapter, "On Shifting Ground: The Conundrums of Participant Observation and Multi-Actor Ethnography in Contemporary Border Research," she reflects on her ethnographic research to raise ethical concerns about having uneven access to legal protection and issues of representational fairness. While there are international agreements to protect political refugees, economic migrants are routinely neglected.[2] Consequently, the terms under which researchers and research participants—as both citizen and subjects—engage on the ground with each other and in the public sphere are changing. Magaña's ethnography emerges as a methodology of exploration and interpretation of this litigious and socially unstable zone of social and state interaction where migrants are simultaneously entangled and abandoned.

Knowing beforehand about the conditions that await migrants is something researchers Martínez, Slack, and Vandervoet wrestled with. In their chapter, "Methodological Challenges and Ethical Concerns of Research Marginalized and Vulnerable Populations: Evidence from Firsthand Experiences of Working with Unauthorized Migrants," they describe in detail the mixed-methods research that reveals how migrants may struggle for days out in the desert, often falling ill from exhaustion, injury, or dehydration. Psychological duress produced by unspeakable assaults to their dignity adds to migrants' pain. However, the compounding effect of multiple border-crossing attempts is skillfully captured by careful research design and planning that is attentive to both the rigors of science and humanitarianism. Preoccupations stem from the heightened awareness of migrant vulnerability, and concern for researcher safety in multiple data gathering sites that are witnessing an escalation of violence as drug cartels become enmeshed with human smuggling.

Issues of researcher safety raised by Martínez and colleagues summon greater appreciation of the final chapter in this section by Guerra, "Entre Los Mafiosos y La Chota: Ethnography, Drug Trafficking, and Policing in the South Texas–Mexico Borderlands." Challenging enough under most circumstances, research in the thick of rising narco violence in the South Texas–Mexico borderlands is infinitely more complicated. In this chapter Guerra also raises the enduring insider/outsider dilemma of conducting ethnographic research on drug trafficking. Key to this research are conventional anthropological techniques that have traditionally included strategies for building rapport with informants. These have been a keystone of most ethnographic fieldwork. However, the issue arising from borderland instability is filtered through the perspective of a "native anthropologist." Conventional anthropological approaches have long reflected preference for research that immerses the researcher amid the unfamiliar, and questions the effectiveness of insiders in conducting research. According to this critique, in being too intimately connected (by sharing the same ethnic origin and language) to the subject culture and community, insider anthropologists may risk taking for granted the significance of many social and cultural processes. Others contend that research by insiders predisposes them to emotional involvement, resulting in biased results (Bilger and Van Liempt 2009b). In reflecting on this issue while completing fieldwork in his community, Guerra also recognizes some of the unique advantages that this type of research may provide: access to a large pool of research informants, established rapport and entrée into the community, an ability to speak to informants about taboo subjects, and the ability to quickly identify important informants who can help the researcher make the most of his or her time in the field. In a community where queries about illicit activities might be unwelcomed and might endanger social scientists, other unique advantages include the knowledge of whom and what to ask. In Guerra's analysis, the advantages are somewhat offset by a series of ethical dilemmas, posed simultaneously and in the course of maneuvering through the different roles in the community (as kin, friend, and neighbor), while remaining true to his role as a scientist and observer, in a part of the world already under high surveillance.

What we know of the border is also largely infused by media reports, and in this regard, journalists very often provide the first reports and images that shape our perceptions of the border, and often at great risk. In the chapter by Chavez, Whiteford, and Núñez Garcia, the authors focus on the development of journalistic practices of the Mexican news media, enriched at times by academic insight and practices. In fact, the authors credit the long-standing moral imperative of migration research scholars on the Mexican side of the border with stimulating journalistic interest on the topic. This has contributed to a diversity of views and migrant stories and voices that ultimately inform the public, thus helping shape public opinion. This scholar-journalist fusion has offered important counternarratives of the border as monolithically perilous and chaotic; but while the authors argue that it is incumbent on journalists to offer balanced and a bilateral approach to border reporting, "resisting the temptations of sensationalism" is unfortunately easily undermined by a chronic neglect of the state peripheries by the distant centers of power.

The chapters in part 3, "Field Work among Entrapped Communities," are grouped to illustrate the methodological and ethical dimensions of working in and among populations that defy, albeit covertly, politico-legal attempts to control their movement. Núñez and Heyman (2007) refer to this process by which populations are immobilized by government forces as "entrapment," and such conditions have significant methodological and ethical implications for those who research these quasi-hidden populations. Conceptually, although immigrant populations suffer great "inequality of movement" (Núñez and Heyman 2007: 354) with increased policing, they also exhibit a great deal of agency and resourcefulness to circumvent movement controls. In this regard, this volume contains an excellent example by Careaga, whose reflexive ethnography is implicitly ethical (Greenhouse 2002), as she considers her responsibilities as a researcher during her fieldwork in a remote migrant staging outpost, where migrants await the arrangements made by smugglers to take them into the United States. Her research aligns well with Hannerz's (1998) suggestion for conceptualizing transnational research in which, in many cases, the social field is delimited—albeit temporally—by impeded mobility (see also O'Leary 2008; 2009). It is in this interstitial space, carved out by precariousness and the unknown, that Careaga demonstrates how iterative observations function as a methodological tool for working in isolation through difficult ethical issues and help her deal with these issues as they arise.

Recorded as field notes, this fieldwork technique proves to be critical for the analysis and interaction with populations made acutely vulnerable by their impending undercover journey through the Sonoran desert, toward an existence of living in the shadows of the United States.

Picking up from this important staging place and time, the chapter by O'Leary, Valdez-Gardea, and Sanchez addresses several related methodological and ethical issues that emerged from the research conducted in a binational research project in Altar, Sonora (where Careaga's research also took place), and Tucson, Arizona. The goals of the research included the documentation and analysis of the reproductive health-care strategies of those they term "im/migrant" women and their access to reproductive health care services in these two sites. In Tucson, Arizona, with the state's growing antagonism towards immigrants, entrapment is a quotidian struggle. The methodological problem that arises is that of recruiting participants for the study amid the fear that increased policing invokes. As researchers grow increasingly sensitive to these fears, they consider their impact on the resultant sample, and resultant answers to questions that respondents provide. Interestingly, this conundrum resonates with the dilemmas faced by Montoya Zavala and described in her chapter, "Women, Migrants, Undocumented Business Owners: Methodological Strategies in Fieldwork with Vulnerable Populations." This chapter, like the one by O'Leary and colleagues, describes contending with respondents' apprehension and reluctance to divulge information that may place them at risk of punitive policy measures. The researchers in these two cases were influenced by the political sensitivity and the precarious lives of their respondents (Manderson and Wilson 1998). The resultant data must thus be analyzed within the overarching conditions of entrapment. In the same vein, the chapter by Goldsmith summarizes survey research and data analysis in two studies of the conditions faced by unauthorized migrants from Mexico who reside in the United States. To be sure, asking respondents within two "entrapped" communities about information that could be incriminating raised issues of confidentiality. Added to this were concerns raised by the immigrant advocacy organization that requested the research in the first study about protecting the rights of the community it served. As a result, great care was taken to design a survey instrument that did not contain any data that could be traced to individuals, and this included formulating questions that could not be used in combination with others to identify individuals. In the second study, the examination of secondhand data, disconnected from information that could be linked to individuals, provided a unique opportunity to answer questions about injustice that had not been asked very often by those using quantitative methods about the relationship between racial profiling and legal status. Consequently, the study succeeded in revealing the perspectives of the oppressed silenced by policing, and enabled researchers to engage in a process of envisioning a better future.

Part 4 takes as a point of departure the central object that has preoccupied BREM participants, both materially and symbolically. Indeed, the border wall separating the United States from its neighbor Mexico has served as a flash point for activists, border residents, officials, entrepreneurs, and the media. It is on the border wall separating Nogales, Arizona, from Nogales, Sonora, that someone—perhaps inspired by other graffiti—lent his or her perspective on the matter by writing, "A fence on its side is a bridge." These words reflect more than an opinion. They appeal to the imagination, an alternative logic, and a way of envisioning a solution through metaphor. These words also capture an idea that threads the chapters together in this final section of the book, which centers on triumph over barriers posed by international borders, boundary enforcement, and nationalism, to strengthen connections between researchers, communities, and stakeholders from both sides.

Valenzuela Camacho, from the Universidad Autónoma de Sinaloa (UAS), discusses his research in "Methodological and Ethical Implications in the Design and Application of the Mexican Household Survey in Phoenix, Arizona (EHMPA 2007)." In this study, the author describes research conducted in Arizona, and the difficult task of locating and surveying a specific immigrant population, *sinaloenses* living in Phoenix, many of whom are undocumented. Working from basic statistical sources (U.S. Census records), he has been aided by organizations such as the Latino Health Council and the National Alliance for Hispanic Health, along with the Mexican Consulate in Phoenix and a small army of UAS students. The team has built on research by other UAS researchers who have over the years, created inroads and bridges (to continue with the metaphor), to enjoin compatriots living abroad. These students from the Department of International Studies and Public Policy received training and were provided with a uniform specially designed to make their identity, their origin, and their institution clear to potential respondents. Thus, elements of coethnicity and familiarity with a well-known Mexican institution of higher learning alleviated concerns of distrust amid anti-immigrant hostilities in Arizona, resulting in a very low rate of refusals during the survey research.

A mirror example comes from "Lessons for Border Research: The Border Contraceptive Access Study" by Amastae and colleagues from the University of Texas–El Paso, who point out the limitations of using community health workers (*promotores*) for their research. In this regard, they have a slightly different perspective on the use of coethnicity for enhancing research goals, and the reader can compare this chapter with the discussion of insider/outsider dilemmas addressed in the chapter by Guerra in part 2 of the book. Having supervised community health workers in a multiyear and binational research study, Amastae and colleagues caution that there are both advantages and disadvantages to incorporating community health workers who are "insiders" to gather data from subjects within their own community. Whereas the very characteristics that enable their success in the field (such as having personal acquaintances, a common language, and knowledge of community dynamics and interaction style) are desirable and valuable (see also the chapter by O'Leary, Valdez-Gardea, and Sanchez), other less advantageous factors may impact outcomes. This cross-border research, designed to explore the use of contraceptives across the U.S.–Mexico border, also revealed a mismatch between community health workers and academically trained researchers responsible for the management of a research study. It is largely accepted that better data are acquired through reciprocal relationships. The authors call for greater discussion of how personal and even emotional involvement as an "insider" might pave the path toward greater in-depth knowledge.

Following the overarching "researcher as bridge" theme of this section, a perceptive case study of the challenges of binational scholarly collaboration is offered by the coauthored chapter by Corbett (Portland State University) and Cruz Martínez (Centro Medico Nacional de Occidente). Aptly titled "Social Research and Reflective Practice in Bi-national Contexts: Learning from Cross-Cultural Collaboration," this chapter looks at two cases of binational research team efforts. As this chapter illustrates, successful binational collaboration depends on understanding and overcoming institutional cultural differences forged by bureaucracies and educational systems. The authors examine one case on the Mexican side of the border and one on the U.S. side. Both cases illustrate how institutions of higher education structure both opportunities and frustrating obstacles for collaboration. Among one of the important lessons from this chapter is that as researchers, we often need to be creative, and be the bridge that connects Mexican institutions and researchers with the "near sacred" protocols necessitated by institutional review boards in the United States.

Final Considerations

As Garofalo and Geuras (2006) argue, the fundamental task of institutions of higher learning is to create and sustain coherence between the academy and society. However, as this book resoundingly demonstrates, more than coherence, conviction is needed to address the ethical and methodological issues that should define the relationship between scholarship and the pressing issues of today. The rich variety of approaches to methodological and ethical issues discussed by contributors to this book underscores the evolving development of scholarship addressing the movement of people and ideas across borders and the policies that enhance or impede them. In the border region, for many researchers engagement with the world around them has increasingly led to the investigation of policies and perspectives that impact the achievement of greater social justice for populations progressively more discredited due to migration and legal status. This volume offers a snapshot of that educational and intellectual process that engages the challenges and difficulties scholars have experienced in implementing their research.

As the BREM project progressed and the collection of papers developed, the advantage of binational spaces for research became ever clearer. However, one of the limitations of achieving a truly binational collaboration and audience comes from the need to have both Spanish and English versions of published texts. The cost of translation to produce a publication in both English and Spanish is certainly a challenge in a time of budget constraints. In spite of this, we agree that whenever possible, every effort should be made to support the elusive goal of binational publishing. Many scholars from the border region as well as those who research border issues are bilingual and increasingly publish in both languages. The Mexican SNI (Sistema Nacional de Investigación) has moved to give incentives to Mexican scholars who publish internationally. In addition, institutions that engage in border research, especially the Colegio de la Frontera Norte (COLEF) and the Universidad Nacional Autónoma de México (UNAM), including its Centro de Investigación de América del Norte (CISAN), publish in both English and Spanish. The Colegio de Sonora (COLSON) has also fostered cross-border scholarship through publications in Spanish and English. In many ways, Mexican social scientists have been more proactive than their U.S. counterparts in promoting publication in both languages. Comparative and cross-border collaborative research also proves challenging. A final recurring theme among the papers relates to issues of binational collaboration that the authors tease out. They agreed on the many factors that offer opportunities and that facilitate cross-border collaboration based on shared interests. However, they point to a longer list of factors that hinder it. We are encouraged that several chapters in this volume are the products of research between researchers from institutions on both the United States and Mexican sides of the border. We look forward to a new era of international collaborative research that transcends barriers, while maintaining sensitivity and respect for the many regional variations, cultures, and topographies that we know as the U.S.–Mexico border.

Notes

1. Although both of these terms are imprecise and their meanings are varied, there are real and symbolic consequences for those who are labeled as such. For most living in the United States, it means that they entered the country without inspection (at a place other than a port of entry) and are thus present in the country without authorization. Others may have entered legally but subsequently overstayed the term limit of their visas. Either way, as unlawful residents they are not entitled to employment or public benefits and increasingly are the focus of law enforcement scrutiny. For an in-depth discussion of the various terms used historically, see Plascencia (2009).

2. For example, international agreements that provide for the safe and orderly repatriation of Mexican nationals, signed in 1997 and 2009 by U.S. Border Patrol officials and officials from the Mexican State of Sonora, "*Procedimientos para la Repatriación Segura y Ordenada de Nacionales Mexicanos,*" are routinely ignored (O'Leary and Sánchez 2011). In addition, the results of a survey undertaken by a community-based organization of more than 13,000 Mexican nationals who had been held in short-term Border Patrol custody (No More Deaths, 2011), documents the overwhelmingly systematic abuse of power by U.S. authorities.

References

Andre, Claire, and Manuel Velasquez. 1987. What Is Ethics? *Issues in Ethics* 1, http://www.scu.edu/ethics/publications/iie/v1n1/whatis.html.
Barsky, Robert F. 2009. Methodological Issues for the Study of Migrant Incarceration in an Era of Discretion in Law in the Southwestern USA. In I. Van Liempt and V. Bilger, eds. *The Ethics of Migration Research Methodology: Dealing with Vulnerable Immigrants.* Pp. 25–48. Brighton, England: Sussex Academic Press.
Bilger, Veronica, and Ilse Van Liempt. 2009a. Introduction: Methodological and Ethical Concerns in Research with Vulnerable Migrants. In I. Van Liempt and V. Bilger, eds. *The Ethics of Migration Research Methodology: Dealing with Vulnerable Immigrants.* Pp. 1–24. Brighton: Sussex Academic Press.

——. 2009b. Methodological and Ethical Dilemmas in Research among Smuggled Migrants. In I. Van Liempt and V. Bilger, eds. *The Ethics of Migration Research Methodology: Dealing with Vulnerable Immigrants.* Pp. 118–140. Brighton: Sussex Academic Press.

Bourdieu, Pierre. 1998. The "Globalization" Myth and the Welfare State. In *Acts of Resistance: Against the Tyranny of the Market.* New York: The New Press.

Chin, Gabriel J., Carissa Byrne. Hessick, and Mark. L. Miller. 2012. Arizona Senate Bill 1070: Politics through Immigration Law. In O. Santa Ana and C. González de Bustamante, eds. *Arizona Firestorm: Global Immigration Realities, National Media & Provincial Politics.* Lanham, MD: Rowman & Littlefield.

Cornelius, Wayne A. 1982. Interviewing Undocumented Immigrants: Methodological Reflections Based on Fieldwork in Mexico and the U.S. *International Migration Review* 16(2): 378–411.

——. 2001. Death at the Border: Efficacy and Unintended Consequences of U.S. Immigration Control Policy. *Population and Development Review* 27(4): 661–685.

Dunn, Timothy J. 1996. *The Militarization of the U.S.–Mexico Border, 1978–1992: Low-Intensity Conflict Doctrine Comes Home.* Austin: University of Texas Press.

Erfani, Julie A. Murphy. 2009. Crime and Violence in the Arizona-Sonora Borderlands. In K. Staudt, T. Payan, and Z. A. Kruszewski, eds. *Violence, Security, and Human Rights at the Border.* Tucson: University of Arizona Press.

Eschbach, Karl, Jacqueline Hagan, Nestor Rodriguez, Rubén Hernández-León, and Stanley Bailey. 1999. Death at the Border. *International Migration Review* 33(2): 430–454.

Farmer, Paul. 2003. *Pathologies of Power: Health, Human Rights, and the New War on the Poor.* Berkeley: University of California Press.

Galtung, Johan. 1969. Violence, Peace, and Peace Research. *Journal of Peace Research* 6(3): 167–191.

Garofalo, Charles, and Dean Geuras. 2006. *Common Ground, Common Future: Moral Agency in Public Administration, Professions, and Citizenship.* Boca Raton, FL: Taylor and Francis.

Goldsmith, Pat, Mary Romero, Raquel Rubio Goldsmith, Miguel Escobedo, and Laura Khoury. 2009. Ethno-Racial Profiling and State Violence in a Southwest Barrio. *Aztlán: A Journal of Chicano Studies* 34(1): 93–124.

Goldsmith, Raquel Rubio, Melissa M. McCormick, Daniel Martínez, and Inez Magdalena Duarte. 2006. A Humanitarian Crisis at the Border: New Estimates of Deaths among Unauthorized Immigrants. In *Immigration Policy Center.* Washington, D.C.: Immigration Policy Center.

Greenhouse, Carol J. 2002. Introduction: Altered States, Altered Lives. In Carol J. Greenhouse, Elizabeth Mertz, and Kay B. Warren, eds. *Ethnography in Unstable Places.* Pp. 1–36. Durham, NC: Duke University Press.

Greenhouse, Carol J., Elizabeth Mertz, and Kay B. Warren, eds. 2002. *Ethnography in Unstable Places.* Durham, NC: Duke University Press.

Hannerz, Ulf. 1998. Transnational Research. In H. R. Bernard, ed. *Handbook of Methods in Cultural Anthropology.* London: Sage.

Hayes, Wayne. 2009. The Public Policy Cycle Web Site Vol. 2012, ©Wayne Hayes, Ph.D.,™ ProfWork. http://profwork.org/pp/study/define.html, accessed August 9, 2012.

Heyman, Josiah McC. 1999. United States Surveillance over Mexican Lives at the Border: Snapshots of an Emerging Regime. *Human Organization* 58(4): 430–442.
———. N.d. "Political-Ethical Dilemmas Participant Observed." In Carl Maida and Sam Beck, eds. *Public Anthropology in a Borderless World.* Berghahn Press, forthcoming.
Heyman, Josiah McC., Maria Cristina Morales, and Guillermina Gina Núñez. 2009. Engaging with the Immigrant Human Rights Movement in a Besieged Border Region: What Do Applied Social Scientists Bring to the Policy Process? *NAPA Bulletin* 31: 13–29.
Heyman, Josiah McC., and Jason Ackleson. 2009. United States Border Security after September 11. In John Winterdyck and Kelly Sundberg, eds. *Border Security in the Al-Qaeda Era.* Pp. 37–74. Boca Raton, FL: CRC Press.
Hinkes, Madeleine J. 2008. Migrant Deaths along the California–Mexico Border: An Anthropological Perspective. *Journal of Forensic Sciences* 53(1): 16–20.
Levitt, Peggy. 1998. Social Remittances: Migration Driven Local-level Forms of Cultural Diffusion. *International Migration Review* 32(4): 926–948.
Manderson, Lenore, and Ruth P. Wilson. 1998. Negotiating with Communities: The Politics and Ethics of Research. *Human Organization* 57(2): 215–216.
Markova, Eugenia. 2009. The "Insider" Position: Ethical Dilemmas and Methodological Concerns in Researching Undocumented Migrants with the Same Ethnic Background. In I. Van Liempt and V. Bilger, eds. *The Ethics of Migration Research Methodology: Dealing with Vulnerable Immigrants.* Pp. 141–154. Brighton: Sussex.
Núñez, Guillermina Gina, and Josiah McC. Heyman. 2007. "Entrapment Processes and Immigrant Communities in a Time of Heightened Border Vigilance." *Human Organization* 66(4): 354–365.
López-Hoffman, Emily D. McGovern, Robert G. Varady, and Karl W. Fliessa. 2009. *Conservation of Shared Environments: Learning from the United States and Mexico: the Edge, Environmental Science, Law and Policy.* Tucson: University of Arizona Press.
O'Leary, Anna Ochoa. 2008. Close Encounters of the Deadly Kind: Gender, Migration, and Border (In)Security. *Migration Letters* 15(2): 111–122.
———. 2009a. The ABCs of Unauthorized Border Crossing Costs: Assembling, Bajadores, and Coyotes. *Migration Letters* 6(1): 27–36.
———. 2009b. In the Footsteps of Spirits: Migrant Women's Testimonios in a Time of Heightened Border Enforcement. In K. Staudt, T. Payan, and Z. A. Kruszewski, eds. *Violence, Security, and Human Rights at the Border.* Tucson: University of Arizona Press.
O'Leary, Anna Ochoa, and Azucena Sánchez. 2011. Anti-immigrant Arizona: Ripple Effects and Mixed Immigration Status Households under Policies of Attrition Considered. *Journal of Borderland Studies* 26(1): 115–133.
O'Leary, Anna Ochoa, and Andrea J. Romero. 2011. Chicana/o Students Respond to Arizona's Anti–Ethnic Studies Bill, SB 1108: Civic Engagement, Ethnic Identity, and Well-being. *Aztlán: A Journal of Chicano Studies* 36(1): 9–36.
Plascencia, Luis. 2009. The "Undocumented" Mexican Migrant Question: Reexamining the Framing of Law and Illegalization in the United States. *Urban Anthropology* 38(2–4): 378–344.

Reich, Robert B. 2010. *Aftershock: The Next Economy and America's Future*. New York: Vintage.

Romero, Mary. 2008. The Inclusion of Citizenship Status in Intersectionality: What Immigration Raids Tells Us about Mixed-Status Families, the State, and Assimilation. *International Journal of the Family* 34(2): 131–152.

Santa Ana, Otto. 1999. "Like an Animal I Was Treated": Anti-Immigrant Metaphor in U.S. Public Discourse. *Discourse & Society* 10(2): 191–224.

Shirk, David A. 2003. Law Enforcement and Security Challenges in the U.S.–Mexican Border Region. *Journal of Borderland Studies* 18(2): 1–24.

Slack, Jeremy, and Scott Whiteford. 2011. Violence on the Arizona-Sonora Border. *Human Organization* 70(1): 11–21.

———. 2012. Caught in the Middle: Undocumented Migrant Experiences with Narco Coyotaje, Backpacks and Bandits. In Tony Payan, ed. *The Many Labyrinths of Illegal Drug Policy*. Tucson: University of Arizona Press.

Velasquez, Manuel, Claire Andre, Thomas Shanks, and Michael J. Meyer. 1996. Thinking Ethically: A Framework for Moral Decision Making. *Issues in Ethics* 1. http://www.scu.edu/ethics/publications/iie/v7n1/thinking.html.

Whiteford, Linda, and Robert Trotter II. 2008. *Ethics for Anthropological Research and Practice*. Long Grove, IL: Waveland Press.

Wimmer, Andreas, and Nina Glick Schiller. 2003. Methodological Nationalism, the Social Sciences, and the Study of Migration: An Essay in Historical Epistemology. *International Migration Review* 37(3): 576–610.

PART ONE

The Big Picture

CHAPTER ONE

Vulnerable Immigrant "Subjects"

Definitions, Disparate Power, Dilemmas, and Desired Benefits

Jessie K. Finch and Celestino Fernández

Over the past few decades, there has been a growing interest in and concern with unauthorized immigration as a topic of research in several disciplines, including but not limited to sociology, political science, economics, psychology, anthropology, history, law, Mexican American studies, and women's studies. As political, cultural, and economic interests continue to focus on and expand the topic of immigration, research in this area will continue to raise questions of methodology and ethics. A growing focus on research involving human "subjects" specifically calls forth concerns about the vulnerability of immigrants, particularly poor, unauthorized immigrants, who participate in research projects. We refer to the humans involved in research from this point on not as "subjects," as the official codes of ethics refer to them, but primarily as "participants," assuming and encouraging the active participation of those people who assist researchers in their study of human phenomena. Whereas other methods not involving human participants directly (archival studies, statistical analysis, literature reviews, content analysis, etc.) may not have as many substantial ethical implications for these immigrant populations, instances of abuse of research participants have raised the subject of vulnerability. Although it is vital, and unquestionably good research methodology, that scholars should apply the same ethical principles to all human participants in order to maintain quality in research and in order to keep expediency from taking precedence over ethical concerns, unfortunately this has not always been the reality. These ethical issues have been insufficiently studied, possibly due to the multidisciplinary nature and methodological diversity of research on immigrant populations. Therefore, in this chapter, we seek to answer the call of Van Liempt and Bilger (2009), who contend that due to the "growing power and legal marginalization of ever-larger immigrant populations and increasing overlap of research and policy agendas," it is time, now more than ever, to expand our understanding of the vulnerability issue (Van Liempt and Bilger 2009: 1). Specifically, we will examine the varying definitions of vulnerability, both historically and contextually, based on disparate power in research relationships, how vulnerability presents dilemmas for researchers, and how researchers can be sensitive to this topic while still achieving the desired benefits of the research. These factors all interrelate and should make the issue of vulnerability a concern and top priority of immigration researchers who are utilizing human participants, particularly those studying unauthorized immigrants as well as other highly vulnerable immigrant groups such as migrant (forced) sex workers, smuggled children, refugees, and asylum seekers. Specifically, these populations tend to be of greatest importance around the southwestern U.S. border region.

A Definition of Vulnerable Based on a History of Research Ethics

Based on historical accounts of abuses, there have been growing efforts in the social and medical sciences to protect human participants. Famous cases of abuse in biomedical contexts tend to be better known and more egregious. Examples include the Nazi experimentation on Jewish prisoners during the Holocaust; the Willowbrook State Hospital incident, in which mentally handicapped children at a New York state hospital were intentionally infected with hepatitis as a condition of being admitted; the Tuskegee case, in which the U.S. Public Health Service continued a study for 40 years of poor, poorly educated African American males with syphilis who were denied medical care for this disease after they had been diagnosed in order to conduct autopsies to determine the full effects of the disease,[1] and the Jewish Chronic Disease Hospital study, in which patients were implanted with cancer cells without their knowledge or consent (Jonsen 1999: 108–9). Additionally, in September 2010, it was brought to light that from 1946 to 1948, American public health officials intentionally, but without the participants' knowledge, infected about 700 Guatemalans with syphilis and gonorrhea in order to test the effectiveness of penicillin. Both Kathleen Sebelius, secretary of health and human services, and Hilary Clinton, secretary of state, issued apologies to Guatemala, and President Barack Obama issued a renewed call for the protection of human subjects (McNeil 2010).

In the social sciences, there are also well-known examples of maltreatment of human participants, such as Laud Humphrey's *Tearoom Trade*, in which the author deceived over 100 participants in public homosexual encounters in numerous ways, including observing said acts, obtaining private information about participants, following participants, and surveying them under false pretenses (Beauchamp et al. 1982: 11–12). The overriding ethical concern that these cases share is the exploitation of a vulnerable population. Children, prisoners, the mentally incapacitated, members of certain racial or ethnic groups, the poor, those with no or little formal education, and participants in socially stigmatized behavior all represent vulnerable populations in research.

Based on these and other ethical violations by scholars, professional and ethical codes and definitions became increasingly popular and often federally required for research institutions. Governments, corporations, and universities all became progressively more interested in conducting ethical research that protected the interests of "human subjects." The first official document specifying the ethical concerns of such research emerged out of the Nuremburg trials that were conducted after World War II. The Nuremburg Code of 1945 established ethical guidelines applying mostly to biomedical research that, without specifically mentioning vulnerable populations, uphold the ideals of informed consent and avoidance of participant suffering or harm. Following in the biomedical footsteps of the Nuremburg Code, in 1964 the World Medical Association created the Declaration of Helsinki, which helped to reinforce the standards of informed consent and no harm to human participants. Article I.10 states: "When obtaining informed consent for the research project the physician should be particularly cautious if the participant is in dependent relationship to him or her or may consent under duress" (Declaration of Helsinki 1964). This particular addition to the code helped to pave the way for the examination of disparate power relationships between the researcher and the researched. This awareness of the social (and psychological) pressures and contexts under which research participants find themselves leads the way to making vulnerability an explicit concern of research ethics and methodologies.

On April 18, 1979, the (U.S.) National Commission for the Protection of Human Subjects of Biomedical and Behavioral Research issued the Belmont Report, which has become the standard guideline for all researchers intending to work with human participants. Its three basic ethical principles of respect for persons, beneficence, and justice have become the standard for Institutional Review Boards (IRBs) and other bodies that evaluate the ethical nature of research and the impact on human subjects. In terms of vulnerability, the Belmont Report was the first to specifically delineate the special considerations of vulnerable groups:

> One special instance of injustice results from the involvement of vulnerable subjects. Certain groups, such as racial minorities, the economically disadvantaged, the very sick, and the institutionalized may continually be sought as research subjects, owing to their ready availability in settings where research is conducted. Given their dependent status and their frequently compromised capacity for free consent, they should be protected against the danger of being involved in research solely for administrative convenience, or because they are easy to manipulate as a result of their illness or socioeconomic condition. (C.3)

According to this document, the vulnerable are readily available, dependent, compromised, and easily manipulated groups, and therefore are in need of special attention when involved in research. This first mention of specific groups needing special consideration in research begins our examination of how the modern-day codes continue to specify vulnerable populations.

The U.S. Food and Drug Administration, under the U.S. Department of Health and Human Services, upholds the Code of Federal Regulations for research and the specific protection of vulnerable populations. These guidelines specify that the selection of research participants should be equitable—based on the purpose and setting of the research in question. Similarly, it instructs IRBs to be "particularly cognizant of the special problems of research involving vulnerable populations, such as children, prisoners, pregnant women, handicapped, or mentally disabled persons, or economically or educationally disadvantaged persons" and that "when some or all of the subjects . . . are likely to be vulnerable to coercion or undue influence additional safeguards have been included in the study to protect the rights and welfare of these subjects" (Code of Federal Regulations 2009: 56.111:3:7b). As such, special protections of the vulnerable are to be included in any research design and methodology using populations that are disadvantaged or easily coerced.

The U.S. government and its agencies continue to issue regulations regarding working with research participants. As recently as January 2010, the National Science Foundation (NSF) instituted a new policy requiring all students (both undergraduate and graduate) and postdoctoral researchers (including faculty members) supported by NSF grants to complete training in the responsible conduct of research. Also in January 2010, the National Institutes of Health (NIH) announced new training requirements. The University of Arizona has developed a Participants' Bill of Rights (Research Participant 2010) to inform and protect human participants; it notes, "The most important person in research is the participant."

Internationally, the issue of vulnerable populations has also been raised. The International Conference of Harmonization (ICH) produces the guidelines that specifically speak to the use of vulnerable populations in pharmaceutical research. This organization unites Europe, Japan, and the United States under its guidelines. This organization first met in 1991 in Brussels, Belgium, and most recently in 2003 in Osaka, Japan; regional meetings are held regularly, most recently in St. Louis, Missouri, in October 2009 (History and Future of ICH 2010). When speaking of vulnerable populations, ICH (2010) states, "Special attention should be paid to trials that may include vulnerable subjects" (IHC Guidelines 2010: 3.1.1), where vulnerable is defined as, "Individuals whose willingness to volunteer in a clinical trial may be unduly influenced by the expectation, whether justified or not, of benefits associated with participation, or of a retaliatory response from senior members of a hierarchy in case of refusal to participate" (IHC Guidelines 2010: 1.61). This very broad and encompassing definition affords extra attention to the issue of just who is vulnerable. The guidelines list students, subordinate employees (especially in the medical field), members of the military, prisoners, the terminally ill, the unemployed, the impoverished, ethnic minorities, the homeless, and minors as examples. The special addition of workers and hierarchal concerns of the division of labor is an important expansion of vulnerable populations. The examples given are particularly expansive, as is the open-ended delineation of anyone whose consent is not totally free, but biased by the power of the researcher.

Another international organization that specifically addresses non-medical research of vulnerable populations is the RESPECT Project, publishers of the *EU Code of Ethics for Socio-Economic Research* (2004).

RESPECT was funded by the European Commission's Information Society Technologies Programme (IST) in order to develop these guidelines and principles based specifically on socioeconomic research. The code includes special provisions requiring that:

> All research studies must take into account the treatment of under-represented social groups by ensuring that they are appropriately treated in all aspects, from research design to reporting the findings. It is important that these groups are not excluded from research, but also that research findings do not lead to their further marginalization. Equally, it is important that vulnerable or marginalized groups are not over-researched so that participating becomes a burden for them. (RESPECT 2004: x)

The special focus here on "under-represented social groups" and attempts "to avoid their marginalization or exclusion" speaks to the issue of vulnerable participants and specifically to giving them special attention and consideration in research projects. In addition, the code also clearly calls for research to be commissioned and conducted with special attention to gender differences, and "with respect for all groups in society regardless of race, ethnicity, religion or culture," in an "attempt to alleviate potential disadvantages to participation for any individual or category of person" (RESPECT 2004: ix, x, xiv). This code appears to be the most progressive of its kind in alerting researchers to the special circumstances and conditions of vulnerable groups. It holds that participation decisions should be voluntary, made from an informed position, and made without coercion. Examples of vulnerable populations listed in the code include women; torture victims; the elderly; people with an incomplete grasp of the language; those with mental, learning, or other disabilities; children or gatekeepers to their consent; and victims of domestic violence. By far, this is the most expansive and encompassing definition and inclusion of vulnerable participants found in international codes.

This broadest definition leads specifically into how we will define vulnerability in this chapter and in particular in the case of unauthorized immigrant research participants. We can see, based on the broader definitions offered in later codes of ethics, that under certain circumstances, every group could be considered vulnerable; however, certain groups, because of their status in society, are clearly always vulnerable. For the purposes of this chapter, any person or group who can be easily taken advantage of due to disparate power relations in the context of the specific research project provides the most basic definition of vulnerability. We expand below how this definition applies specifically to immigrants. We also explore applications of this definition in research designs and methodologies that take special care to avoid manipulation of human participants through receiving truly informed consent, consent that is fully informed and voluntary without any coercion, compulsion, or intimidation.

Disparate Power Leads to Compounding Vulnerability in Immigrants

It is important to note early on that while we refer to immigrants as a group being especially vulnerable, individuals (and subgroups) within this larger group will certainly vary in their potential exploitability. We do not mean to imply that all immigrants are poorly educated or have low socioeconomic status, for that is certainly an inaccurate generalization. However, we do wish to call attention to, and alert researchers to the increased probability of, compounding vulnerabilities when using immigrants as research participants, particularly unauthorized immigrants in the southwestern U.S. border region.

We have identified seven categories in which immigrants can be defined as vulnerable: racial/ethnic group membership; immigrant/citizenship status; stigmatized position in society; socioeconomic status; educational and language disadvantages; social and cultural exclusion and isolation; and psychological and emotional duress. Based on the above vulnerabilities, we can see that the common issue of disparate power between the researcher and the researched is what makes immigrants so vulnerable. Whether it is racial, legal, cultural, economic, or psychological power that is unequally distributed, there is always potential for abuse in research relationships. Examining more closely each of these areas helps describe immigrants' special status as vulnerable, as well as explain what is meant by disparate power.

Racial/Ethnic Group Membership

Starting in the early 1970s, codes of ethics such as the Belmont Report discussed above as well as various research organizations began to include members of particular racial or ethnic minorities in their descriptions of possible vulnerable research participants. Many of the most famous cases of abuse, including the Tuskegee case and the Jewish Chronic Disease

Hospital study, involved a particular racial/ethnic group that was seen as either expendable or accessible, or that could easily be manipulated due to the race/ethnicity of its members.

Immigrants moving from one nation to another frequently are of racial or ethnic groups different from the majority of the people living in the new host country. Specifically in the United States, the most common conception of an immigrant, particularly during the past 50 years, is a Latino/a person and in particular a Mexican. The inequality of races and ethnic groups in the United States is well established and places Latinos very close to the bottom (Palmer et al. 1998; Ma and Henderson 1999). Access to health care and education, income levels, and employment and law enforcement discrimination are just some of the many obstacles faced by minority ethnic/racial groups in the United States. Immigrants, including Latinos, merely by being of a different racial or ethnic group are also exposed to this risk, making them vulnerable, perhaps especially to researchers of the majority race/ethnic group.

Immigrant/Citizenship Status

A second kind of vulnerability that many immigrants find themselves faced with is their legal status in the host nation. The most obvious example of this is when immigrants enter the country without proper documents; due to the threat of imprisonment or deportation, such immigrants may find themselves easily exploitable. Again, in the case of the United States, the centrality of legal issues, particularly in the borderlands, may put immigrants in a parallel position with vulnerable prisoner populations who are officially described as vulnerable in research codes of ethics.

Even with legal entry to a host country, immigrants are still in a precarious position. Many immigrants may enter the country on a semi-permanent basis with specific conditions they must follow to remain eligible for permanent residency and later for citizen status. Many immigrants who are not yet naturalized are also disenfranchised, with little political influence. This may lead to a sense of powerlessness and interpretation of disparate power between oneself and a potential researcher. Michael Jones-Correa explains that "immigrant political socialization and behavior," such as voting habits, are differentiated based on gender and other potential immigrant vulnerabilities, such as language, employment, economic status, and education (Jones-Correa 1998: 326). In the case of the U.S. southern border, many immigrants are especially at risk for this political disenfranchisement, evident in hostile laws like Arizona's SB1070 as well as in the Dream Act's failure to pass.

In combining legality with racial/ethnic status, the embedded racism/ discrimination in the legal system is particularly exploitative of immigrants. In an article in the *Columbia Law Review*, Shie-Wei Fan incorporates critical race theory (which "endeavors to account for the voices of people of color by exploring the systemic and pervasive nature of racism in society") to criticize how immigrants are treated by, and studied in, law (Fan 1997: 1202). She contends that "[i]mmigration scholars could better account for the complex intersections of race, alienage, and other identity characteristics by more carefully considering the racial biases intrinsic to the context of immigration law and by highlighting the inability of contemporary scholarship to recognize the depth and breadth of the immigrant experience" (Fan 1997: 1202). This discussion of legality and racism/discrimination highlights the particular disadvantages that pertain to immigrants. Translated into a research setting, these factors again clearly result in disproportional distribution of power.

Stigmatized Position in Society

Certainly not in all host nations, but in general, there is a potential for immigrants to become the targets of unfair social stereotyping due to their status as "new arrivals" and as "different." Many immigrants may experience discrimination, intolerance, and stigma as part of their experience in a host country. Take the United States, for example, where there is a popular opinion that immigrants "steal jobs" or "take advantage" of public systems and programs such as education and healthcare. While these opinions are most often misinformed—that is, not supported by systematic empirical research—there still exists the possibility of unequal interpersonal power dynamics experienced by immigrants who may be subject to threats or violence due to these prejudices. This is especially apparent near the southern border where "Minutemen" and other vigilantes specifically target immigrants.

Keogan (2002) completed a comparative study of how immigrants were characterized in newspapers in New York and Los Angeles. Using content analysis of the *Los Angeles Times* and the *The New York Times*, researchers found "the social construction of an exclusive 'threat' narrative in Southern California, and an inclusive 'immigrant as victim' narrative in the New York metropolitan area" (Keogan 2002: 223). In both of these cases, immigrants are either stigmatized by a "present-future 'threat' narrative" in Los Angeles or by a "sympathetic, 'victim' narrative" in New York (Keogan 2002: 248). The article examines the causes of divergence, mostly based on "sharp focus on the U.S.–Mexico Border" as "a deviant symbol of immigration" (Keogan 2002: 248). Both of these empirically proven narratives exemplify the stigma that may be attached to being an immigrant in the United States, be it as threat or as victim, especially in reference to the border.

Social stigmatization of immigrants may also be unduly compounded for members of an already stigmatized gender group. Thus, female immigrants may be especially vulnerable to discrimination and manipulability. Many studies have characterized immigrant women as especially likely to be taken advantage of and as vulnerable due to their gender status. Women whose immigration status is tied to their marriages, for example, face an elevated threat of abuse (Narayan 1995). Also, in "Trafficking, Migration, and the Law: Protecting Innocents, Punishing Immigrants," Chapkis (2003) examines the relationship between forced sexual labor and undocumented immigrants. In sum, the potential for exploitation is increased by stigmatizing factors, which may cause unforeseen issues in a research situation in such a way as to affect the voluntary consent of participants. This also may be tied to gendered violence occurring in a country of origin, such as the murdering of hundreds of women in and around Ciudad Juárez, Mexico.

Socioeconomic Status

Frequently, immigrants will have low socioeconomic status in their host country. Oftentimes immigrants migrate from a poorer nation seeking to improve their life conditions in the new nation. The impoverished status of many immigrants can lead to their vulnerability through unemployment, poor housing, limited healthcare, lack of education, and other issues associated with poverty. This has certainly been the case for many immigrant groups in the history of the United States, such as the Irish during the potato famine or the Southern and Eastern Europeans who migrated in the late 1800s and early 1900s, and it is clearly the situation in which many Latin American immigrants, particularly from Mexico and Central America, now find themselves, particularly in the U.S.–Mexico border region.

Wood (1994) compares the situation of immigrants who appear to be migrating by choice with the situations of refugees who are forced to migrate. Wood concludes that the extreme poverty and vulnerability of many immigrants, which has forced them to migrate, is comparable to that of officially labeled refugees, and therefore these immigrants are just as subject to government and other types of exploitation. Wood contends that while "[r]efugees are forced to flee . . . [i]mmigrants are supposed to have a degree of choice, but when their livelihood is so miserable, I don't know what the level of choice is. It may be that they too should then be looked at as people forced to flee by poverty" (Wood 1994: 607). If immigrants moving to a host nation are as impoverished as refugees, it can be assumed that they may not easily find relief from their poverty in the new country. This can be seen especially in the economic displacement of Mexican *maquiladora* workers near the border.

Once in a new nation, it might be expected that immigrants would find jobs and be able to improve their life situation. This, however, is not usually the case, especially for immigrants who enter without proper documents, like many border crossers in modern times. The difficulty of finding work in a new country where presumably one has fewer contacts, in addition to other compounding vulnerabilities, can impede economic progress. Merino (1988) analyzes the role that laws in a host country can play in the employment of undocumented immigrants. Through an analysis of the Immigration Reform and Control Act (IRCA) of 1986, Merino contends that the 1982 eligibility date established by the law created a division between immigrants. This division makes those who immigrated after 1982 an especially vulnerable group or "a substantial underclass" (Merino 1988: 426). This has exacerbated the problem of illegal employment and left many immigrants in a position of extreme vulnerability due to their socioeconomic conditions and the limited opportunities available to them. This problem can be compounded where there are large groups of people in this same situation, as is usually the case in the southern border region of the United States. Being in poverty may very well influence a participant in research, especially if a direct benefit, such as a voucher coupon or other compensation, is offered; the research participants may perceive that they have less choice in participating in a study.

Educational and Language Disadvantages

Often, immigrants are not in a particularly informed position when they enter a new country. They may be quite unfamiliar with the language, laws, and/or culture of the new nation. Due to an uneducated, undereducated, or ill-informed position or lack of experience, they can easily be in a position to be readily manipulated. There can also be major linguistic challenges when immigrants are not familiar with the host nation's language. As a reminder, we are not suggesting that all immigrants are under-educated, but if, as Wood (1994) suggested above, they have been forced to immigrate, the chances of them having been educated in the ways of their host nation seem highly unlikely, particularly if they are poor. The Pew Hispanic Center estimates that 41.6 percent of foreign-born Mexicans in the United States have below a ninth-grade education compared to only 3.5 percent of all Americans born in the United States (Statistical Portrait of the Foreign-Born Population in the United States). For a significant proportion of this population, low education is a realistic vulnerability. Not knowing the laws, culture, and/or language can leave immigrants easily exploitable, coercible, and controllable.

Additionally, studies have shown that children who immigrate are particularly vulnerable when trying to adapt to a new educational system. Jones (1987) and Cahan et al. (2001) have both found that age of immigration and educational attainment are linked. Generally, immigrant children have lower educational attainment than native-born children. In reviewing the literature, it becomes clear that "[i]n research on the social adjustment of immigrants, the fact of immigration is given a prominent place as a determinant of various kinds of behavior, whether it be educational attainment, family conflict, career development, behavior or personality disorders, or juvenile delinquency" (Jones 1987: 70). Although this chapter focuses on educational attainment, it makes way for the next vulnerability we will discuss.

Social and Cultural Exclusion and Isolation

In addition to the lack of formal education and host-language skills, immigrants also may suffer from the lack of socialization to a host country's culture, including its values and norms. Social integration, or lack thereof via social isolation, is a type of vulnerability that immigrants are especially likely to experience. Social exclusion is a common problem for immigrants, particularly those who are in the country without proper documents and are forced to live a clandestine existence. These individuals frequently are isolated into areas where only other immigrants reside, and they are not able to integrate with the larger culture of the host nation, as frequently happens near the border. Yoshikawa et al. (2008) help us to define what we mean by social exclusion: "The concept of social exclusion was developed to capture dimensions of the experience of immigrants that go beyond poverty to issues of lack of access to political, social, and health systems. Exclusion can occur with reference to public institutions, such as government policies and service systems, as well as social institutions, such as social networks or community organizations" (Yoshikawa et al. 2008: 64). Access to community resources and cultural inclusion can affect the status and well-being of immigrants just as much as formal education and political resources.

While Yoshikawa specifically addresses the issue of child cognitive development and educational attainment, Bask (2005) has shown that a multitude of areas can be influenced by social exclusion, in particular for immigrants. The author documents that there are at least six major areas where immigrants are especially vulnerable to social exclusion: "long-term unemployment, economic problems, health problems, experience of violence or threats, crowded housing, and lack of interpersonal relationships" (Bask 2005: 74). While we have addressed some of these issues separately above, Bask links them all to the fundamental problem of social exclusion of immigrants. These compounding issues place researchers in acutely more powerful positions than potential immigrant research participants. Being in the position of a person with a high level of education, both formal and social, the researcher is therefore in a position to make a participant of lower educational and cultural attainment feel especially inferior.

Psychological and Emotional Duress

A final contributor to immigrant vulnerability explored here is the mental toll that the factors discussed above and others relating to the immigrant experience can take on individuals. Emotional, psychological, and mental distress can lead to feelings of fear, lack of trust, stress, depression, and isolation in immigrant populations, particularly for those individuals who are in the country without the required documentation. Emergency situations that can affect mental status, such as refugees may experience when leaving their home country, can be expanded to include the experience of unauthorized immigrants who are under considerable mental and physical distress when crossing the border.

Ornelas et al. (2009) contend, "Mexican immigrant mothers face many challenges that put them at increased risk for poor mental health" (Ornelas et al. 2009: 1556). These mental health risks include depression and anxiety caused by both "economic stressors" (financial obligations, work, and child care) as well as "social stressors" (family separation, social isolation, and discrimination) (Ornelas et al. 2009: 1556). Similar results have also been found for Yemeni immigrant women (Volk 2009).

In general, any of the factors, independently or combined, discussed above can lead to vulnerability among immigrant populations. These compounding vulnerability factors and a general sense of fear or lack of understanding can affect the mental stability of an immigrant who may agree to participate in research without complete voluntary consent. Overall, then, through our exploration of the many facets of immigrants' vulnerabilities, we can see that there is much overlap in these categories. Frequently there are causal cycles that lead to the compounding of these factors. For instance, in the United States, the typical experience of a Mexican immigrant makes him/her vulnerable in all of these categories. Being of a different race/ethnicity, coming from a country where a language is spoken that is different from the dominant language in the United States, and being generally worse off economically and educationally, as well as entering into a society that has attached a negative stigma to Mexican immigrants all can produce effects of social and cultural exclusion that lead to psychological distress, whether the immigrants entered legally or not. While not all Mexican immigrants enter the country without the required documents, Mexican immigrants are automatically subject to this suspicion and are stereotyped because of it. Thus, although these seven factors can be discussed separately, in reality they overlap a great deal and can clearly be found when considering the specific case of unauthorized Mexican immigrants in the United States.

Exploring Research Dilemmas to Gain Desired Benefits

Based on the characteristics described above, we can see how vulnerabilities are regularly present when one undertakes research using immigrants as participants. In almost every research project, scholars will need to consider at least one, and most likely several, of the seven issues described above when conducting research on immigrants. Dilemmas due to vulnerability must be addressed in order to allow for desired benefits for both the researcher and the researched. For researchers, the desired benefits involve obtaining information from the research population for the development of academic work that can build both literature and theory in their given field, and of course, academic presentations and publications contribute to career development. However, the researcher's desired benefits, particularly when working with vulnerable populations, should be balanced with giving back to the population studied—that is, by assisting those being researched. This can be accomplished by employing suitable research designs and methodologies and by using the results of the studies appropriately so that vulnerable populations, in this case immigrants, are empowered. Empowerment comes from two areas: through interaction and collaboration with participants on the micro level, and through transmission of the research to general audiences and influence on policy-making on the macro level. In the following section, we discuss research designs, methodologies, and research transmission that effectively empower the vulnerable immigrants being studied, and examine a research counter-example to illustrate some of the main ideas.

Research Designs and Methodologies

First, when deciding to conduct research on immigrants, the investigator should ask him/herself: "What is my interest in studying the immigrant population?" As mentioned above, immigration is of growing national interest. Are the researcher's reasons for studying immigrants simply based on a desire to include currently popular topics? Because of the topic's popularity, there may be calculating careerist motives at stake in studying immigration due to access to grant funds and attainment of status as a result of the attention given to this research area. In some situations, there may also be a danger of using immigrants as participants due to easy access to them, as they may be vulnerable and thus easily manipulated and controlled. All of these and similar reasons for conducting research on immigrants present ethical conflicts in studying this population. The dangers of becoming involved in a research area for reasons other than genuine academic and/or policy interests motivated by study of that particular group should be avoided. Therefore, the first part of designing empowered research lies in assuring that the reason immigrants are being studied are to better understand this group and, ideally, to assist this vulnerable population.

Next, when designing research projects with immigrant research participants, one should allow for a methodology that considers the fact that this is a vulnerable population and, ideally, that empowers this group. A main criticism of much research on vulnerable populations is the low degree to which participants are involved in all stages of the research. Many traditional methods do not allow for the incorporation of the researched in the design process. On the other hand, many newer methodological techniques used in other areas of research can be applied to immigration studies in order to involve immigrant participants in the research design. Acknowledging and incorporating research participants into the research design can help in many areas, including translation issues and the "insider-outsider" debate that questions the faithful representation of participants. These issues can be minimized through improvements in research design, enabling studies to incorporate multiple perspectives and accuracy checks by participants.

Some current research designs and methodologies that incorporate participants in the design process include critical race theory, feminist approaches, liberation anthropology, international collaboration techniques, and community-based approaches. Below we explore some of these methods and their main foci.

Critical Race Theory. Critical race theory (CRT) began in the 1970s mostly as a legal movement that questioned the institutionalized racism present in the United States. It quickly spread to the field of education, as well as to political science and areas of ethnic studies. The theory is focused on the questioning of traditional views of race: "Unlike traditional civil rights, which embraces incrementalism and step-by-step progress, critical race theory questions the very foundations of the liberal order, including equality theory, legal reasoning, Enlightenment rationalism, and neutral principles of constitutional law" (Delgado and Stefancic 2001: 3). This framework of CRT, then, suggests methodologies for conducting research that differ from those of traditional race and ethnic studies.

Solórzano and Yosso (2002) use the assumptions of CRT to create a specific methodology for educational research. The authors question traditional methods, saying, "Although social scientists tell stories under the guise of 'objective' research, these stories actually uphold deficit, racialized notions about people of color." They seek to challenge this by using CRT to provide a "space to conduct and present research grounded in the experiences and knowledge of people of color" (Solórzano and Yosso 2002: 23). The "counter-stories" used by CRT methodology are a "tool for exposing, analyzing, and challenging the majoritarian stories of racial privilege. Counter-stories can shatter complacency, challenge the dominant discourse on race, and further the struggle for racial reform" (Solórzano and Yosso 2002: 32). While the authors go on to apply their research specifically to education, we argue here that these methods can improve the research conducted on immigrants. Since, as discussed above, immigrants are usually vulnerable on various dimensions, including both their racial/ethnic and cultural differences, CRT methodology, which is designed to empower minorities, can effectively help vulnerable immigrants feel more empowered by research. In other words, research on immigrants grounded in the daily experiences of this population is likely to result in rich data based on genuine stories, thus resulting in better understanding of their situations, on the basis of which more equitable public policy may be enacted. Limitations of the approach, however, may include overfocusing on the race of immigrants. This could be detrimental in terms of profiling or stereotypes that may prevail about immigrants and race.

Feminist Approaches. Similar to CRT, feminist approaches to research methodology often call into question the institutional bias of traditional research. Renzetti and Lee (1993) explain that in researching sensitive topics, it can often be useful to bring in feminist methods as a critique of traditional research practice: "The feminist reformulation of the research process calls for (a) open acknowledgement by the researcher of her or his assumptions, beliefs, sympathies, and biases, especially those for emanating from her or his sex, race, social class, and/or sexual orientation; (b) rejection of the traditional separation of the researcher form the researched; and (c) adoption of the goals of the research as consciousness-raising and empowerment" (177). These goals of feminist approaches in research are aimed at empowerment, social justice, and service to the research participants. While there are several specific methods of feminist research, much of it tends to be qualitative, in-depth interviewing and observation. However, the larger goal of feminist research is to embody the principles of empowerment and to question the researcher's relationship to the researched, focusing specifically on the power dynamic or differential.

Thus, feminist approaches are extremely helpful when dealing with vulnerable immigrant populations. While clearly not all immigrants are women, we commented above on how many immigrant women are especially vulnerable. Furthermore, although feminist research is supposed to be women-centered, the overall principles regarding researchers examining their own biases and power relationships between the investigator and the participants can serve as powerful lessons for all investigators conducting research on immigrant populations and are particularly helpful in efforts to overcome potential biases and vulnerabilities. Again, there are limitations to this framework, including focusing too much on women to the point of overrepresenting their experiences as equivalent to that of all immigrants.

Liberation Anthropology. Named by Jennifer Hirsch around 2003, this particular brand of anthropology applies specifically to immigrants and it is a framework and methodology designed to assist researchers. Hirsch contends: "Our ethical obligations to migrants who are the subject of our research stems from three sources: (1) our general ethical responsibility as social science researchers to avoid harm to our subjects, (2) *the ways in which the particular vulnerabilities of our immigrant subjects may facilitate entrée into their communities* [emphasis added], and (3) the dependence of Americans on the exploitation of immigrant labor for our very high standard of living" (Hirsch 2003: 232). Drawing specifically on Latin American experiments in liberation theology, liberation anthropology, designed for immigrant groups, is a research approach that assures that research that may present risks to participants will have greater benefits to those participants. Specifically applying to health and medical research, Hirsch points out that liberation anthropology is "not just a sensitive form of ethnographic storytelling and a keener ear for community member's pain . . . it would also involve . . . a commitment to social analysis that reveals the underlying causes of suffering and health, including the pathogenic role of social inequality" (Hirsch 2003: 231). This methodological approach calls for the researcher to "embrace the role of spokesperson and advocate" (Hirsch 2003: 230). We will address this issue further in the section below on presenting research results in an empowering way.

While not specifically using the terms liberation anthropology or focusing on immigration, Speed (2006) also addresses the issue of the changing role of human rights as a focus for anthropological research. Incorporating other frameworks that criticize the exploitation of research participants, such as postcolonial, feminist, postmodern, and critical race theories, she suggests "that an approach of collaborative research that merges activism and cultural critique — although it doesn't fully resolve these questions — is precisely what is needed in the current moment for the anthropology of rights" (Speed 2006: 67). By examining the researcher's role and the inherent creation of an "other" in research, Speed suggests that recognizing the biases and social "situatedness" of the researcher can effectively help create research that is more considerate of human rights and potentially, for our purposes, both limit manipulation of vulnerable populations and lead to research that benefits these populations. Though Speed does not specifically address immigrant issues as Hirsch does, the same messages and lessons can be learned and applied when conducting research on immigrants by focusing on the absolute (as opposed to conditional) human rights of the research participants.

Some concerns about this method include the fear of "going native." If researchers become too concerned on the human status of their subjects, they may lose track of the research questions at hand. A special balance is needed to keep from going too far from the traditional methodological approach while still emphasizing a participatory research method.

International Collaboration. Hamnett (1984) discusses the issues of ethical social research, including the "myth of neutrality" and issues with positivism and pragmatism. The author includes a critical history of the reigning paradigm of international research that leads him to develop a new framework for research that can be more productive and ethical when addressing international issues and migrant populations. He focuses on three specific issues: critical thinking, international collaboration, and participatory research. His focus on critical thinking delves into the researcher's use of his or her expert knowledge when working with international participants. He contends that "the most efficacious means for the enlightenment and liberation of both the individual and society" is the spread and sharing of knowledge (Hamnett 1984: 63). He encourages researchers not only to create knowledge but also to share it as part of the research process, and to do so through international collaboration.

Hamnett describes the need for international collaboration at all stages of the research process involving cross-national and cross-cultural studies. This approach also leads to a discussion of the concepts of insider and outsider, as well as indigenization. Hamnett proposes that due to the unique cultural system of each society, developed and underdeveloped nations might have difficulty reconciling their ideas regarding research. He thus contends that while the research methods of developed nations are invaluable, inclusion of researchers from other nations is imperative to avoid misinterpretation and the possibility of inaccurate results. In a similar way, Van Liempt and Bilger (2009) note that research can be "particularly interesting when researchers (or part of the research team) are themselves migrants or even exponent of the populations, community and/or identity group they are constructing studies with" (Van Liempt and Bilger 2009: 4). Therefore, one of the best ways to avoid indigenization, exploitation, and inaccurate portrayals is through participatory research, which is discussed in greater depth below.

Community-Based Participatory Research (CBPR). Defined as "efforts along several lines to develop research approaches that involve those persons who are the expected beneficiaries of the research process," participatory research can be key to accurate, empowered research (Hamnett 1984: 102). This includes the participation of the research population in all levels of the research process. Hamnett claims that in order to be most effective, "A research project should involve the community of research subjects in the entire research project, from the formulation of the problem to the discussion of how to seek solutions and in the interpretation and use of findings" (Hamnett 1984: 103). Starting from the basic issue of how to frame the research question, participants should be involved in the design and implementation of the entire research process.

These issues have also been addressed by other researchers in the medical field. While Hamnett speaks mostly in terms of the social sciences, CBPR has also been applied to health and environmental research. According to the U.S. Agency for Healthcare Research and Quality, CBPR has been shown to benefit researchers, research participants, and health care practitioners. According to this report:

> CBPR creates bridges between scientists and communities, through the use of shared knowledge and valuable experiences. This collaboration further lends itself to the development of culturally appropriate measurement instruments, thus making projects more effective and efficient. Finally, CBPR establishes a mutual trust that enhances both the quantity and the quality of data collected. The ultimate benefit to emerge from such collaborations is a deeper understanding of a community's unique circumstances, and a more accurate framework for testing and adapting best practices to the community's needs. (Community-Based Participatory Research: Assessing the Evidence 2004: 1)

As we can see, CBPR has been shown to assist in helping participants of research gain just as many benefits as the researchers. Used in immigration research, CBPR can be a method that takes into account the compounding vulnerabilities of immigrants and allows for the mutual benefit of research projects—that is, for benefits to both the researcher and the researched. Some methods based on CBPR have already been implemented with immigrant communities with positive results (van der Velde et al. 2009). Downsides to this approach include the extra time and coordination needed to make research more community friendly.

Empowerment Evaluation. Closely related to CBPR is the empowerment evaluation method. This approach "is an invaluable tool for those of us convinced that community residents have collective insights, wisdom, and experiences that can and should be mined to inform programs and policies" (Fetterman and Wandersman 2005: v). Less specifically related to research and more so to programs and policies, empowerment evaluation still has much to offer researchers. Its ten principles of improvement, community ownership, inclusion, democratic participation, social justice, community knowledge, evidence-based strategies, capacity building, organizational learning, and accountability offer valuable insight on research design and methodology. Specifically related to immigration, these evaluation techniques can lead to improved use of research results that empower and otherwise benefit immigrant communities, though again the extra time and organization needed to implement these processes can be limiting. We turn to this issue in our next section.

Research Transmission

As seen above, research designs and methodologies can be specifically implemented on the micro level in ways that empower immigrant research participants. However, on a macro level, researchers are just as obligated to control for the vulnerability of research participants, including, for example, in publications and in terms of possible influence on policy. Due to the politically sensitive nature of immigrant research, particularly with unauthorized immigrants, there is the possibility that although research conducted on immigrant groups may cause no harm to the specific individuals who participated, there is a potential that the results can affect the well-being of the group as a whole. Therefore, researchers need to consider such impacts and consequences in the process of publishing the results. Advocacy-driven and empowering research can help keep scholars from exploiting their vulnerable participants. In a continued exploration of liberation anthropology, Hirsch contends, "It is equally urgent to consider how the knowledge we produce fits into broader political economies of knowledge, serving certain political agendas and silencing others" (Hirsch 2003: 230). After research is completed, researchers should avoid using victimization frameworks, since "exaggerating the importance of culture as a determinant of health outcomes can do a real disservice to those for whom we presume to speak" (Hirsch 2003: 231). To avoid exploitation, then, scholars should not use overly victimizing frameworks and also should use their own status as researchers to enhance the voices of those they research.

Historically, we know that research can have a large effect on public policy. In fact, "[m]any of society's most articulate and vehement spokespersons of topics of ethnic change and immigrant incorporation have been academics" (Foner et al. 2000: 9). In order to appropriately assure that no harm comes to individuals or the group from the publication of research, scholars should use their less-vulnerable status to empower participants. Speed (2006) also addresses this issue: "Here, one would expect advocacy to be the prescription: If our research subjects are in danger, then anthropologists should use their positions—and whatever prestige or power they might afford—to defend and make known their subjects' rights against violation," while all the time continuing to "maintain a critical analytical focus" (Speed 2006: 67). This perspective can clearly apply specifically to the area of policy.

In a recent book devoted to political uses of expert knowledge in the area of immigration, Boswell (2009) found that policy-makers use research "as a way of lending authority to their preferences" and as a tool to "signal their capacity to make sound decisions" (Boswell 2009: i). In particular, areas of high risk (national security) or high contention (human rights), such as unauthorized immigration, are more likely to see appointed and elected officials call on research in an attempt to try to legitimize political decisions. Boswell asks: "Does increased governmental interest in research reflect the fact that research is being valued for its instrumental, legitimizing or substantiating function?" (Boswell 2009: 11). She examines European immigration policies to show the complex and often unpredictable interaction between research and policy. She explains that "the focus on policy adjustments obscured other forms of knowledge use," which creates a knowledge gap that exists between researchers and policy-makers (Boswell 2009: 247). While she offers no specific suggestions to researchers in her book for addressing this issue, the examination of the relationship between research results and public policy is an important concern for researchers, particularly social scientists, to regularly bear in mind.

The relationship between the researcher and his/her regulating or sponsoring institutions should also be examined in order to maintain the researcher's integrity with the participants. Policy-makers often use research to push their political agendas, which may be contrary to the interest of the researchers, or worse, contrary and even harmful to the groups studied. Speed again addresses this issue, saying that recently, "[a]ttention was drawn to the ways that the myth of scientific objectivity had served to conceal both indirect, unintended effects of anthropological research and work with obvious political ends, such as spying for government agencies under the guise of fieldwork. Thus, scientific objectivity was not only an impossible goal but also potentially something more insidious: a cover for the harmful political effects of our work on those about whom we researched and wrote" (Speed 2006: 66).

We should, then, account for any political ends for which our research may be used. The fact that much immigration research, particularly on unauthorized Mexican immigrants, has become increasingly policy oriented "has encouraged researchers to take the categories, concepts and priorities of policy makers at the core of their research design. This privileges the worldview of the policy makers in constructing the research, constraining the research questions asked, the subjects of study and the methodologies and analysis adopted" (Van Liempt and Bilger 2009: 2). When policy is used in this way to orient research, it is possible that the results will be harmful to immigrant communities.

A Counter-Example

To end our investigation of empowering research methodologies, we turn to a counter-example to help illustrate the importance of accounting for vulnerability in immigrant research. DaVanzo et al. (1994) provide a methodological resource for researchers interested in surveying immigrant communities with the intent of influencing policy. Their book does not at all address the idea of vulnerability. Specifically, they call for a national survey of immigrants from many nations and over time in order to get statistically significant data on this group. They detail a pilot project of Salvadorian and Filipino immigrants in Los Angeles as a model to be followed. However, we question their model on several fronts.

First, the reason for the survey is to influence policy—their main focus in collecting data on immigrants is to provide these data to policy-makers. They claim that in future years "policymakers will need to make fundamental decisions: How many immigrants can the nation productively absorb? What types of immigrants should be encouraged? Should the government help immigrants adjust to life in the United States? If so, which ones and how?" (DaVanzo et al. 1994: 4). Contrary to our suggestions of having the research participants as the first priority and first beneficiaries of research, their book places "America's" interests over that of immigrant research participants. Its focus is on how the government can get better data on immigrants.

Second, there was no participation of the research participants in design of the study. In their very thorough description of their pilot study, they describe the importance of bilingual interviewers of the same race as interviewees, some of them even immigrants themselves. However, neither interviewers nor participants had any say in the actual questions being asked. Interviewers were trained to ask questions designed by "higher-ups" in the research process and participants remained only "subjects" of the research.

Once researchers had designed the study without immigrant input and trained interviewers to ask only the questions they had given them, contact with the immigrant population began through a selection and screening process. In screening, the immigrant participants were chosen based on semi-randomized sampling and judged on criteria of cooperativity, the amount of effort it would take to interview the selected respondent, and answers to the question of "would a $5.00 grocery certificate be an effective incentive payment?" (DaVanzo et al. 1994: 28). There is little individual attention paid to the participants in the screening process, which is focused on response rates and randomizing the sample as much as possible.

On a positive note, the explanation of the $5 grocery card incentive does emphasize the importance of giving added benefits to minority research participants. The authors quote Marín and VanOss Marín (1991) saying that minority status of participants may result in low socioeconomic status, which results in more difficult home situations and thus a greater burden for taking time to complete a survey. The authors then summarize as follows: "Thus, the conventional wisdom is that to maximize participation, surveys of ethnic and minority groups should include an appropriate incentive payment" (DaVanzo et al. 1994: 32). Notice how the authors' focus is not on the benefit of the participants, but on the benefit to the research being done—improved participation. They did discuss with interviewers the appropriateness of a card to see what the perception of this benefit would be, a step in the right direction. Still, compensation in the amount of $5.00 is so minimal as to be insulting; it does not constitute a meaningful incentive or "thank you" to participants.

After screening, main interviews were conducted with participants who met the above-listed screening criteria. An appendix is included with the questionnaires, but not any kind of informed consent, as if it were not relevant to provide future researchers with this essential information. In analyzing the data from the main interviews, the researchers do focus on potentially sensitive topics and response rates, including immigration status, family income, and tax contributions. Their attention to these issues is based on the idea of nonresponse rates being detrimental to their study, not on the idea that these topics might have been sensitive to responders. They make no special notice of immigrants' vulnerability in responding these questions, only that their nonresponse rates were "comparable to what is found on general population surveys" (DaVanzo et al. 1994: 36).

The authors then summarize their findings based on questions framed for policy-makers. In this section, the authors are slightly more sensitive to immigrants as research participants by focusing on distinctions between types of immigrants. They conclude the book with lessons learned from their pilot that they state can be applied to a national survey. However, most suggestions are about access and strategies of reaching immigrant populations and focus less on empowering the participants or asking for their assistance in creating the study or specifically the survey.

Overall, this study does not center on the potential vulnerabilities of immigrant populations. It is what we term "non-concerned" methodology of immigrant research. It takes no account of vulnerabilities, it does not have the interest of immigrants as a focus in design, it does not encourage immigrant participation in design or distribution of results, and it does not allow for immigrants to form their own responses but rather limits their responses to questions based on the ideas of researchers alone. This example demonstrates the methodological concerns that can arise when vulnerability is not addressed as a central focus of design. We encourage readers to introduce special measures when researching immigrants that address immigrants' concerns and answer questions participants also deem valuable.

Conclusion

Immigration research with human participants, particularly unauthorized immigrants, presents an enhanced possibility for exploitation of a vulnerable research population. Because of this, care must be taken in both research design and methodology, as well as in the distribution of research findings. By examining the historical development of vulnerable groups in research, we arrived at a definition of vulnerability that includes any person or groups who can be easily taken advantage of due to disparate power relations in the context of research. We then examined seven ways that immigrants, particularly unauthorized immigrants, are especially vulnerable in society and thus in research practices. The compounding factors of racial/ethnic group membership, immigrant/citizenship status, stigmatized position in society, socioeconomic status, educational and language disadvantages, social and cultural exclusion and isolation, and psychological and emotional duress require that special attention be focused on research designs and methodologies when studying immigrants. Examination of different methodological approaches, including liberation anthropology, feminism, critical race theory, community-based participatory research, and empowerment evaluation, provide helpful directions for researchers to begin examining how they can better account for and address the vulnerability of immigrants in their research designs. We also discussed the need for researchers to consider the potential political and social impacts of their research, particularly in times when immigration is a hot political issue.

Best research practices challenge scholars to pay close attention to all of the issues identified in this chapter when working with human participants, particularly vulnerable populations. By providing a definition of vulnerability dependent on disparate power, we examined the dilemmas of and potential solutions to accounting for vulnerability in order to receive and extend desired benefits to both researcher and researched, specifically to highly vulnerable immigrant communities, particularly unauthorized immigrants.

Note

1. Even today, the University of Arizona's website on human subjects research makes reference to this case as justification for federal regulations on human participants in research: "Our process for protecting human research subjects reflects federal regulations developed in response to such cases as the Public Health Service syphilis study and the U.S. government radiation experiments" (Human Subjects Research and IRB, 2010).

References

Bask, Miia. 2005. Welfare Problems and Social Exclusion among Immigrants in Sweden. *European Sociological Review* 21(1): 73–89.

Beauchamp, Tom L., Ruth R. Faden, R. Jay Wallace, Jr., and LeRoy Walters. 1982. *Ethical Issues in Social Science Research*. Baltimore: Johns Hopkins University Press.

Boswell, Christina. 2009. *The Political Uses of Expert Knowledge: Immigration Policy and Social Research*. Cambridge, UK: Cambridge University Press.

Cahan, Sorel, Daniel Davis, and Rachel Staub. 2001. Age at Immigration and Scholastic Achievement in School-Age Children: Is There a Vulnerable Age? *International Migration Review* 35(2): 587–595.

Chapkis, Wendy. 2003. Trafficking, Migration, and the Law: Protecting Innocents, Punishing Immigrants. *Gender and Society* 17(6): 923–937.

DaVanzo, Julie, Jennifer Hawes-Dawson, R. Burciaga Valdez, and Georges Vernez. 1994. *Surveying Immigrant Communities: Policy Imperatives and Technical Challenges*. Santa Monica, CA: Rand.

Delgado, Richard, and Jean Stefancic. 2001. *Critical Race Theory: An Introduction*. New York: New York University Press.

Fan, Shie-Wei. 1997. Immigration Law and the Promise of Critical Race Theory: Opening the Academy to the Voices of Aliens and Immigrants. *Columbia Law Review* 97(4): 1202–1240.

Fetterman, David M., and Abraham Wandersman. 2005. *Empowerment Evaluation Principles in Practice*. New York: The Guilford Press.

Foner, Nancy, Rubén G. Rumbaut, and Steven J. Gold. 2000. *Immigration Research for a New Century: Multidisciplinary Perspectives*. New York: Russell Sage Foundation.

Hamnett, Michael P. 1984. *Ethics, Politics, and International Social Science Research: From Critique to Praxis*. Honolulu: University of Hawaii Press.

Hirsch, Jennifer S. 2003. Anthropologists, Migrants, and Health Research: Confronting Cultural Appropriateness. In *American Arrivals: Anthropology Engages the New Immigration*. Nancy Foner, ed. Pp. 229–258. Santa Fe, NM: School of American Research Press.

International Conference on Harmonisation of Technical Requirements for Registration of Pharmaceuticals for Human Use. 2010a ICH Guidelines for Good Clinical Practice, Section E6. http://www.ich.org/cache/html/250-272-1.html, accessed January 20, 2010.

———. 2010b. History and Future of ICH. http://www.ich.org/cache/compo/276-254-1.html, accessed February 11, 2010.

Jones, Frank E. 1987. Age at Immigration and Education: Further Explorations. *International Migration Review* 21(1): 70–85.

Jones-Correa, Michael. 1998. Different Paths: Gender, Immigration and Political Participation. *International Migration Review* 32(2): 326–349.

Jonsen, Albert R. 1999. *A Short History of Medical Ethics*. New York: Oxford University Press.

Keogan, Kevin. 2002. A Sense of Place: The Politics of Immigration and the Symbolic Construction of Identity in Southern California and the New York Metropolitan Area. *Sociological Forum* 17(2): 223–253.

Ma, Grace Xueqin, and George Henderson, eds. 1999. *Rethinking Ethnicity and Health Care: A Sociocultural Perspective*. Springfield, IL: C.C. Thomas.

Marín, Gerardo, and Barbara VanOss Marín. 1991. *Research with Hispanic Populations*. Applied Social Research Methods Series 23. Newbury Park: Sage Publications.

McNeil, Donald G., Jr. 2010. U.S. Apologizes for Syphilis Tests in Guatemala. *The New York Times*, October 2, A1.

Merino, Catherine L. 1988. Compromising Immigration Reform: The Creation of a Vulnerable Subclass. *The Yale Law Journal* 98(2): 409–426.

Narayan, Uma. 1995. Male-Order Brides: Immigrant Women, Domestic Violence and Immigration Law. *Feminist Ethics and Social Policy* 10(1): 104–119.

National Institute of Health: Office of Human Subjects Research. 1945. Nuremburg Code. http://ohsr.od.nih.gov/guidelines/nuremberg.html, accessed January 15, 2010.

———. 1964. Declaration of Helsinki. http://ohsr.od.nih.gov/guidelines/helsinki.html, accessed January 20, 2010.

———. 1979. Belmont Report. http://ohsr.od.nih.gov/guidelines/belmont.html, accessed January 20, 2010.

Ornelas, India J., Krista M. Perreira, Linda Beeber, and Lauren Maxwell. 2009. Challenges and Strategies to Maintaining Emotional Health: Qualitative Perspectives of Mexican Immigrant Mothers. *Journal of Family Issues* 30: 1556–1575.

Palmer, John L., Timothy Smeeding, and Barbara Boyle Torrey, eds. 1988. *The Vulnerable*. Washington, D.C.: Urban Institute Press.

Pew Hispanic Center. 2009. Statistical Portrait of the Foreign-Born Population in the United States. http://pewhispanic.org/factsheets/factsheet.php?FactsheetID=69, accessed February 20, 2011.

Renzetti, Claire M., and Raymond M. Lee, eds. 1993. *Researching Sensitive Topics.* London: Sage.

RESPECT Project. 2004. *An EU Code of Ethics for Socio-Economic Research.* http://www.respectproject.org/ethics/412ethics.pdf, accessed January 20, 2010.

Solórzano, Daniel G., and Tara J. Yosso. 2002. Critical Race Methodology: Counter-Storytelling as an Analytical Framework for Education Research. *Qualitative Inquiry* 8(1): 23–44.

Speed, Shannon. 2006. At the Crossroads of Human Rights and Anthropology: Toward a Critically Engaged Activist Research. *American Anthropologist* 108(1): 66–76.

University of Arizona Office for the Responsible Conduct of Research. 2010a. Human Subjects Research and IRB. http://orcr.vpr.arizona.edu/irb, accessed February 11, 2010.

———. 2010b. Research Participant. http://orcr.vpr.arizona.edu/irb/research_partici pant, accessed February 11, 2010.

U.S. Agency for Healthcare Research and Quality. 2004. *Community-Based Participatory Research: Assessing the Evidence.* Evidence Report/Technology Assessment no. 99. http://purl.access.gpo.gov/GPO/LPS54051, accessed January 29, 2010.

U.S. Department of Health and Human Services: U.S. Food and Drug Administration 2009 Code of Federal Regulations, Title 21. http://www.accessdata.fda.gov/scripts /cdrh/cfdocs/cfcfr/CFRSearch.cfm?fr=56.111, accessed January 20, 2010.

Van der Velde, Jeannette, Deanna L. Williamson, and Linda D. Ogilvie. 2009. Participatory Action Research: Practical Strategies for Actively Engaging and Maintaining Participation in Immigrant and Refugee Communities. *Qualitative Health Research* 19(9): 1293–1302.

Van Liempt, Ilse, and Veronika Bilger. 2009. *The Ethics of Migration Research Methodology: Dealing with Vulnerable Immigrants.* Portland: Sussex Academic Press.

Volk, Lucia. 2009. "Kull wahad la haalu": Feelings of Isolation and Distress among Yemeni Immigrant Women in San Francisco's Tenderloin. *Medical Anthropology Quarterly* 23(4): 397–416.

Wood, William B. 1994. Forced Migration: Local Conflicts and International Dilemmas. *Annals of the Association of American Geographers* 84(4): 607–634.

Yoshikawa, H., E. B. Godfrey, and A. C. Rivera. 2008. Access to Institutional Resources as a Measure of Social Exclusion: Relations with Family Process and Cognitive Development in the Context of Immigration. *New Directions for Child and Adolescent Development* 121: 63–86.

CHAPTER TWO

The Good, the Bad, and the Ugly

Border Research Collaboration

Kathleen Staudt

"The ethical mind ponders the nature of one's work and the needs and desires of the society in which one lives. This mind conceptualizes how workers can serve purposes beyond self-interest and how citizens can work unselfishly to improve the lot of all. The ethical mind then acts on the basis of these analyses" (Gardiner 2006: 3).

With these words, Harvard psychologist and inventor of multiple intelligences approaches Howard Gardiner provides a guidepost to cultivate broad uses of the mind. Grounded in and for borderland societies and their binational citizens and residents, his remarks can inspire scholars, students, and activists in meaningful work to generate knowledge and social justice. Heretofore, an unexplored vacuum has existed in the writing about border research ethics, methods, and collaboration—a vacuum this volume is intended to fill. In this chapter, I analyze border research collaboration in the U.S.–Mexico borderlands and the multiple borderlines of identity, nationality, organizational affiliation, and class in which partnerships can and should occur.

This chapter is divided into six parts. I begin with brief discussion of the terms collaboration, research, and borders in their rich and multiple forms. Then I provide some background on my own specialized training, after which I engaged in research and activism at the border that involved crossing multiple borders. After that, I outline the cross-border organizing framework put forth in my collaborative research with Irasema Coronado (2002), followed with an update and expansion that focuses on border research collaboration and its special challenges and opportunities. Among some of the challenges, I would include university bureaucracies and their complex procedures and agendas. Finally, after setting forth the mythical ideal for border research collaboration, I lay out the inspiration for the title of this chapter, brief vignettes of the good, the bad, and the ugly in border research collaboration. My closing remarks address the lessons that can be drawn to advance border research collaboration.

"Good" collaboration, I argue in this chapter, occurs across the borderlines of nation-state, identity, and institutions—among campus and community-based organizations (CBOs). People with shared interests meet face to face to develop relationships of trust and interact with respect and directness; labor and funding for such work should be distributed fairly and equitably. The collaboration can be time consuming and labor intensive, but such commitments are well worth it for the knowledge, value, and action gained to advance mutual self-interests and community and/or public interests. "Bad" collaboration is characterized by tension, mistrust, and unarticulated concerns regarding research instruments and interpretation. "Ugly" collaboration breaks down into tension over power and control; it can become politicized and polarized, and result in lower quality or less credible findings (if results are even written and published at all). Alas, too often the real tragedy involves non-collaboration: missed opportunities to collaborate, given people's anxieties about possible risks and/or reluctance to invest the time and labor to collaborate.

Conceptualizing Collaboration, Research, and Multiple Borders

Let me start with the meanings of terms I use. Although *collaboration* is a word with both positive and negative connotations, here I view research collaboration as the sharing of ideas, methods, talents, and work in order to analyze and publish research findings that connect with action and change, including policy change. Collaborative research enriches both process and outcome, given the multiple eyes, brains, hearts, and experiences that can be dedicated to research problems and questions.

By *research*, I mean the methodical application of study, data collection, analysis, and interpretation of particular problems and questions. The reference to data is inclusive, ranging from observation to surveys, interviews, and statistical analyses of databases to embrace mixed methods, triangulation, and both qualitative and quantitative approaches.

The term *border* requires multiple paragraphs. Typically, we view borders as lines that separate sovereign nations and their people in geographic space, such as the Mexico–U.S. border, the Guatemala–Mexico border, and so on. Oscar Martínez offers a four-fold typology in which to explain the hundreds of international borders worldwide: alienated, coexistent, interdependent, and integrated (1994). Martínez views the U.S.–Mexico border as interdependent, given the extensive crossing of family, friends, workers, and shoppers in a context of hierarchy and hegemony between two countries of different wealth and power. Then and now, the income inequalities are large and obscene, whether analyzed in GDP per capita or in minimum-wage terms: a ratio of 5–10:1 (Staudt 1998: chapter 3; 2009). Since the 1996 U.S. immigration reform, the tragedy of 9/11 (September 11, 2001), media-inspired xenophobia, and militarization of the border thereafter, the U.S.–Mexico border seems almost like an alienated border. Yet Mexico and the United States are not at war; rather, both nations (and Canada) are top trading partners.

From Gloria Anzaldúa (1987) and subsequent border theorists, we can also view the borderlands as a special space, a hybridized space of crossing and scars, and multiple languages and cultures. In that space, over 14 million people live (2000 census figures) approximately 25 miles north and south of the line (Staudt and Coronado 2002: chapter 1). For the border researchers among us, it is important to reflect on the border spaces as unique spaces, as bellwethers of national mainstreams, or some of both.

Borders can also refer to people, based on their identities. Martínez identifies those people who live in the borderlands as borderlanders, *fronterizos*, and *fronterizas*. Among them, he differentiates between "nationals" and "transnationals," with the latter identifying with and working with people on both sides of the border (1994). Thus he parts ways with the typical census-labeled breakdown: Hispanic, White, and Black (African American). I have found his distinctions useful in my own work, especially in efforts to collaborate. I seek borderlanders or people open to becoming *fronterizos and fronterizas*, especially for research in the borderlands. The mainstream identities imposed upon people and/or claimed by people are lacking. At the center point of the U.S.–Mexico border, El Paso–Ciudad Juárez, even the cultural-political identities of Latino and Chicano (Latina and Chicana) are claimed less than Mexican/Mexicano/Mexicana or Mexican American and Anglo.

Readers might wonder about the relationship between the border research collaboration I analyze here and the decades-old variations of what is variously called community-based participatory research, community-based research (CBR), participatory action research, action research, and/or even popular education, Paulo Freire style (which Freire writes about in *Pedagogy of the Oppressed*). Rather than undergo a lengthy literature review, I would cite Stoecker (2005) and his useful website and listserv, which contain papers and syllabi on CBR. In the last decade, some U.S. government agencies, especially in health, urban, and housing research in their request for proposal (RFP) grant opportunities, require that scholars build community-based participatory research in proposals for several reasons: to deepen and spread expertise, to generate constituencies and stakeholders who connect research and action, and to increase cooperation with subjects, among other reasons. What sets this broad work apart for my analysis in this chapter is the binational space and location of research analyzed herein, which necessarily complicates CBR and adds nationality, sovereignty, and—in the case of the U.S.–Mexico border region—extreme income inequalities to the collaboration equation.

Scholarly and Activist Border Crossings

For the sake of full transparency, this section outlines the foundations on which my border research experience grew. Born and raised with working-class heritage in the industrial Midwest, I joined the Peace Corps (Philippines) and then moved through higher education amid the activism of the late 1960s and early 1970s in my first academic love, political science. During graduate school at the University of Wisconsin, only the faculty members in international development, comparative politics (those who study politics outside the United States), and the lone political anthropologist valued interdisciplinary research; the majority among 40 faculty did not. At the margins of this male-dominated discipline, I earned my PhD after dissertation research in Kenya at a time when women represented only 13 percent of all political science PhDs in the United States. I was socialized, or perhaps brainwashed is the better word, into thinking that sole authorship was the only publication mode of value. My positivist training made me wary of involvement and/or activism for how it might "taint" the results. Soon, I learned differently, through active experience where my knowledge was deeper than that of colleagues sitting in front of their computers analyzing databases constructed in distant cities and locales.

For 30 years, I taught at the University of Texas–El Paso (UTEP), situated about a quarter mile from the border and next door to Ciudad Juárez, and home to a majority of Mexican-heritage students. This was an ideal location for me: an international border region, where the global meets the local with many opportunities for comparative and collaborative work.

I am an adopted, rather than native-born, *fronteriza*. After receiving tenure, a liberating experience for collaboration, I coauthored research and publication in articles and books, but it was my transition to border studies that moved me toward the collaborative approach and offered opportunities to work with multiple eyes, minds, and complementary skill sets in the research process. I became involved in a series of long-term, multiyear projects with other faculty members and students that included *Free Trade? Informal Economies at the U.S.–Mexico Border* (1998); *The U.S.–Mexico Border: Transcending Divisions, Contesting Identities* (1998), with sociologist David Spener; *Fronteras No Más: Toward Social Justice at the U.S.–Mexico Border* (1998), with Irasema Coronado; *Pledging Allegiance: Learning Nationalism at the El Paso–Juárez Border* (2003), with educational anthropologist Susan Rippberger; and *Human Rights along the U.S.–Mexico Border: Gendered Violence and Insecurity* (2009), with Tony Payan. My 2008 book *Violence and Activism at the U.S.–Mexico Border: Gender, Fear, and Everyday Life in Ciudad Juárez*, involved collaborative research through grant proposals and implementation, with most of the resources going to a large non-governmental organization (NGO) in Ciudad Juárez.

My most recent edited collection, *Cities and Citizenship at the U.S.–Mexico Border: The Paso del Norte Metropolitan Region*, involves a formal collaboration with El Colegio de la Frontera Norte–Ciudad Juárez, in particular with two scholars there (sociologist Julia Monárrez Fregoso and urban planner César Fuentes), and a cross-border group of colleagues (2010). Alejandro Lugo wrote about the book's collaborative process for the back cover, from which I quote:

> This groundbreaking interdisciplinary edited collection embodies the social commitment and the kind of scholarly collaboration deeply indispensable, both within and across nation-states, to more effectively confront the socio-political, cultural, and policy-making challenges associated with global border regions, such as Paso del Norte, around the world.

Ultimately, this fascinating volume is the extraordinary result of a rare and rigorous collective dialogue among and between Mexico- and U.S.-based scholars, all of whom not only have studied the region for years, but have also experienced, either directly or indirectly, the impact of twenty-first century border life in its multiple dimensions: from the absent state to the empty curriculum, from organized crime to disorganized urban planning and border violence, from the triumphs of global capital to local labor and community struggles.

My involvement in community-based organizations (CBOs) and non-profit organizations truly deepened my knowledge of and experience in collaboration. Training with the Alinsky-style Industrial Areas Foundation (IAF) allowed me to "name" processes and gave me the language to clarify the principles and strategies for collaboration (see Orr 2007). I acknowledge these principles here: recognition of mutual or multiple "self-interests"; directness; "one on one" face-to-face meetings; relationality (that is, building relationships of trust); engagement; and the value of diverse leaders and talents in what is essentially a collaborative process. For the IAF and many CBOs, power relations are at center stage, and powerlessness is like poverty in the economy.

Cross-Border Organizing: The Foundational Model

In the book *Fronteras No Más*, Irasema Coronado and I analyzed the first-ever attempt to understand cross-border organizing in the U.S.–Mexico borderlands. We chose the title for the various ways it could be interpreted: No more borders (or: borders, no more—it's only a border). We began by acknowledging people's shared interests in opportunities, living wages, human rights, and clean water and air, on whichever side of the international border they lived. Despite these shared, common interests, people reside in two sovereign countries, with their own political representatives and infrastructure, made complex by two variations of federalism in their governments. Moreover, power relations and access to resources tend to be unequal.

Coronado and I identified conditions under which cross-border organizing became potentially successful in several issue areas: environment, business and labor, and human rights. We began with a discussion of "personalism" in border relationships, including its possible causes, benefits, and drawbacks. We also analyzed the importance of binational "institutional shrouds," such as formal agreements that have the potential to legitimize, facilitate, and/or fund collaboration and cooperation (*or* to symbolize action where none really exists). We chose the word "shroud" for its double meanings: A shroud can be protective support or it can be a funeral covering. Coronado and I also acknowledged various factors that hinder cross-border organizing, cooperation, and collaboration.

Below is a visual that illustrates factors that facilitate and hinder cross-border collaboration.

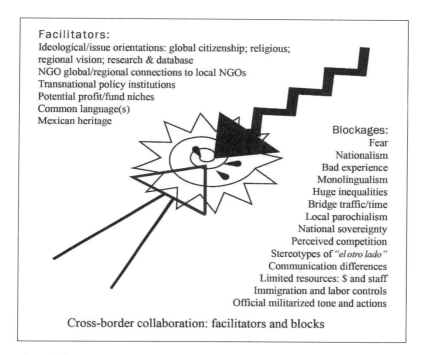

Facilitators:
Ideological/issue orientations: global citizenship; religious; regional vision; research & database
NGO global/regional connections to local NGOs
Transnational policy institutions
Potential profit/fund niches
Common language(s)
Mexican heritage

Blockages:
Fear
Nationalism
Bad experience
Monolingualism
Huge inequalities
Bridge traffic/time
Local parochialism
National sovereignty
Perceived competition
Stereotypes of *"el otro lado"*
Communication differences
Limited resources: $ and staff
Immigration and labor controls
Official militarized tone and actions

Cross-border collaboration: facilitators and blocks

Figure 2.1

As can readily be seen, many factors facilitate cross-border collaboration, from shared language and cultural heritage to idea-based shared interests. But more factors block such collaboration, from such mundane issues as the time it takes for an hour-long meeting across the border turning into a lengthy half-day intimidating experience going through ports of entry and bureaucratic surveillance, to communication differences, such as the digital divide in Internet and email. Once as much stereotyping as fear, now there is genuine fear whether one goes north or south, given the militarization of the border, xenophobia, and Ciudad Juárez's infamy as a site with a high murder rate, 2008–2012.

Predecessors and Complex Additions
to the FNS Model

With this chapter's interest in border research collaboration in mind, let us now go beyond *Fronteras No Más* to examine new and different complications associated with universities, higher education funding, and the university-CBO interface. Researchers must contend with university bureaucracies, in particular their research and grant centers (what at UTEP we call the Office of Research and Sponsored Projects); the institutional review boards (IRBs) for human subjects research clearance; memoranda of understanding (MOUs); and *convenios*, or inter-institutional paper agreements that, in my mind, only come alive with people and collaborative experiences.

Public university ORSP-type offices, generously staffed, exist to facilitate external grant funding in an era of declining state subsidies from state legislatures. The success of such offices is measured in annual terms, with hard numeric indicators and little regard for long-term relationships of trust. Universities sometimes compete with one another for funding; administrators are evaluated in terms of funding amounts generated, particularly awards with high "indirect costs" built into budgets, which form precious discretionary resources in higher education. Alas, more and more administrators seem to evaluate faculty members in dollar terms. On a visit to the ORSP director's office, I was surprised to see a huge TV screen flash my whole history of attempted grants and grants awarded: my primary "worth" and value listed on the screen.

My caution here is linked to the sometimes delicate, precarious, and potentially sensitive long-term relationships with colleagues in Mexico. When I first arrived at the border in the late 1970s, Mexican colleagues expressed reasonable suspicions about "hidden agendas" and potential co-optation: who funded research, why, and for what ultimate aims? In the interim, gradually people opened up to the idea of fair collaboration. However, funding patterns from the U.S. federal government have shifted since 9/11. The U.S. Departments of Homeland Security and of Defense spread new money around to Southwestern universities for national security and intelligence (surveillance) programs, new courses, and curricular certificates in the name of cultural and linguistic diversity for government recruitment and the practicalities of getting buy-in from Southwestern congressional representatives. Remembering President Eisenhower's warning about the military-industrial complex, Payan, Dunn, and I view these new monies as part of the "Border Security Industrial Complex," or BSIC (2009). Dare we refer to these resources as dirty and/or tainted money? It is incumbent upon us to think through funding sources and consequences for more or less accurate interpretations made in contexts of nationalism and (historically violated) sovereignty.

The institutional review board process, designed to protect human subjects, seems as much oriented to protecting the university. The process emerged from health and medical research, after outrageous abuses; these were followed by the requirement of informed consent for clinical trials. As documented in other chapters of this volume, social science and ethnographic research with vulnerable communities often operates with different paradigms. Some IRB procedures appear to sabotage such research.

Many university leaders build risk-avoidant institutional cultures, given the ever-present concerns about offending potential funders and donors, many of whom come from regional economic establishments. If the integrity of an independent IRB process is not protected, there is danger that controversial research projects will be censored with the risk-avoidant fund-raising agendas in mind.

Still other problems exist with health science–origin IRB procedures. I have submitted many IRBs, a few of them returned as "revise and resubmits" because reviewers operated out of positivist, deductive, and hypothesis-testing models, rather than out of grounded, inductive approaches. Language issues can also be problematic and time consuming. In the complicated research with an NGO in Ciudad Juárez that I referred to earlier on violence and activism (2008), the IRB reviewers returned the lengthy Spanish-language survey for the Spanish-speaking respondents asking for an English translation for their review. The complex translation into English was only used for the English-only reviewers.

IRB procedures, for better or worse, are only a first step in ethical border research and collaboration. See the far more comprehensive Code of Personal Ethics for Border Research in English reprinted at the end of this volume.

Beyond the model in *Fronteras No Más*, this section has addressed a host of new, complex factors that complicate border research collaboration. Each institution and organization has its own organizational cultural features to diagnose in order that collaboration move forward. I include here the CBOs that have ideological, turf, and visibility agendas that may part ways with the long-term agendas of advancing knowledge through analysis and publication. We cannot romanticize organizations just because they work in the community and operate with less bureaucracy, volunteers, and clean money. And these entities are not monolithic, but rather spaces of conflict, negotiation, and potential settlements in which there is continuous turnover of personnel. All this adds time and labor to the research process. In a multi-institutional and organizational collaboration, the challenges are the stuff of Rube Goldberg cartoons with their coordination nightmares (http://www.rubegoldberg.com/).

The Vignettes: The Mythical Ideal versus the Good, Bad, and Ugly

Before outlining good, bad, and ugly vignettes, let us begin with the mythical ideal of what border research collaboration might look like. The face-to-face conversations begin with common interests in advancing knowledge and action through publications; policy or budgetary change; and empowering visibility for those who seek such visibility, including from fair media attention. There is potential for changing power relations. Resources are plentiful and divided fairly and equitably, whatever side of the border on which one works and lives. The money is clean, with no long-term taint or surveillance due to origins in the military or border security establishments. The methodology involves mixed methods, with credible, in-depth documentation that satisfies multiple kinds of readers and users of the knowledge. The IRB process is uncensored and quickly clears the way for work to begin. Voices and procedures are developed in a democratic way, and non-burdensome but appropriate memoranda of understandings (MOUs) or formal agreements are signed as necessary. People trust one another and know what to expect at all stages of the project timeline. There is room and space for negotiation over details that can never be fully anticipated ahead of time. Research, after all, is a complex series of major and minor decisions made in shifting contexts.

The mythical ideal is what it is: a probable myth. Let us now reverse good, bad, and ugly, first by turning to some ugly vignettes. These are based on conversations that took place in spring 2010, but with my ethical choice to avoid using names.

Vignette No. 1. In this ugly vignette, all appropriate steps appeared to have been taken prior to the research and data collection. The health science researcher and native Spanish speaker obtained research clearance from both her university and from Mexico City, in the logical secretariat, as suggested and cleared by her research and grant office at the university. She established a local stakeholder advisory committee, a *junta colectiva*, at the local level, with all relevant stakeholders—individuals and organizations. They met periodically to discuss the project.

Mexico is a multiparty, federal system of government, with authority divided across government levels, from the national (Mexico City) to the state and municipal levels. State and municipal government authorities became furious that clearance had not been obtained from them as well. To make matters worse, it was an election year, so partisan politics and competition infused the headline-driven process and undermined it even further. The researcher faced public accusations of collecting samples of controversial and symbolic substances: lead, blood, etc. She was also accused of being a traitor to her Mexican heritage when results contained controversial findings. The stakeholder group caved in to pressure, remaining silent and offering no support or corroboration of the partnership.

Controversy died down once the university president stepped in. Fortunately, the researcher had tenure and a strong funding and research profile.

Vignette No. 2. Sex work and sexually transmitted infections (STIs) generate considerable research interest at the border. Data collection for this research had proceeded with normal agreement and clearance processes. A U.S. state with a regional health body commissioned research and obtained clearance from the Mexican government. The research had intriguing elements, with *promotoras* (health outreach workers) collecting data via pinprick samples to determine whether sex workers carried HIV, herpes, and/or syphilis. A special feature of this research involved the potential for follow up and treatment for those with infections.

Years later, a researcher sought access to the database of the heretofore buried, unused, and unpublished data. Once access was gained through the U.S. state agency, the researcher noticed poorly worded questions throughout the instrument, inconsistencies, and documentation that made follow up impossible for at least a quarter of the sample and probably more. However, the pinprick samples did provide concrete documentation of STI incidence levels among the sample at one point in time. When Mexican authorities discovered that a researcher was analyzing the database, they raised critical questions: Why was access allowed? Why are STIs a priority and not environmental health issues? They insisted on interpreting and publishing findings first. The researcher proceeded.

Multiple tragedies are to be found in this project, the first of which includes the workers' and initial researchers' failures to establish the action component of the research (possibly a feature that made the project appealing to those who decided, among the usual competitive proposals, to fund the project). The burial rather than publication of data is all too common in a variety of fields. Finally, stakeholders differed over research priorities; this issue is always contentious but sometimes based on distant funders' agencies and money rather than borderlanders' agendas.

Vignette No. 3. In this good, or good-enough, collaboration, we find funded research that was proposed and implemented in equitable and collaborative ways. In fact, as proposed, the NGO in Mexico justifiably received most of the resources because of the labor-intensive research-action project. Researchers obtained IRB approvals from institutions on both sides of the border, with the provision that a brochure be provided to participants—a reasonable requirement that was implemented.

In the course of finalizing details about the instrument, the NGO director was reluctant to retain questions about *maquiladoras*, the export-processing factories, because of concerns about offending these firms where the NGO provides workshops and enjoys access. The research collaborators had periodic meetings about the everyday details as the project moved forward. Fortunately, the researcher had allies in the collaborator meetings who argued persuasively for the continued inclusion of such questions.

Later in the project, with data entry of complex questionnaires that the NGO subcontracted to another firm, the researcher noticed some inconsistencies and sought copies of the voluminous questionnaires. The NGO resisted this move, raising control issues, but again, with space for negotiation, the potential conflict was handled with photocopies of the questionnaires for collaborators on both sides of the border. Ultimately, the researcher decided to reenter all the data, a time-consuming effort but one that assured confidence in the laborious data-analysis process.

The border research collaboration was complex, with awkward moments, but time and space existed to negotiate concerns and differences. Full documentation existed for all agreements and money matters. In the end, various publications and presentations emerged from the research, with prospects for action. However, the NGO director seemed to lose interest in the project once the funding was over, reducing prospects for sustained NGO outreach on the research findings. However, a professional staff member in the NGO had continued interest in the project and supported the researcher's presentations at several events in Mexico. Although final reports to the funder and in media outlets could be read in Spanish, the research findings emerged in English-language publications. A huge vacuum exists in translating and publishing findings of border research collaboration into both Spanish and English.

Vignette No. 4. Another good vignette illustrates the utility of a formal collaboration with expectations fully developed at the outset. A Mexico-based think tank advertised a part-time visiting researcher position in order to collaborate on binational research to be published in English. Alas, much fine research in Spanish is not fully read or appreciated among the English-language U.S. student and academic audiences. The application required that prospective candidates outline potential research agendas. Colleagues at the think tank interviewed candidates and made their choice. A token stipend was made available to the selected researcher.

As a government agency, the think tank was required to implement many work-permit procedures. The birth certificate, including its certification as authentic by a U.S. state, and all education transcripts had to be translated by government-certified translators, also an expensive proposition. The entire process took at least six months, but the researcher gained insight into *tramitología* (procedure-ology) and learned lessons about the comparable frustrations that workers from Mexico also face in gaining permission to work in the United States.

A fine process and outcome emerged from this border research collaboration, with a forthcoming edited collection and coeditors who developed not only relationships of trust but firm friendships, given their similar workaholic orientations; efficient e-mail communication (after relationships had developed); and commitment to the region. The three coeditors maintain prolific publication agendas, with the Mexican scholars operating in a highly incentivized national research system under CONACYT (National Council of Science and Technology), with recognition for Level I researchers who publish prolifically. Although English-language publications are valued in CONACYT, without additional funding the book may never be published in Spanish—a loss to Spanish-speaking students, faculty members, and researchers.

The four vignettes analyzed illustrate various conditions under which good or good-enough border research collaboration can be achieved. And the bad or ugly vignettes illustrate what to avoid. Yet ugly partisan and nationalistic tension can emerge, even when researchers plan for and anticipate potential problems, as in the case of Vignette No. 1.

Remembering *Fronteras No Más*, the vignettes show that good or good-enough collaboration operated with equity and power balance among participants. Such balance did not eliminate awkward moments and delays, but participants planned for time and space to address issues as the project moved forward, given the invariable numerous decisions that must be made with ongoing research. All partners in the good cases recognized their self-interests and their mutual, overlapping interests. NGOs are not necessarily interested in academic publications, although their name and visibility in publications can create future advantages. However, many NGOs require constant revenue generation to survive and potentially grow their agendas and visibility. Good cross-border research also involves people who anticipate the time, patience, and tolerance required for bureaucratic hassles, whether crossing the ports of entry after waiting in long lines or seeking multiple IRBs and work permits.

Closing Reflections and Lessons Learned

In this chapter, I have conceptualized research, collaboration, and the multiple meanings of borders. Borders draw lines between people and may result in long-felt "scars" (in Andalzúa's terms), but borders can be crossed for fruitful and ethical research agendas that advance knowledge and stimulate action and policy change. It is a great tragedy when people do not seek opportunities to collaborate across borders, thereby maximizing talent, skill, perspectives, and experiences.

The chapter took the *Fronteras No Más* model as a starting point, examining factors that facilitate and hinder cross-border organizing and collaboration. I then built on this model to analyze the complex challenges of working in university bureaucracies with their revenue-generating, risk-avoidant imperatives—features that can sabotage or censor comprehensive research with populations in peril. Several vignettes illustrated how the minimalist and formalist university and government approaches may not be enough to generate fully collaborative research models. Vignette No. 2 showed the tragedy of an unfulfilled, sloppy project that failed to deliver intended results to human subjects or even publish findings after years of burial in bureaucracy. From that, we see the importance of involving borderlanders who care enough and who empathize with their communities to produce quality findings and action.

From this chapter, we learn some broad lessons about border research collaboration. First, some common interests among collaborators are necessary, though the overlap does not have to be 100 percent identical. Second, we see that good research begins with face-to-face relationships of trust among "binational" people (in Martínez's terms) who transcend borderlines. Third, we can appreciate the importance of creating space and developing allies to "agree to disagree" about the constant, daily decisions in research implementation so that decisions and solutions can be negotiated. Fourth, the vignettes show the importance of seeking approval, but remind us that things can still get misinterpreted, politicized, and ugly. Of course, this can also happen in sole-authored, noncollaborative research far from borders. All nontenured researchers should exercise care, perhaps collaborating with those who can manage risk most optimally. But it is worthwhile to pay attention to political contexts. And finally, for complex partnerships, partners should formalize and document issues relating to money and expectations.

For future directions, borderlanders and mainstreamers should be developing strategies to develop and support border research collaboration. Among them, I would emphasize clearinghouses and translation sites to spread knowledge and action among nonbilingual people. Few formal opportunities exist, save the Border Fulbright, Colegio de la Frontera Norte Visiting Researcher, and North American Mobility programs, among others. Thankfully, the University of Arizona has taken leadership in its conferences on Border Research Ethics and Methods.

Despite analysis of tensions, especially in the ugly vignettes, potential border research collaborators should realize that practice and experience are effective ways to gain prospects for success. Practice may not "make perfect," but it surely enhances skill, learning, research knowledge, and action toward social justice at and around borders.

References

Anzaldúa, Gloria. 1987. *Borderlands/La Frontera: The New Mestiza*. San Francisco: Spinsters/Aunt Lute Press.

Gardiner, Howard. 2006. *Five Minds for the Future*. Boston: Harvard Business School Press.

Martínez, Oscar. 1994. *Border People*. Tucson: University of Arizona Press.

Orr, Marion, ed. 2007. *Transforming the City: Community Organizing and the Challenge of Change*. Lawrence: University Press of Kansas.

Staudt, Kathleen. 1998. *Free Trade? Informal Economies at the U.S.–Mexico Border*. Philadelphia: Temple University Press.

———. 2008. *Violence and Activism at the Border: Gender, Fear, and Everyday Life in Ciudad Juárez*. Austin: University of Texas Press.

———. 2009. "Violence at the Border: Broadening the Discourse to Include Feminism, Human Security, and Deeper Democracy." In K. Staudt, T. Payan, and Z. A. Kruszewski, eds. *Human Rights along the U.S.–Mexico Border: Gendered Violence and Insecurity*. Pp. 1–29. Tucson: University of Arizona Press.

Staudt, Kathleen, and Irasema Coronado. 2002. *Fronteras No Más: Toward Social Justice at the U.S.–Mexico Border*. New York: Palgrave USA.

Staudt, Kathleen, César Fuentes, and Julia Monárrez Fragoso, eds. 2010. *Cities and Citizenship at the U.S.–Mexico Border: The Paso del Norte Metropolitan Region.* New York: Palgrave USA.

Staudt, Kathleen, Tony Payan, and Timothy J. Dunn. 2009. Closing Reflections: Bordering Human Rights, Social Democratic Feminism, and Broad-Based Security. In K. Staudt, T. Payan, and Z. A. Kruszewski, eds. *Human Rights along the U.S.– Mexico Border: Gendered Violence and Insecurity.* Pp. 185–202. Tucson: University of Arizona Press.

Staudt, Kathleen, Tony Payan, and Z. Anthony Kruszewski, eds. 2009. *Human Rights Along the U.S.–Mexico Border: Gendered Violence and Insecurity.* Tucson: University of Arizona Press.

Stoecker, Randy, Moderator. Listserv and Comm-Org: The On-line Conference on Community Organizing. http://comm-org.wisc.edu/.

———. 2005. *Research Methods for Community Change: A Project-Based Approach.* Thousand Oaks, CA: Sage.

CHAPTER THREE

Dilemmas in Immigration Policy Research

Judith Gans

Liberal democrats need to find ways to affirm the genuine value that particular communities have for efforts to realize desirable goals in the world as it is constituted now, but they must do so without denying the dangers of these memberships. The greatest threats come from profound political and psychological tendencies to treat such communities as natural, in ways that seem to legitimate both oppressive internal hierarchies and harsh injustices toward outsiders.

FROM CIVIC IDEALS: CONFLICTING VISIONS OF CITIZENSHIP
IN U.S. HISTORY BY ROGERS SMITH

[W]ith huge differential incomes for equally productive people simply because of where they live; with international and internal migration offering individuals one of the few nearly sure-fire ways to escape poverty, with migrant remittances from rich to poor countries exceeding foreign aid; and with rich countries designing immigration policies to selectively attract the poor world's most talented and motivated people—with all of this, it is obvious that international migration and global labor mobility truly are 'development' issues.

FROM LET THEIR PEOPLE COME: BREAKING THE GRIDLOCK
ON GLOBAL LABOR MOBILITY BY LANT PRITCHETT

Overview

This chapter concerns itself with a specific dilemma in research about the structure of and approach to U.S. immigration policy. This dilemma has to do with how immigration debates get framed, the attendant assumptions about what constitutes a legitimate basis for setting immigration policy, and how this framing shapes research agendas.

Immigration regimes derive from explicitly political processes. Immigration debates are highly charged. Immigration research agendas are inevitably framed so as to address some aspect of those debates. But because immigration debates focus on the interests of those within the political system, they often ignore ethical dimensions of policy that require weighing the interests of immigrants who are outside of the political system against those inside the system.

It doesn't have to be this way. Academic researchers are in a position to step back from immigration debates that focus exclusively on the interests and perspectives of those within the political system and to perform analyses that shed light on the complexities of immigration policy from broader perspectives. By articulating conceptual frameworks that do not derive directly from national political interests, academic researchers can illuminate the consequences of immigration regimes in wealthy countries for human beings in poor countries and bring moral and ethical questions to bear on immigration debates.

Framing

What is the "right" U.S. immigration policy? On what basis should U.S. immigration policy be determined? Which interests are salient? Are there other interests that should be salient? If so, on what basis? In short, what constitutes legitimate grounds for lining up guns at the border to keep people out? Is the *fact* of nationhood sufficient justification? How should competing interests of people within a nation be considered? Do people outside a nation have moral standing when considering a country's immigration policy? Is the use of force to keep migrants out morally legitimate in the face of humanitarian crises? These are not straightforward questions.

The nature of these questions might lead one to consider immigration policy in moral and ethical terms. Deeply embedded in American civic identity are egalitarian liberal democratic values that stress the inalienable right of an individual to "life, liberty, and the pursuit of happiness." These values imply sympathy for immigrants seeking a better life, yet the inscription on the Statue of Liberty aside, such sympathy has waned more than waxed throughout American history. In fact, moral and ethical dimensions of immigration policy—especially with regard to immigrants themselves—are notably absent from most immigration debates. Rarely do immigration debates focus on the plight of poor people seeking to migrate to wealthy countries. In fact, when poverty around the world is discussed, the focus is on solutions such as foreign aid that keep the poor in their home countries.

There is a central asymmetry in discussions of immigration policy. An individual's right to leave a country is generally understood as a basic right and is specifically enumerated in the United Nations Universal Declaration of Human Rights. Attempts by governments to interfere with this right are widely seen as totalitarian acts and illegitimate uses of state power. However, the question of where an individual might go is *not* typically addressed in terms of human rights. There is no widely accepted right to enter a country, and the use of force to keep people out is generally accepted as a legitimate use of state power. Hence the asymmetry with regard to migration: Decisions to emigrate—to leave a country—are made by individuals and embedded in notions of personal agency, freedom, and basic human rights. Decisions to immigrate—to choose one's destination country—are conditioned on the laws of each destination country, which laws the immigrant has little or no say in establishing.

Immigration regimes—the rules governing entry of people into the geographic boundaries of a country—are adopted by nation-states through political processes. In the United States, as in other democracies, this means that the interests and opinions of voters largely drive immigration policy. At their simplest level, these interests are economic, and in fact, much debate is focused on the economic costs and benefits of immigration. A country's citizenship and immigration laws are also a codification of its social and cultural identity—its sense of itself—and social and political interests of voters also shape immigration policy.

Because the economic, social, and political interests of voters in the United States centrally drive immigration policy, debates are about what approach to immigration is "good for America." Immigration policy research inevitably considers the various dimensions of this question. These include the economic impacts of immigrants on wages and economic output; the fiscal impacts of immigrants on social service costs and on (native-born) taxpayers; and the social impacts of immigrants on issues of culture and national identity and what it means to be "American." While these interests are not monolithic within a society—any immigration regime creates winners and losers by privileging some groups at the expense of others—immigration debates focus on the interests of those within the polity and accord little standing to those of the immigrant. This chapter will explore framing dilemmas relating to the economic and fiscal impacts of immigrants.

Framing the Economic Impacts

There is a vast literature on the impacts of immigrant workers on the wages of native-born workers and economic theory is clear as to the nature of those impacts: To the extent that immigrant workers possess skills that are similar to those of native-born workers, increased immigration will unambiguously lower the wages of those native workers whose skills are similar to those of immigrants; to the extent that immigrant workers possess skills that are different from those of native-born workers, immigration will unambiguously raise the wages of those native-born workers whose skills are different from but mesh well with those of immigrants.

Harvard economist George Borjas has devoted much of his professional work to measuring the extent to which immigrants have lowered the wages of American workers. In one paper, Professor Borjas concludes that immigration to the United States during the 1980s and 1990s lowered the wages of most American workers and that the effects were most significant for workers at the bottom and the top of the native-born educational distribution.[1] Specifically, Borjas found that immigration:

- lowered the wages of native-born high school dropouts by 7.4 percent;
- lowered the wages of college graduates by 3.6 percent; and
- reduced the wages of the typical native worker by 3.7 percent

These impacts translated to annual earnings that were about $1,800 lower for native-born workers without a high school diploma and a reduction in earnings of native-born college graduates of about $2,600 per year. Borjas characterized these results as "sizeable."[2]

Other economists have asked slightly different questions and argued for more nuanced measurements of the impacts of immigrants on native-born workers, in effect saying, "Wait a minute, the impacts aren't that bad." Professor Borjas and UC–Davis economist Giovanni Peri have engaged in an ongoing professional debate on the magnitude of the impacts of immigrants on the wages of native-born workers with whom immigrants compete and on the wages of native-born workers whose skills are complementary to those of immigrants (see Ottaviano and Peri, Immigration and National Wages: Clarifying the Theory and the Empirics, July 2008). The following graph illustrates Ottaviano and Peri's conclusions as to these impacts:[3]

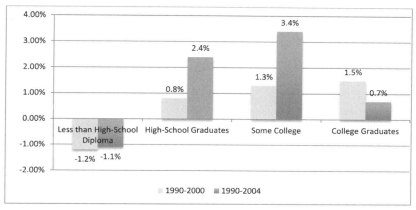

Figure 3.1

In this analysis, the authors conclude that some native-born workers benefit from immigration through higher wages while others are hurt by it through lowered wages. And, while the *magnitude* of the impacts varies depending on the time period considered (1990–2000 versus 1990–2004), the *nature* of the impact of immigrants on native-born wages is unaffected by the time period considered and therefore the results of the analysis can be seen as robust.

In another study, Professor Peri examines the impacts of immigration on U.S. "state employment, average hours worked, physical capital accumulation, and, most importantly, total factor productivity, and its skill bias."[4] The study concluded that there was no evidence of immigrants crowding out employment and hours worked by natives. Further, the study found robust evidence that immigrants increased total factor productivity while decreasing capital intensity and the skill bias of production technologies. On average, the study found that the combined effect of immigration was to increase employment by 1 percent and income per worker by 0.5 percent.[5]

While these analyses are interesting and Professor Peri's results can be understood as more favorable to immigrants than those of Professor Borjas, both approaches look at immigration from the perspective of Americans. Missing from both analyses is the perspective of immigrants themselves. The following graph of 2004 data from the World Bank's World Development Indicators illustrates differences in standard of living around the world. We see that in 2004 the vast majority of people in the world—approximately 5 billion—lived in countries where annual per capita income was $5000 or less, while relatively few—about 800 million—lived in wealthy countries.

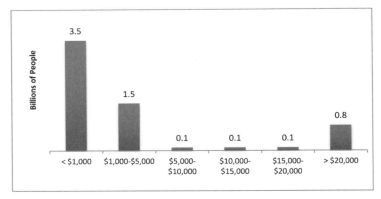

Figure 3.2

Economists have estimated that the potential wage gap between sending (poor) countries and receiving (wealthy) countries is often as high as 10:1.[6] The wage impact of migrating from the perspective of the immigrant can be as high as 1,000 percent, and in a global economy, the wages a worker can earn are much more a function of where he or she lives than of the skills or education that worker possesses:

> [R]ecent data on the earnings of migrants before and after migrating show that when they move, their wages are almost identical to those of workers in the country they move to and almost nothing like those in the country they move from. Jasso, Rosenzweig, and Smith (2003), using data on worker earnings before and after immigration to the United States, show an increase of $17,000 to $39,989 (in PPP) for the same worker—or, in other words, wages nearly doubled just by moving across the border.[7]

Advocates for limiting immigration to the United States focus on the "sizeable" negative wage impacts on native-born workers, ranging from $1,800 to $2,400 per year, while giving little or no weight to benefits for the immigrant that are orders of magnitude larger. This omission is understandable in light of commonly accepted prerogatives of nations to set immigration policy, and in fact, many would argue that the interests of the immigrant are irrelevant to this issue. But there is, with few exceptions, a striking absence of meaningful discussion of the ethical issues involved in using of the full legal and military might of the United States to protect $1,800 to $2,400 per year in earnings of American workers at the expense of $17,000 to $39,989 in earnings for mostly poor immigrants. This absence is a direct consequence of the fact that the political processes that determine immigration policy dictate how immigration debates are framed, and researchers are invariably drawn to weigh in on the claims and counter-claims that arise from political debates as to the economic costs and benefits of immigration for Americans.

Framing the Fiscal Impacts

There is also a vast literature on the impacts of immigrants on public coffers. UC–San Diego professor Gordon Hanson's research suggests that the economic and fiscal consequences of immigration significantly shape public opinion on immigration and that taxpayers in states with large immigrant populations bear most of the costs of immigration.[8] He states, "Generating greater political support for open immigration policies would require reducing immigration's adverse effects on the labor-market earnings and on the fiscal burdens of U.S. residents."[9]

Attempts to measure the fiscal impacts of immigrants focus on the differences between direct taxes paid by immigrants and the cost of social services provided to immigrants. Precise measurements of these net fiscal impacts are difficult to obtain because most of the fiscal costs of immigration are incurred at the state level and net costs depend on the specific structures of state public finance systems, the specific skill and earnings profile of immigrants in each state, the time period analyzed, and the proportion of undocumented immigrants in each state. It is generally held, however, that low-skilled immigrants (many of whom are undocumented) consume more in services than they directly pay in taxes.

The Center for Immigration Studies (CIS) (http://www.cis.org/), an advocacy group dedicated to restricting immigration to the United States, quotes National Research Council estimates that immigrant households in total impose a net fiscal burden of $20.2 billion annually and that an immigrant without a high school diploma creates a lifetime fiscal burden on American taxpayers of $89,000.[10] Such calculations are used as prima facie evidence in arguments for restricting immigration, especially of low-skilled immigrants.

However, these estimates of the net fiscal burden of immigrants do not take into account something called the Earnings Suspense File (ESF). This "file" is a fund that holds reported wages where the Social Security number either is not valid or does not match the name associated with that number. There is evidence that a significant portion of the wages in the ESF and their associated Social Security taxes were paid by undocumented immigrants, and these immigrants are unlikely to receive the benefits that they would otherwise be entitled to upon retirement. In fact, in 2007, the U.S. Senate passed an amendment to immigration legislation under consideration that would have explicitly barred undocumented immigrants from receiving retirement benefits from these taxes paid. The amount of money involved is significant. As of July 2002, the Social Security Administration estimated that the ESF contained approximately $374 billion in wages and that in the year 2000 alone, $49 billion in wages were posted to the ESF.[11] An April 2010 CNN iReport (available at http://www. ireport.com/docs/DOC-430297) reported that since 2000, the ESF has been growing by more than $50 billion per year and generating $6 to $7 billion in Social Security tax revenue and about $1.5 billion in Medicare taxes. These data are generally *not* part of the "net fiscal burden" calculus of those who would restrict immigration.

Analysis of data on 100 employers in the ESF file from 1993 to 1996 revealed that almost 75 percent of them were in industries that employ large numbers of low-skilled immigrants.[12] The results of this analysis are shown in figure 3.3.

There are ironic asymmetries in political debates over the fiscal impacts of immigrants. While much attention is paid to the fiscal costs imposed on native-born taxpayers by low-skilled immigrants, there has been little concern for or discussion of the implications for high-skilled immigrants of the fiscal *surplus* they generate.

To the contrary, it is frequently suggested that immigration policy be crafted to increase high-skilled immigration in order to maximize these fiscal surpluses. Thus, an opportunistic approach that minimizes fiscal costs of low-skilled immigrants while maximizing the fiscal surplus generated by high-skilled immigrants is widely understood as a legitimate approach to crafting immigration policy. There is a striking absence of discussion of the ethical issues involved in using of the full legal and military might of the United States to generate these net fiscal surpluses.

Further, even in the face of opportunistic attempts to generate these fiscal surpluses from high-skilled immigrants, little or no consideration is given to the ethical issues raised by federal policies that restrict access to certain public services by immigrant taxpayers. To the contrary, these policies have been enacted to reduce "moral hazard," to discourage an inducement to immigrate in search of public assistance.

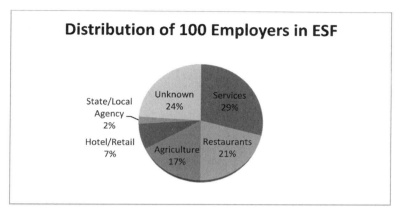

Figure 3.3

Debates over the net fiscal impacts of immigrants are framed from the perspective of American taxpayers. Since immigrants are coming *to* the United States this makes the consequences for the receiving country salient. And these debates are complicated by the fact that low-skilled immigrants, many of whom are undocumented, impose the largest fiscal burdens. This reality adds an element of moral outrage to debates that serves to justify punitive measures such as prohibiting immigrants who entered illegally from receiving Social Security benefits regardless of their legal status upon retirement and in spite of their having paid taxes that would otherwise result in benefits.

But there is a bigger picture. Because political debates on U.S. immigration policy and on the fiscal impacts of immigrants are framed in terms of the (fiscal) interests of Americans, they are strikingly devoid of a discussion of the ethical issues around policies such as:

- denying specific social service benefits to legal residents of the United States strictly on the basis of their immigration status in spite of requiring these same immigrants to pay taxes, which taxes fund social service costs;
- attempting to structure immigration policy so as to generate a net fiscal surplus from high-skilled immigrants while avoiding the fiscal costs of low-skilled immigrants;
- attempting to structure policy to encourage immigration by high-skilled (i.e., highly educated) foreign-born individuals without regard to the fiscal costs incurred by the sending countries to educate them.

As with the economic impacts of immigrants, political debates have largely shaped research agendas with regard to the fiscal impacts of immigrants. Research in this area is largely focused on the implications of immigration for Americans and little attention is paid to the perspective of immigrants or issues of basic fairness and equal protection under the law.

Concluding Comments

The central dilemma for the immigration policy researcher is the following: Conducting research on the economic and fiscal impacts of immigrants that speaks to policy debates has the effect of legitimizing the framing of those debates. Conducting research that measures the economic and fiscal impacts of immigrants on Americans gives credence to the notion that immigration policy should be decided on the basis of the economic, fiscal, and social interests of Americans. Elected representatives in a democracy do have to be responsive to the interests and opinions of their constituents. But immigration policy also has ethical dimensions relating to the rights and interest of immigrants themselves. The challenge for the researcher is how to conduct research that is relevant to policy debates without ignoring its ethical and moral dimensions.

Notes

1. George Borjas, Increasing the Supply of Labor through Immigration: Measuring the Impact on Native-born Workers. Center for Immigration Studies Backgrounder, April 2004. Available at http://www.cis.org/LaborSupply-ImmigrationEffectsNatives.

2. Ibid.

3. Giovanni Peri, Rethinking the Effects of Immigration on Wages: New Data and Analysis from 1990–2004. *Immigration Policy in Focus* 5(8), October 2006. Immigration Policy Center, Washington, D.C.

4. Giovanni Peri, The Effects of Immigration on Productivity: Evidence from U.S. States, NBER Working Paper 15507, November 2009.

5. Ibid.

6. Lant Pritchett, *Let Their People Come: Breaking the Gridlock on Global Labor Mobility*. Baltimore, MD: Brookings Institution Press, 2006, 6.

7. Ibid., 21.

8. Gordon Hanson, Why Does Immigration Divide America? Public Finance and Political Opposition to Open Borders. University of California–San Diego and NBER, March 2005.Available at http://irps.ucsd.edu/assets/022/8793.pdf

9. Ibid., 1.

10. Steven Camarota, Immigration's Impact on Public Coffers: Testimony Prepared for the House Judiciary Committee Subcommittee on Immigration and Claims, August 24, 2009. Available at http://www.cis.org/.

11. Social Security Administration, Status of the Social Security Administration's Earnings Suspense File, Congressional Response Report A-03-03-23038, November 2002, 1.

12. Ibid, 3.

PART TWO

The Border as an Unstable Place

CHAPTER FOUR

On Shifting Ground

The Conundrums of Participant Observation and Multi-Actor Ethnography in Contemporary Border Research

Rocío Magaña

That the United States–Mexico border is portrayed as a site of recurrent crises and ongoing lawlessness that requires ever increasing, if slightly changing, intervention, policing, and analysis is of little novelty. Still, many would agree that those very conditions that enable this field to be continuously perceived as broken anew themselves merit analysis. Paradoxically, perhaps, contemporary border research practice is challenged at its core by that intrinsic quality of apparent instability and perpetual emergency that defines much of what happens on the U.S.–Mexico border today. One way to examine the processes by which such popular understandings of crisis, emergency, and insecurity or lawlessness renew their claim to this landscape, I argue, is by focusing on the terms of social engagement among competing actors and how those change over time. Like most ethnographers engaged in qualitative research, I employed a methodology based on embedded work and adapted participant observation in my research in the region. Adaptations and limitations to data collection methods and techniques were unavoidable because of the multiplicity of subjects and actors involved. In order to capture the range of legal, political, and moral claims about the legitimacy of local border policing and migrant rescue practices, which my research aimed to explicate, I needed to understand this border space from the perspective of a series of individuals, agencies, and organizations who were frequently on antagonistic and competing terms with each other, and whose actions were subject to changing security practices, policies, and paradigms. The questions this chapter contends with emerge from challenges I faced while doing fieldwork among them. More specifically, in the pages that follow I address the tension between the methodological need to chart competing efforts central to the Arizona–Mexico border region—namely those regarding border protection and migrant rescue—and the ethical obligation to ensure that my research among such actors did not compromise anyone involved.[1]

By way of this reflection on border research and methods, I argue here that the ethnographic examination of contemporary social fields framed by conflict and tension requires the disambiguation of participant observation for practical, ethical, and analytic reasons. Participant observation has been understood by anthropologists as a data collection method based on the researchers' full immersion in the everyday life of cultural groups in ways that "informants," as Malinowski would put it, "ceas[e] to be interested or alarmed, or made self-conscious by [the researchers'] presence" ([1922] 1999: 6). Opposite to traditional cultural research, the study of social fields—like borders—cannot simply privilege full immersion with any one single group, institution, or actor without sacrificing a more comprehensive and dynamic understanding and potentially exposing those people, institutions, or actors to greater risks and undue scrutiny from others in that field. Because ethics and methodology are never divorced, particularly in contexts as socially, politically, and legally complex and volatile as these borderlands, the contemporary participant observer must be capable and willing to disambiguate the quality of his engagement in that setting. In other words, in contexts in which researchers understand that subject risks may change or increase, they should make clear to their "informants" that they are treating them as such, and their engagement is qualified and always mediated by the collection of data on them, from them, and through them.

In this chapter, I outline the significance of the disambiguation of participant observation to multi-actor ethnography first by contextualizing the shifting social and political landscape in which I conducted fieldwork, then by examining the limitations and need for adaptation of the method, and finally by discussing a series of specific scenarios and solutions from my own field research. To illustrate the challenges of conducting fieldwork under changing policies and political climates let us turn at once to the U.S.–Mexico border.

On Shifting Ground

Throughout the time I conducted doctoral research (between 2002 and 2008) in the Arizona–Sonora border region, spikes in law enforcement presence along key desert corridors were common on either side of the boundary. In the process of moving between field sites and countries, I had my vehicle searched more times that I care to remember. Stops in the desert soon became routine, although for the most part I would pass through checkpoints without incident or delay, have cordial encounters with agents on remote roads and even stop to make small talk with them — common desert courtesies that benefited my research.

A shift in these dynamics of policing normalcy became clear on a mid-summer day in 2005. It was a bright Tuesday morning and I was returning to Tucson from Altar, Sonora, a small Mexican town from which most migrants launched their cross-border journeys at the time. As I often did, I drove up on the same 60-mile dirt road that local ranchers as well as most migrants and their smugglers use to get to the town of Sasabe and eventually the United States. At the port of entry I had a friendly 10-minute conversation about human rights and Mexican migration with a veteran female Customs and Border Enforcement official. The conversation, remarkable in itself, was one of many I had at this entry port, especially when traveling by myself.

About 12 miles into the United States, I encountered the Border Patrol trucks that routinely sit at the intersection of Arizona 286 and Arivaca Roads. As desert driving manners dictate, I acknowledged the agents by making eye contact and slightly lifting my hand from the steering wheel in a minimalistic waving gesture. Whether or not they nodded back, I cannot say. I kept driving north in my dusty two-door, forest green Jeep Cherokee with Illinois plates. A couple of minutes later I noticed a Border Patrol truck in my rear view mirror. As I got into the section of Highway 286 characterized by rolling hills, I realized that it was not just one truck tailing me, but three. Roads in this part of Arizona are so few and far between that driving amid law enforcement is an everyday occurrence. Still, it was not until I saw four other Border Patrol vehicles approaching from multiple directions that I gave the situation some thought. I was surrounded. Law enforcement lights went off.

I was particularly relieved that my Jeep had untinted windows all around and that I had nothing but the essentials for my research with me: a bag with my computer and fieldwork equipment, a small backpack with clothes and personals, a couple of water jugs, granola bars, a first aid kit. I was search-ready indeed. Perhaps this is why I took the excessive manpower around me with more curiosity than concern. The agents exchanged messages through their radio receptors. Although at that point I had been crisscrossing the boundary north and south and the desert east and west several times per week in that same vehicle for about a year, I imagine that my out-of-state plates were the reason for the delay. An agent I recognized finally approached. He first looked inside through the rear window, then inspected the Jeep's undercarriage with a special mirror device, and then carefully moved toward me. I rolled down my window and turned to him with a smile. He jumped back. "It's you!" he said in an exclamation of mixed surprise and disappointment. Agent Rivera[2] stepped back and whispered a few inaudible commands onto to his radio, then took another long look inside the vehicle through the rear side window before approaching me. "Anything inside the car, ma'am?" he asked me in an overly formal tone, which surprised me. Rivera and I had had a few desert conversations before, some of them about migration, some about the desert and the impossible weather, even some about ethnography and the risks of doing border research. "Why did you stop me?" I asked him. "It's just a routine stop," he replied, a rehearsed-sounding statement. "Routine?" I pressed half jokingly as I looked around at the law enforcement vehicles that were then beginning to pull away. He took his sunglasses off, grinned discreetly, and sent me on my way, telling me to "drive safely."

While many anthropologists are able to point to communities and villages as their field sites, a handful of roads stand out as some of my most important research locations. Along the span of this very road—from where it starts at the intersection with Arizona Road 86 in Three Points all the way south to Sasabe and its subsequent dirt stretch ending at the gas station outside Altar in Mexico—I conducted many an interview and got to see and experience the effects of the desert-turned-border. There were many encounters with migrants waiting along its shoulders for Border Patrol to detain them because they were too injured, tired, or lost to continue. Along this road, I met a smuggler with a Cuban accent and heard vandalism complaints from newcomer ranchers. From here, the National Guard took position along the desert hills, and after unknown gunmen chased them out, I witnessed Chris Simcox rally and deploy a dozen of his "Minutemen" in solidarity. Off this road, I asked private security contractors about their role in protecting the "Virtual Fence" watchtowers, and got to know the Quaker and the Jesuit arrested for trespassing them to pray in protest. In the pursuit of an ethnographic analysis based on a complex and comprehensive portrayal of this border region, I came to know this road and the kinds of people who use and inhabit it well enough not to be surprised by the unexpected—including my own momentary detention.

I did not know it at the time, but just three days before the morning in which I found myself literally at the center of law enforcement attention, two volunteers with the humanitarian organization No More Deaths had been detained while "medically evacuating" three migrants with varying degrees of heat-related illness from the desert. The arrest of Daniel Strauss and Shianti Sellz on July 9, 2005, and the felony charges pressed against them for allegedly conspiring to transport "illegal entrants" reverberated throughout the region. Pro-migrant activists called for intensified humanitarian presence and intervention in the desert. Anti-immigrant groups planned to step up their own patrols. Journalists were on standby. Law enforcement was—as it became evident to me—on high alert. Everyone prepared to engage in what would become a highly public legal battle over the right to render lifesaving aid to unauthorized border crossers in lethal distress. As parties marshaled arguments in favor and against the two then 23-year-old volunteers, the humanitarian and pro-migrant organizations to which they belonged transformed the uncertainty brought about by their legal battle into a collective call for the legal recognition that "humanitarian aid is never a crime," as their campaign motto asserted.

The sudden expansion of the field of intervention from the border and the desert to the courts made the rules of ethnographic engagement with and among border actors more elusive, the production of knowledge about this border and its dynamics potentially incriminatory, and the stakes higher. In retrospect, I should have been alarmed by the dozen agents blockading me in the desert that morning—if not as a young woman, visibly and verifiably traveling by herself on a remote road on the nicest of summer days, then most certainly as a researcher aware of an obvious permutation in this landscape. If anything was certain, it was that the terms of engagement among border actors had changed and that they were enough to render the familiar unrecognizable and treacherously untrustworthy. The legal landscape was shifting right under my feet, and the implications were unclear and potentially dire for everyone involved.

Participant Observation in Multi-Actor Border(line) Engagements

Throughout the history of the U.S.–Mexico boundary, fear and protection have been at the core of the border's operational framework to separate, subject, and classify people and commodities. Particularly at moments of rupture, history has shown that fear and anxiety activate powerful forces that call for the border to operate as a secluding membrane filtering undesirable subjects from those deserving of protection and safe passage. Because the application and efficacy of social and cultural research methods in settings like this are greatly affected by political climate and context, I would like to consider how American anxieties and securitization politics over the last decade change the conditions of ethnographic border research practice. In keeping with the famous Benjaminian thesis that "the 'state of emergency' in which we live is not the exception but the rule," and that "we must attain to a conception of history that is in keeping with this insight" (Benjamin 1969: 257), border researchers ought to develop methodological and analytical tools to assess what invocations of rupture, emergency, and exceptionality reveal about permanent systemic structures of seclusion that both drive and derive their potency from the mobilization of border fears and migration anxieties. As researchers trying to comprehend border phenomena, the challenge at hand is to study the practices that give rise to the border as a social field—which may include border crossing and policing, migrant smuggling and rescue, injuring and healing, exposing and protecting—without exposing practitioners to undue risk and danger. This involves taking the necessary protective measures from research design and conception through its implementation and write-up, as well as keeping a watchful eye over anything that may affect the terms under which researchers and research participants engage as both citizens and subjects on the border, with each other and in the larger public sphere.

One response to changing subject risks ought to be the reconceptualization of participant observation and its practice. This methodological approach has traditionally been understood as involving the investigator's total immersion within a group, with the purpose of arriving at an understanding of its social and cultural worlds. Kathleen DeWalt and Billie DeWalt write that "participant observation is a method in which a researcher takes part in the daily activities, rituals, interactions, and events of a group of people as one of the means of learning the explicit and tacit aspects of their life routines and their culture" (2002: 1). To this notion, Russell Bernard adds the caveat that the method requires practitioners to learn both to immerse themselves in a culture and "to *remove* [themselves] every day from that immersion so [they] can intellectualize what [they have] seen and heard" (2006: 344, emphasis added). Even so, as I have suggested elsewhere, "some projects and settings require the constant reassessment of the marriage between 'participation' and 'observation,' and how [research-ers] convey that balance to those [they] study" (Magaña 2008: 47). The reasons for which we, as researchers, ought to disambiguate participation from observation to our subjects and to ourselves are of methodological importance and analytical consequence; they also speak to concerns about ethics and research practicalities.

In order to explore these, it is paramount to approach the question of participant observation from an entirely different angle—moving away from "ego."

Qualitative researchers have long considered the method's limitations. Some have discussed the effects immersion has on researchers by expos-ing them, for example, to violence (e.g., Nordstrom and Robben 1995), or to uncomfortable and contradictory relationships with informants (Hume and Mulcock 2004). Others, left wanting by the ambivalent position of the participant-observer, have responded by reflexively turning the analytic focus on themselves (e.g., Briggs 1970; Belmonte 1979; Salzman 2000). A significant number of these analyses are researcher focused, as can be observed, for example, in Lynne Hume's and Jane Mulcock's assertion that "[p]articipant observation is primarily an 'advanced' exercise inform-ing and maintaining intimate relationships for professional purposes. And therein lie its greatest strengths and its greatest weakness" (2004: xii). Yet instead of pursuing cost-benefit analyses of embedded qualitative research and all its complexities, I would like to pause here to agree with Renato Rosaldo that the benefits of the method come from the "position or struc-tural location" it affords the scholar (1993: 19). Rosaldo's emphasis on structure allows a shift away from the researcher and his or her "intimate relationships" to the larger field in which those relations take place.

With the exception perhaps of scholars who privilege single infor-mants for their analyses—like Ruth Behar with Esperanza (1993); Joao Biehl with Catarina (2005); and, to a certain degree, Victor Turner with Muchona (1967)—field researchers engage multiple subjects who may not be on friendly terms with one another. Complex webs of relations complicate the fieldworker's presence and methods. To say the least, the ethnographer on the U.S.–Mexico border cannot ignore the conflict-ing interests and relations that shape social interactions in the region. In such context, the kind of unqualified full immersion that participant-observation is predicated upon can be methodologically problematic and ethically irresponsible. Allen Feldman (1991) offers perhaps the sharpest critique of such forms of ethnographic immersion when reflecting on his research in Belfast during the Irish Troubles when he writes, "In a culture of political surveillance, participant observation is at best an absurdity and at least a form of complicity with those outsiders who surveil" (Feldman 1991: 12). Opposite to other ethnographers of the conflict whose participant observation limited their research to a given group, Feldman suggests his approach, based on very controlled and clearly delimited interactions,[3] granted him the kind of access and data needed to develop a theory on the cultural construction of violence (283). The U.S.–Mexico border cannot be equated with Northern Ireland despite its increasing militarization and violence (Dunn 1997; Payan 2006), but Feldman's methodological critique applies to border research.

If the ultimate goal of border scholarship is to understand the cultural practices of a particular group like border residents, or migrants, or law enforcement, as some have skillfully done (e.g., Velez-Ibañez 1996; Chavez 1992; and Heyman 1995, respectively), then full-immersion participant observation may be appropriate and necessary. However, if the goal is to expand our understanding of the border to other forms of phenomena, the study of social fields that involve or affect multiple actors is essential. In that case, at the very minimum our research practices should remain transparent to our field interlocutors.

As the legal, social, and/or political ground changes under the fieldworker's feet, data collection methods and techniques must be reassessed and adjusted accordingly. In what follows, I outline five of the most salient ethical and methodological issues I encountered over the course of my own field research, as well as the practical ways in which I addressed them. Like the challenges themselves, my responses were shaped by context and availability of resources. I do not offer them here as a prescription, but rather as an invitation to think critically about the multiple implications of our research presence and practice and come up with creative, effective solutions that may contribute to making our work more rigorous, accessible, and fair to everyone involved. The following scenarios exemplify some of the difficulties of conducting research on shifting ground.

Specific Challenges, Responses, and Outcomes

Research with Vulnerable Populations in Dire Situations

When I decided to pursue research on the politics surrounding border-crosser injury and death in the Sonoran Desert, I understood the project would be difficult and taxing on many levels. Phyllis Palgi and Henry

Abramovitch open their overview of anthropological studies on death by citing Hortense Powdermaker's reflection of the difficulties of research in the face of tragedy. Powdermaker writes about her field experience in Lesu, "'How can you take notes in the midst of human sorrow? Have you no feelings for the mourners?' I had a quick vision of a stranger walking into the living room of my Baltimore home at the time of a death. The notebook went back into my pocket. But I continued, 'Are you not an anthropologist? . . . A knowledge of these rites is absolutely essential.' I took the notebook out and wrote what was happening. The Lesu people understood. . . .'" (Palgi and Abramovitch 1984: 386).

Not to undermine how "essential" knowledge about the Lesu death rites might be, almost a century after Powdermaker's assertion of her ethnographic mission, scholars who encounter vulnerable populations in particularly difficult or tragic moments are forced to deal with the dilemma. My own "Powdermaker moment" came in the summer of 2005, the day I found myself in a Mexican consular vehicle sitting next to a 19-year-old girl who had been granted humanitarian parole, a rare exception resulting from personal tragedy that enabled her to stay in the country for a few days, not illegally, but without admission status. The duration of the sanctioned stays is typically just long enough to help bring legal closure to a migrant death, be it by identifying the body of a loved one or by granting permission to cease life support. For any anthropologist interested in the intersection of power, vulnerability, and exceptional legal domains, meeting these parolees presents a rare opportunity.

Looking at the teenager, whose body bore the marks of a difficult and depleting several-day walk in the desert and whose sorrow was readily visible, I also asked myself questions about my position as an anthropologist and the importance of understanding that moment. What was "essential" to understand about this teenager's situation was not going to come from peppering her with questions or painstakingly taking inventory of the blisters on her feet or the skin peeling off her lips. Her condition was and remains duly noted. Unlike Powdermaker, in the "midst of human sorrow," I did not take my recorder out, but that does not mean I did not take note. The anthropological insight from this situation came as much from my realization of the teen's needs as from my awareness of the context that made it possible for us to be sitting next to each other in a vehicle that carried diplomatic protection. This insight opened a line of investigation that I took up with consular representatives, legal experts, and U.S. authorities.

Vulnerable people in desperate situations are also exposed to research exploitation. Indeed one of the challenges of scholarship and advocacy on the vulnerability of migrant populations involves exploring such a condition without exploiting it. Focusing on the vulnerable alone exacerbates their exposure and limits the analytic reach and scope of any study. Because of this, ethnographic fieldwork on the U.S.–Mexico border ought to be multi-actor, multisited, multifocal, and multiscalar.[4]

Unsuspecting Subjects and the Challenge of Continuously Informed Consent

While the vulnerability of migrants as research subjects tends to be readily acknowledged by most border actors, it can be a challenge to make non-migrant subjects understand and remember the risks they might incur as research subjects. In my practice, insisting on my role as an ethnographer collecting data at all times was a way I tried to maintain transparency and awareness of the main reasons for my engagement with my interlocutors. It was also an effort to create some balance between the kind of access and information given to me by those who supported my work wholeheartedly and those less welcoming. For instance, reviewing research protocols with unsympathetic and suspicious participants granted my work a kind of transparency of the terms and risks of participation not as easily achieved and maintained with those who saw me in friendly terms—as a colleague or potential ally. In a context in which rights and restrictions are continuously contested and redefined, it was crucial to my research and to me that everyone understood that my presence among them meant that they were most likely being observed, and that they had the right withdraw as participants. Despite my constant and overt disclosure as a researcher, there were moments that revealed to me how much more work I needed to do on this front. The clearest manifestation of this came during the 2006 Border Forum.

Coalición Derechos Humanos agreed to let me join a delegation of college-age activists going to the border's spin-off of the World Social Forum being held in Ciudad Juárez. Although most of us already knew each other, introductions were made; I talked about being an ethnographer at work and we chitchatted during the six-hour drive to Juárez. One night after dinner, I overheard a discussion among a subsection of the group sitting next to me. "The problem with anthropology," one of them said, "is that you always have white men going off somewhere to study people of color." The statement concerned me. For close to two years, then, not only I had introduced myself week after week as an anthropologist doing research, but I had also delivered letters of introduction and provided hard copies of my research protocols; I made it a habit to distribute business cards and even created a website detailing my project; I asked people for consent to record and permission to photograph every time I pulled out a camera or recorder; I had even requested and done interviews with some of them. In what turned out to be an incredibly awkward moment, I interjected, "You do realize that *I* am an anthropologist and that I've been studying *you* for two years now, right?" It was not the idea that a woman of Mexican descent, who was an American-trained researcher, would focus on white college-age activists in the United States that I was after; rather, I wanted them to be as aware of my presence, my work, and its implications as were, for instance, the anti-migrant activists with whom I was also in contact. Such uneven appraisals of my position seemed unfair to me and potentially unethical if left unaddressed.

Because border populations are always in flux, border researchers face challenges unseen by researchers in settings that are socially, culturally, and geographically bounded in straightforward ways. On the Arizona–Sonora border, not only migrants are transient; so are volunteers, journalists, and political figures. Even within agencies and institutions there is significant turnover. This requires that ethnographers be transparent to the point of redundancy about the nature of their activities and their protocols. Such influx also demands that precautions be taken for research-driven interest not to be misconstrued or mistaken (Kulick and Wilson 1995; Cupples 2002), and for newcomers to be introduced to the research being done with the agencies and organizations to which they belong. Above all, however, researchers must remain conscious that in a context that changes, the value and significance of the data they collect may also change in ways that may be risky and detrimental to others.

Fair Access and Engagement with Structurally Unequal Subjects

Making basic information about my research and its protocols available to all subjects was also a challenge. The members of the institutional review board that oversaw the protocols for my doctoral research had plenty of questions regarding how I would ensure that consent among such dissimilar subjects was equally willful and informed. They granted me a waiver for signed consent after some deliberation. Although verbal disclosure and consent facilitated my work, it did not always lead to fair and productive engagements in the field. It became necessary to find a way to provide more information to those I encountered as a border researcher, but print forms in the desert were impractical and disadvantageous, and would most likely end as debris.

A major incentive was to provide information to migrants, the most elusive category of people in my study, but two events augmented the urgency of this effort. First, I learned that a couple of local journalists had come across an early conference paper in which I cited some of their writing and they wanted to know more about the overall framework of my interests. Secondly, after the initial deployment of the Minuteman Project, some Minutemen circulated photographs of my vehicle and me together with a description of my work pieced together from information online. It became obvious that I needed to offer information to those I felt might need it, but also to those who actively sought it.

My solution was to develop a website with a domain name easy enough to be remembered, so I used my name.[5] With contents in Spanish and English, the site offered a description of my research project and its funding, IRB protocols, and consent scripts, as well as my curriculum vitae and contact information for me, my advisers, and the University of Chicago offices in which inquiries and complaints could be filed.[6] I added the site's address to my contact information in the business cards I had made and distributed those generously to just about everyone I met. An interesting trend emerged. While most English-speaking participants and interested parties emailed me, I began to receive phone calls from Spanish-speakers and migrants I encountered on the border. Sometimes they would call to verify who I was, to check if I had given them an accurate number, to tell me how they had fared in the desert, to ask questions, or just to stay in touch.[7] Although I cannot claim this fully solved the problem of access, it added layers of transparency and accountability that would have been otherwise impossible.

Representational Challenges and Vulnerabilities

Representation issues have long been foci of scholarly debate. French philosopher Guy Debord argued that "spectacle is not a collection of images; rather it is a social relationship between people that is mediated by images" (1995: 12). Through ethnographic work with media on the border, I became hyper-aware of the ways in which this place, its peoples and problems were depicted and of how such representations affected local dynamics. I also learned that the politics of representation begin in the field. While they are determined in large part by practical concerns and constraints, the consequence of such representations is far reaching. In her reflections on violence and social change, Hannah Arendt posits, "In the realm of human affairs, being and appearance are indeed one and the same" (2006: 88; see also Virilio 2002). When images of migrants are deployed to illustrate the abstract notion of a vulnerable border, migrants are made to embody the source of vulnerability and danger itself. In seeing how locals engaged both the reporters and the reported stories, the power of those who determine what enters the domain of visibility and public concern became undeniable.

In considering the effects of this dynamic for border research, its methods, and ethics, three points regarding visibility and representation seem essential, for me at least. First, because I engaged conflicting parties through my research, the visibility of my work to all my interlocutors was of utmost importance. For the most part I believe that people knew I was as likely to visit with migrants, humanitarians, doctors, and church people as I was with smugglers, law enforcement, journalists, attorneys, and diplomats. I was also concerned that my own visibility as a researcher would not harm anyone. For instance, because I knew that those in the migrant trade—"guest house" keepers, taxi drivers, smugglers, etc.—are wary of migrants who might "snitch" on them for their practices, I made it a point not to be seen talking with any person or group in ways that might have seemed secretive or exclusive, which would have put that person or group at risk.

This issue of managing perceptions brings me to the second point: When it comes to depicting the injured and the dead, who has the authority their representation? Two issues stand out. The first concerns the practical aspects of portrayal of migrants, their bodies, and their death, as well as the justifications and audiences used to frame their depiction. This is in part the question of exposure versus exploitation explored in the first point above. The second set of issues concerns the commodification of the injured migrant body, which is perhaps best illustrated by looking at how it manifests in the case of documentary production. In the summer of 2009, John Carlos Frey showed a preview of his documentary *The 800 Mile Wall* at the church that houses the headquarters of Humane Borders in Tucson. Both in the film and in the discussion that followed, Frey justified his decision to depict the semi-dismembered, decomposing body of Prudencia Martín Gómez, a 19-year-old indigenous Guatemalan woman,[8] stating that it was the desire of her fiancé for the world to know what had happened to Prudencia on the border. On the screen Prudencia is reduced to her body, and her objectified body on display is made to convey misery. Her persona, her family, and her world are erased as she is turned into an object of representational desire—the desire of the "fiancé," of the documentarian, of the audience. In my own research and writing, the depiction of migrant deaths and their bodies has been a constant preoccupation. By privileging the visual impact of decaying corporeality, the emphasis shifts away from any sense of common humanity these images might evoke (Scarry 1985) to their spectacularly extraordinary character. Because of this, their objectification, I fear, reproduces and exacerbates the kind of divides that lead to these deaths in the first place.

This points to a third, and much more complicated, issue pertaining to representation: the tension between visibility and invisibility. Visibility has problematic implications in the context of migration, unauthorized border crossing, and border enforcement and, consequently, on the research about them. On the one hand, the researcher must contend with the vulnerability that living in the "shadows" entails (Chavez 1992), and yet Mexican migration and the illegality in which it has been sustained are systemically conditioned on imposed invisibility (De Genova 2002, 2004). On the other hand, when migrants are made visible, the results are often vitriolic and repressive (Inda 2006; Chavez 2001). Negotiating this tension is not an easy task—not during fieldwork, not during data analysis, not in the presentation of findings. And yet, it is from this tension—the systemic creation of subjects denied legal recognition and protection, and the political effects of their visibility—that much border research derives its import. As social scientists practicing grounded field research, we must remain aware that our work will most likely enter and shape this field of representation, a fact we will do well to keep in mind as we design and execute our projects.

"Engaged Anthropology" and the Public's Appropriation of Research Outcomes

The applicability of border research is a mixed blessing to social scholars with a focus on the U.S.–Mexico borderlands. For instance, as anthropologists debate the politics and means of developing an "engaged anthropology," the option of "unengaged" work is not really available to border scholars. At the most basic level, "engaged border scholarship" can be more a descriptive than a prescriptive term. Long before we can effectively determine the domains of knowledge and practice that we hope our research will inform and contribute to, our work can be engaged, appropriated, and diffused by others, like local residents, activists on all sides of the debates, law enforcement, journalists, and other stakeholders. In a context in which research subjects possess the skills and resources to obtain and deploy expert knowledge, and at a time in which electronic access has broken the barriers that used to seclude scholars in the ivory tower, U.S.–Mexico border scholarship is to some degree always already "engaged."

From my own experience, while my peers joked about dissertations gathering dust in the basement of libraries, my work entered circulation quickly. Soon after filing my electronic copy with the ProQuest Dissertation Database, I began receiving emails from students within the United States and Europe who had come across my work. Upon my return to the Arizona–Sonora region, as part of the ethnographic tradition of "giving back," I intended to distribute hard copies of the dissertation among the various actors who had supported my fieldwork. Much to my surprise, copies of the dissertation were already in circulation.

While such a liberalization of academic expertise is most welcome as an effective way to keep scholars accountable, it also stands as a cautionary tale of the ways in which ethnographic depictions and anthropological analysis stand to circulate and be appropriated by subjects independent of the researcher's control or input. One can only hope that this development toward a grassroots circulation of knowledge will contribute to a better understanding of the conditions that characterize everyday life and exceptional death on this border. And yet, given the social and cultural climate and the trend to reduce rights and increase policing and restrictions that we have seen since the turn of the century, border researchers cannot but be concerned about how the appropriation of the knowledge we produce may be operationalized to exacerbate conditions that, in the name of national protection, already result in much suffering and sorrow.

Conclusion

Ethics and methodology are never divorced, especially for research projects carried out in contexts as socially, politically, and legally complex and volatile as those that have characterized these borderlands, and particularly under escalation of the security state. Ethics and methods are Janus-faced elements of knowledge production, from the minutiae of everyday fieldwork encounters to the conceptual conundrums tied to representational practices. In this chapter I discussed some of the challenges I encountered as an ethnographer in the Arizona–Sonora region of the U.S.–Mexico border to insist that, as the ground changes under the fieldworkers' feet, the effectiveness and ethical implications of their research methods and techniques must be continuously reassessed and adjusted accordingly. In my case, such adjustments involved a range of practices, from the constant, if repetitive, disclosure of my position as an anthropologist collecting data to my decision of when to abandon the ambiguity of "participant-observer" paradigm in favor of explicit engagement either as a participant or as an observer. It is impossible for me to claim that my methodology was always effective, but I can at least say that I strived to remain ethical and transparent, even when it taxed my research. As policies and practices that create conditions and spaces where rights can be suspended—or worse, when their temporal suspension becomes the norm—it is paramount that as producers of knowledge with direct responsibilities to the people in these places and under such conditions, we remain as critical of the dynamic and the challenges that we and our research participants face.

Notes

1. The project from which this chapter emerged received generous support at various points of the research process from the Wenner-Gren Foundation, Dartmouth College, the American Anthropological Association, and the American Academy of Arts and Sciences. My gratitude goes out to them for their support; the responsibility for this piece remains with the author.

2. Pseudonyms are used in lieu of real names in this chapter. An exception to this is made in the case of migrants who died while crossing the desert and whose names are publicly available either at the request of their families or due to the process of their repatriation.

3. Feldman writes, "In a culture of political surveillance, participant observation is at best an absurdity and at the least a form of complicity with those outsiders who surveil. I avoided residing in the communities of my informants for these reasons. Neutral spaces were best for talking about the items we agreed to deal with. Long-term visual appropriation of any social milieu was not welcomed. Too much mobility between adversarial spaces, which my nationality facilitated, also proved to be subjectively disturbing. As I became familiar with the topography of confessional communities, I realized that the only other people who were publicly moving back and forth in such manner were the police and the army. I had to constrain the body as well as the voice. Finally, in order to know I had to become expert in demonstrating that there were things, places, and people I did not want to know" (1991: 12).

4. This methodological approached is informed by Saskia Sassen's (2006, 2007) theorization of the global and the multiplicity of ways and levels in which actors like corporations, but also states, operate.

5. That website remains active and can be accessed at www.rociomagana.com.

6. The only complaint I ever received concerned my use of "biopolitics" as a term not in conversation with its usage in American political science in the 1960s, which privileges the politics of the life sciences (Caldwell 1964), not the politics of life as exemplified, for instance, by Foucault's work.

7. On four occasions, this also landed me with phone calls from fraudulent smugglers who alleged to have nonexistent relatives of mine in their custody.

8. Prudencia died in Ironwood Forest in 2007. Documentarian Juan Carlos Frey portrays her remains next to a full-body photograph he claims was provided by Prudencia's "fiancé."

References

Arendt, Hannah. 2006. *On Revolution*. New York: Penguin Classics.

Behar, Ruth. 1993. *Translated Woman: Crossing the Border with Esperanza's Story*. Boston: Beacon Press.

Belmonte, Thomas. 1979. *The Broken Fountain*. New York: Columbia University Press.

Benjamin, Walter. 1968. *Illuminations: Essays and Reflections*. New York: Schocken Books.

Bernard, Harvey Russell. 2006. *Research Methods in Anthropology: Qualitative and Quantitative Approaches*. Lanham, MD: Alta Mira Press.

Biehl, Joao. 2005. *Vita: Life in a Zone of Social Abandonment*. Berkeley: University of California Press.

Briggs, Jean L. 1970. *Never in Anger: Portrait of an Eskimo Family*. Cambridge, MA: Harvard University Press.

Caldwell, Lynton. 1964. Biopolitics. *Yale Review* 56: 1–16.

Chavez, Leo R. 1992. *Shadowed Lives: Undocumented Immigrants in American Society*. Fort Worth, TX: Harcourt Brace Jovanovich College.

———. 2001. *Covering Migration: Popular Images and the Politics of the Nation*. Berkeley: University of California Press.

Cupples, Julie. 2002. The Field as a Landscape of Desire: Sex and Sexuality in Geographical Fieldwork. *Area* 34(4): 382–390.

Debord, Guy. [1967] 1995. *The Society of the Spectacle*. Trans. D. Nicholson-Smith. New York: Zone Books.

De Genova, Nicholas P. 2002. Migrant "Illegality" and Deportability in Everyday Life. *Annual Review of Anthropology* 31 (2002): 419–447.

———. 2004 The Legal Production of Mexican/Migrant "Illegality." *Latino Studies* 2: 160–185.

DeWalt, Kathleen Musante, and Billie R. DeWalt. 2002. *Participant Observation: A Guide for Fieldworkers*. Lanham, MD: Alta Mira Press.

Dunn, Timothy. 1996. *The Militarization of the U.S.–Mexico Border, 1978–1996*. Austin: CMAS Books.

Feldman, Allen. 1991. *Formations of Violence: The Narrative of the Body and Political Terror in Northern Ireland*. Chicago: University of Chicago Press.

Heyman, Josiah M. 1995. Putting Power in the Anthropology of Bureaucracy: The Immigration and Naturalization Service at the Mexico–United States Border. *Current Anthropology* 36(2): 261–287.

Hume, Lynne, and Jane Mulcock. 2004. Introduction. In L. Hume and J. Mulcock, eds. *Anthropologists in the Field: Cases in Participant Observation*. Pp. xi–xxvii. New York: Columbia University Press.

Inda, Jonathan Xavier. 2006. *Targeting Immigrants: Government, Technology, and Ethics*. Malden, MA: Blackwell.

Kulick, Don, and Margaret Wilson. 1995. *Taboo: Sex, Identity, and Erotic Subjectivity in Anthropological Fieldwork*. London: Routledge.

Magaña, Rocío. 2008. The Undercover Anthropologist and the Smuggling of Field Data. *Anthropology News* 49(4): 47–48.

Malinowski, Bronislaw. [1922] 1999. *Argonauts of the Western Pacific: An Account of Native Enterprise and Adventure in the Archipelagoes of Melanesian New Guinea*. London: Routledge.

Nordstrom, Carolyn, and Antonius C. G. M. Robben, eds. 1995. *Fieldwork under Fire: Contemporary Studies of Violence and Survival*. Berkeley: University of California Press.

Palgi, Phyllis, and Henry Abramovitch. 1984. Death: A Cross-Cultural Perspective. *Annual Review of Anthropology* 13: 385–414.

Payan, Tony. 2006. *The Three Border Wars: Drugs, Immigration, and Homeland Security*. Westport, CT: Praeger Security International.

Rosaldo, Renato. 1993. *Culture and Truth: The Remaking of Social Analysis*. Boston: Beacon Press.

Sassen, Saskia. 2006. *Territory, Authority, Rights: From Medieval to Global Assemblages*. Princeton, NJ: Princeton University Press.

——, ed. 2007. *Deciphering the Global: Its Scales, Spaces and Subjects*. New York: Routledge.

Salzman, Philip Carl. 2002. On Reflexivity. *American Anthropologist* 104(3): 815–813.

Scarry, Elaine. 1985. *The Body in Pain: The Making and Unmaking of the World*. New York: Oxford University Press.

Turner, Victor. 1967. *The Forest of Symbols: Aspects of Ndembu Ritual*. Ithaca, NY: Cornell University Press.

United States General Accounting Office. 2004. *Data Mining: Federal Efforts Cover a Wide Range of Uses*. Washington, DC: GAO.

Velez-Ibanez, Carlos G. 1996. *Border Visions: Mexican Cultures of the Southwest United States*. Tucson: University of Arizona Press.

Virilio, Paul. 2002. *Desert Screen: War at the Speed of Light*. Trans. M. Degener. London: Continuum.

CHAPTER FIVE

Methodological Challenges and Ethical Concerns of Researching Marginalized and Vulnerable Populations

Evidence from Firsthand Experiences of Working with Unauthorized Migrants

Daniel E. Martínez, Jeremy Slack,
and Prescott Vandervoet

Being located in the most active U.S. border patrol enforcement sector (U.S. Citizen and Immigration Services 2010) has led to a substantial focus on the study of unauthorized migration among a group of scholars at the University of Arizona. The authors of this article were involved in two different projects that helped them gain a better understanding of unauthorized migration in the Arizona–Sonora region. The projects, which utilized different methodological approaches, raised comparable concerns regarding the sensitivity of conducting research with unauthorized migrants. Despite the obvious difficulties of researching the events surrounding an activity that is essentially "illegal" (i.e., unauthorized border crossings), we also struggled knowing that our respondents were either about to attempt a potentially dangerous journey or had just undergone a strenuous and unsuccessful crossing attempt. This chapter serves to combine our experiences and highlight some of the challenges associated with researching a vulnerable and often already highly marginalized population such as unauthorized migrants. We begin by providing examples of some of the contextual factors related to increased border enforcement that have directly contributed to the heightened vulnerability of unauthorized migrants. Next, we outline and connect some of the extant literature on marginalization and vulnerability to the case of unauthorized migration. We follow by describing the methodological designs of the two studies that gave us our insights. We conclude by discussing how issues of marginalization and vulnerability influenced the selection of our research sites, participant recruitment, incentives to participate, and the general data collection process. In our experiences, we found that recognizing and being attentive to the needs of a marginalized and vulnerable population while also maintaining high methodological standards is challenging, yet possible.

Background

Recent increased border militarization efforts have played a significant role in redistributing migratory routes into remote and dangerous areas along the border (Andreas 1998; Dávila, Pagán, and Soydemir 2002; Eschbach, Hagan, Rodriguez, Hernández-León, and Bailey 1999; Cornelius 2001, 2005; Rubio Goldsmith, McCormick, Martínez, and Duarte 2006). As a result of these efforts, the overall proportion of U.S. border patrol apprehensions that occur in the Tucson Sector have increased drastically. In the early 1990s, roughly one of every twenty border patrol apprehensions occurred in this sector (U.S. Citizen and Immigration Services 2010; Martínez forthcoming). This ratio has narrowed substantially over the past 10 years. On average, one in every 2.7 border patrol apprehensions has occurred in the Tucson Sector since 2000 (U.S. Citizen and Immigration Services 2010; Martínez forthcoming), making southern Arizona the single most traversed unauthorized crossing corridor along the entire U.S.–Mexico border.

Border enforcement efforts have not only shifted unauthorized crossing routes into southern Arizona (Rubio Goldsmith et al. 2006), but have also completely changed the nature of the unauthorized crossing experience. In addition to geographical location, the unauthorized crossing experience has changed in recent years in terms of the greater amount of time a typical crossing requires, the treacherous terrain where crossings occur, the increased risks and fees associated with the journey, and the elevated possibility of encountering thieves who prey on migrants in remote areas while crossing. These factors have all certainly increased the vulnerability of unauthorized migrants who continue to attempt to cross despite intensified border enforcement efforts. In the end, researchers working with this population or others like it must be aware of this increased vulnerability and take it into consideration when planning and executing their research designs.

The ever-present possibility of death is well understood by many migrants and is perhaps one of the most salient issues related to unauthorized border crossings, as the number of known deaths has increased exponentially since the implementation of the border militarization efforts. The remains of over 2,200 unauthorized migrants have been recovered from southern Arizona alone; a majority of these deaths have occurred since 2000. This underlying theme and notable public health concern not only makes research on unauthorized migration and with unauthorized migrants important, but also extremely sensitive. The rugged terrain of the Arizona–Sonora borderlands is harsh for migrants, as many of their movements take place at night and/or through some of the most difficult landscapes to navigate. Many people suffer some form of physical or psychological depredation whether or not they succeed in reaching their desired destination in the United States. This, coupled with the constant pressure to evade border patrol or vigilante civilian groups, causes the unauthorized border crossing experience to be a potentially dangerous and deadly one. While it is believed that a small proportion of all migrants actually die while crossing, this number is high enough for nearly all those who cross to realize that death is a very real possible consequence. The possibility of death undoubtedly impacts migrants' psychological well-being while in transit, thus contributing to a heightened state of vulnerability.

Another reason this type of research is sensitive is that it addresses an issue within a space and time racked by violence. Increased enforcement efforts have caused drug and human smuggling activities to overlap within areas of the Arizona–Sonora borderlands, creating intense competition on the part of smuggling organizations for control of certain corridors (STRATFOR 2008). All too often migrants find themselves caught in the middle of turf disputes, as this competition has manifested itself in the form of violence in rural and urban border areas alike. The indiscriminate nature of these acts of violence has created an atmosphere of trepidation for researchers, respondents, and local community members. This is yet another factor that contributes to migrants' vulnerability while on their clandestine journeys and needs to be considered when working with this population.

Clearly, increased border enforcement efforts have redirected migration routes into southern Arizona, making this region the most important area along the entire U.S.–Mexico border for unauthorized crossings. In the process, border enforcement efforts have also contributed to unauthorized migrants' vulnerability by forcing them to cross for longer periods of time through some of the most remote, inhospitable, and contested areas along the border, thus increasing the risk of injury, victimization by various actors, and death along the way. Throughout this chapter we will highlight some of the ethical and methodological challenges associated with conducting research with unauthorized migrants who find themselves in heightened and intersecting states of vulnerability and marginalization. We hope that the issues discussed here will be given consideration by future researchers working with similar populations when creating and carrying out their methodological designs.

Participant Marginalization and Vulnerability

Having an understanding of the concepts of marginalization and vulnerability, as well as how they are related to migrants and the unauthorized migration process, is crucial when engaging in this type of research. At first glance, the notions of marginality and vulnerability seem rather analogous to one another. However, while these concepts are undoubtedly interconnected, we argue that an important distinction must be made between them. Marginalization is directly related to the socioeconomic conditions migrants face in their communities of origin (Anzaldo and Prado 2005), many times *causing* migration, while vulnerability is a "social condition of powerlessness" *resulting* from migration (Bustamante 2002). Although a migrant's vulnerability may be contextual or situational, it may also be further heightened by his or her level of marginalization, something that has become evident to us while working with this population. Researchers must find a delicate balance between executing a research design and being sensitive to the needs of simultaneously marginalized and vulnerable study participants.

Marginalization

According to a report by Mexico's Consejo Nacional de Población (CONAPO), marginalization is "a structural phenomenon that has its origins in historical modes, styles, and patterns of development" (Anzaldo and Prado 2005: 11). Essentially, marginalization is a consequence of unequal patterns of development within or between countries. The United

Nation's Human Development Index (HDI) is used by researchers to examine varying levels of development or marginalization on a global level, specifically in terms of "a long and healthy life; access to knowledge, and a decent standard of living" (UNDP 2007: 224). Similarly, the Marginalization Index (MI), which was instituted in Mexico by CONAPO, is used to measure varying levels of development within the country. The MI was created using a principle components method (Anzaldo and Prado 2005) and summarizes municipal and state levels of schooling, housing conditions, population density, and income characteristics (Anzaldo and Prado 2005; López-Córdova, Tokman, and Verhoogen 2005). Marginalization is a structural factor that can increase a person's social risks and vulnerability (Anzaldo and Prado 2005). In addition to measuring development, the concept can be useful when assessing which segments of a population may be at higher risk for vulnerability during the unauthorized migration process (i.e., migrants from communities with high marginalization index scores).

While previous scholars have used the concept of marginalization on a community, state, or national level (López-Córdova et al. 2005; Lindstrom and Lauster 2011), we expand this concept to include analysis at the individual level. By marginalization we are still referring to the same measures that make up CONAPO's MI (education, housing, population density, and income), but also conceptually extend the understanding of marginalization to include the intersection of various migrant characteristics including gender (females), education (the illiterate), income (the impoverished), age (juveniles and the elderly), economic sector of employment (*campesinos*), and ethnicity or culture (indigenous peoples of Mexico). Our conceptual framework includes a notion similar to the idea of intersectionality used by Patricia Hill Collins in the sociological study of race and ethnicity (1998, 2000). We argue that it is precisely the intersectionality of multiple characteristics or factors, at various levels, that constitutes people's levels of marginalization—an outcome in which the whole is greater than the sum of its parts.

Generally speaking, many unauthorized migrants traveling through Mexico to the border tend to be some of the most marginalized members within their society. For instance, nearly half (49 percent) of the respondents in the quantitative study that will be discussed later originated from the four Mexican states with the highest levels of marginalization according to CONAPO's 2000 MI (Veracruz, Oaxaca, Guerrero, and Chiapas), while only 5 percent were from the four Mexican states with the lowest levels of marginalization (Mexico City, Nuevo León, Baja California, and Coahuila). We argue that migrants' marginalized status within Mexico and the United States adds to their vulnerability and increases the likelihood of them experiencing exploitation during their travels to and across the border. More specifically, for us as researchers, this status also played a role in deciding how, or if at all, respondents would be remunerated for their participation in the studies. The following vignette is one respondent's firsthand experience of crossing. Javier, who originates from an extremely impoverished area of Mexico and can be described as experiencing multiple forms marginalization, insists he will attempt another crossing despite being pushed to the limit physically and psychologically. As we will discuss shortly, his marginalized status may have actually played a role in increasing his vulnerability to various forms of exploitation near the border.

Javier, a single 19-year-old *campesino* from Oaxaca, is one of 23,000 remaining Chatino language speakers in Mexico. Life in his hometown of 120 inhabitants was very difficult. Javier had never been to school and spent his youth working alongside fellow community members on an *ejido*. Javier's family earned less than $250 per month and relied mostly on subsistence farming to survive. He decided his only option was to travel *al norte* in search of a better life for himself and his family.

Javier eventually made his way to central California where he worked harvesting lettuce for about a year. However, his luck ran out and he was apprehended and repatriated to Baja California, Mexico. In an unfamiliar border area thousands of miles from Oaxaca, Javier scrambled to find a way back across the border.

After a couple of failed attempts, he finally met a *coyote* in Mexicali through a friend who agreed to a take him across the border for $1,300. Javier, the coyote, and a group of 10 other migrants attempted to cross the border near Sonoyta, Sonora. The group traveled for seven days and nights through the rocky terrain near Organ Pipe Cactus National Monument. Along the way the group encountered *bajadores*, or bandits that prey on migrants while crossing. Javier was beaten and robbed of all his money—a mere $40. It was unclear to Javier whether or not his coyote had been in on the robbery. The group managed to avoid apprehension and was eventually picked up and transported to a drop house in Phoenix, Arizona, where they were held with 20 other migrants. After several days, the drop house was raided by Maricopa Sheriff's deputies and the group was eventually turned over to Immigration and Customs Enforcement (ICE). Javier, who was still dehydrated and exhausted from his desert trek, was very nervous when the home was raided. Although he did not resist, he was physically and verbally abused by the apprehending officers.

After spending two months in a detention facility, Javier was repatriated to Nogales, Sonora, the day before we interviewed him. The whole deportation process made him very nervous, especially since he did not have any money. What would he do? Where would he go? Despite the physical and psychological stress of his most recent attempt, Javier was certain that he would try to cross again in the near future.

Vulnerability

Sociologist Jorge Bustamante has applied the notion of vulnerability to the context of immigration, specifically with regards to the human rights of immigrants in their host countries. In contrast to the concept of marginalization, he asserts that "vulnerability is not a condition brought by an immigrant to a country of destination" and therefore "the causes of vulnerability should not be confused with the causes of immigration" (2002: 340). Marginalization, as discussed in this chapter, may be a significant factor contributing to the initiation and perpetuation of migration flows, but it should not be mistaken as the root cause of vulnerability. Rather, vulnerability should be understood as a "social condition of powerlessness ascribed to individuals with certain characteristics that are perceived to deviate from those ascribed to the prevailing definitions of a national" (Bustamante 2002: 340). While marginalization is one of many possible factors contributing to migration flows, we view vulnerability as a social condition exacerbated by the experiences of the actual unauthorized crossing and apprehension, detention, and repatriation by U.S. authorities. Migrants indeed experience a true sense of powerlessness during various stages of the migration process, especially once in the custody of U.S. authorities, as they are limited in their access to legal and political representation at that time.

Overall, Bustamante (2002) uses a broad understanding of vulnerability relating to power differentials between immigrants and the state as well as to issues of human rights. However, he clearly asserts that immigrants can also be vulnerable in their country of origin, something that was evident to us in our research with unauthorized migrants in Sonora, Mexico. In this context, according to Bustamante, vulnerability is "likely to be related to the distance that separates the internal migrant from his or her community of origin" (2002: 314). The logic here is that migrants have fewer resources, weaker social capital (in the form of network ties), and less financial capital the further they are from their communities and the longer they are in limbo near the border. Resources such as Grupos Beta, the Comisión Nacional de los Derechos Humanos, and various church-operated and private shelters have been established throughout Sonora to attempt to deal with precisely this issue and reduce migrants' vulnerability. The following vignette describes some of the factors that have contributed to the increased vulnerability of one of our respondents, Marisol.

Marisol, a 22-year-old single woman from Veracruz, Mexico, has attempted to cross the border without documents a total of five times—none of which has been successful. Although she has never lived or worked in the United States, she was desperately trying to get to Savannah, Georgia, to be reunited with family members as well as to secure employment. In the past, few women would have attempted such a crossing without being accompanied by family members or friends. But times are changing. Marisol is a perfect example of a new cohort of women who are now trying to undergo the journey north on their own.

Marisol made her way north from Veracruz to Nogales, Sonora. There she met a coyote who agreed to smuggle her into the United States for $1,000—a true bargain by today's standards. She, her coyote, and a group of 22 migrants attempted to cross into the United States through the tall grass and rolling hills on the outskirts of Nogales, Sonora. The coyote claimed the journey would take less than two days, but it actually lasted three, and only because they were detected and apprehended by border patrol. The trek could have been longer. However, before being apprehended, the group was assaulted, beaten, and robbed by bajadores. Marisol lost everything.

Marisol was quickly processed by the border patrol and voluntarily repatriated to Nogales, Sonora, less than 12 hours after being apprehended. She was repatriated by the private security company Wackenhut at 2 a.m. Being deported to a relatively unfamiliar border city in the middle of the night is enough to put anyone on edge. Yet Marisol's status as a young woman thousands of miles from home most likely exacerbated her vulnerability upon repatriation. With no money and nowhere to go, she was fortunate that Grupos Beta transported her to the private shelter where we later interviewed her. When asked whether or not she planned on attempting another crossing, Marisol stated, "No, the journey is simply too difficult, too dangerous."

One major reason we chose migrant shelters as our research sites was that they provided a safe space where migrants would hopefully feel a lower sense of vulnerability and therefore be more willing to share their experiences with us than they might have if we had chosen to conduct our work in public spaces. For this reason, we believe conducting our research in shelters ultimately resulted in greater validity. Evidence of this was clear to Vandervoet when he compared his experiences working in public spaces, such as in Altar's main plaza, to the interviews he conducted within the confines of the shelter.

Our conceptualization of vulnerability relates to Bustamante's discussion of migrants within their own country and the relationship between the distance from their community of origin and access to resources to prevent exploitation. Furthermore, we agree that vulnerability, unlike marginalization, is not something that is brought by migrants from their community of origin, but rather is a socially ascribed condition relating to power differentials (Bustamante 2002). However, our understanding of vulnerability deviates from Bustamante's in that we use it to describe a social context resulting from proximate conditions relating to an immediate migration experience. We understand vulnerability to be the result of various conditions that increase a person's susceptibility to exploitation. Like Bustamante, we believe such conditions are related to limited access to financial and social resources (e.g., cash, social contacts, and networks) that are disrupted during the migration process the farther one is from his or her community of origin. However, we extend this notion and add that vulnerability can also be the result of physiological stress from a strenuous crossing experience (e.g., dehydration, sleep deprivation, injuries, or exhaustion) or psychological trauma endured during apprehension, processing, detention, and repatriation by U.S. authorities.

It is precisely the intersection of marginalization and vulnerability migrants experienced that proved to be a significant challenge when it came to the recruitment of potential respondents while also making sure their immediate needs were addressed upon arrival at the shelter. Further, as we will later discuss, the execution of a systematic random sample as well as the administration of the structured survey instrument also proved to be challenging, yet possible, given these factors.

Methodologies of Specified Studies

This section briefly describes the purpose, research questions, and methodologies of two projects (one quantitative and the other qualitative) that were conducted to examine migrants' perceptions of risks and experiences while crossing the border. Both studies were conducted in migrant shelters in Sonora, Mexico. We specifically draw on our research experiences from these projects to offer some insight on the challenges of recruiting and working with a marginalized and vulnerable population such as unauthorized migrants. While neither the quantitative nor qualitative studies discussed below were solely designed to specifically assess migrants' levels of marginalization and vulnerability, these issues did influence our decisions to conduct our research in shelters. Further, as will be noted, these issues impacted how we dealt with issues of sampling, data collection, and the difficult decision of whether or not to compensate study participants.

Migrant Border Crossing Study (MBCS)

The Migrant Border Crossing Study (MBCS) is a quantitative study created and led by Daniel E. Martínez with the aim of identifying and understanding the sociological factors that contribute to the unauthorized crossing experience in southern Arizona. The three authors of this article played significant roles in creating, translating, and administering the survey instrument. The overarching purpose of the MBCS was to complement extant qualitative research of the crossing experience by collecting a large random sample of quantitative survey data. One major advantage of this methodological design is that quantitative studies yield data that can be used to conduct systematic multivariate analyses that, in turn, can be used to test and refine existing theories shaped by previous qualitative work. In addition, if weighted properly, results from quantitative studies can be used to generalize to a larger population of unauthorized migrants. Currently, very few quantitative studies exist that specifically examine the unauthorized crossing experiences of migrants in southern Arizona in an era of increased border enforcement. This may be due in part to the challenges associated with locating members of this population and securing a safe space and time in order to be able to administer a survey.

The MBCS was administered at a migrant shelter in Nogales, Sonora, on multiple trips to the shelter over the course of 18 months. Hundreds of unauthorized migrants are repatriated to Nogales on a daily basis, a majority of whom are just as far from their communities of origin as they are from their desired destination in the United States. Shelters provide a safe place where many recently repatriated migrants can take refuge from the elements and escape the noises and traffic of this bustling border city.

Criteria for inclusion include having attempted an unauthorized cross-ing along the Arizona–Sonora border, having been apprehended by U.S. authorities, and having been repatriated to Nogales, Sonora. Further, in order to account for issues that may be associated with memory recall, all of these experiences must have taken place within six months of the time the survey was administered. Eligible respondents also needed to be at least 18 years of age during the time of study and be able to speak Spanish well enough to complete the survey.[1] Most importantly, migrants needed to be willing to participate in the study. Respondents were not coerced into taking the survey and their stay at the shelter was not contingent upon their participation in the study. This was made clear to all potential partici-pants during the informed consent process.

All potential participants were randomly sampled using a spatial sam-pling technique. The shelter was divided into four previously defined areas and every X person within each space was asked to participate and screened for eligibility. Researchers avoided sampling from the shelter's bed-list as a means to protect the anonymity of potential participants. A total of 688 migrants were screened; of those, 47 were eligible to partici-pate. In the end, a total of 415 surveys were completed with a response rate of 97 percent. Table 5.1 illustrates the unweighted descriptive statistics for several demographic characteristics of MBCS respondents.

Table 5.1. Demographic Characteristics of MBCS Respondents (Unweighted Data)

Demographic Characteristic	Mean	Std. Dev.	Min	Max	N
Female	0.12	0.32	0	1	415
Age	30.46	8.51	18	58	415
Indigenous Language	0.21	0.41	0	1	413
Years of Education	6.93	3.59	0	15	406
Monthly Household Income ($US)	720.13	947.03	0	6,000	376
Northern Mexico	0.09	0.29	0	1	411
West-Central Mexico	0.20	0.40	0	1	411
Central Mexico	0.20	0.40	0	1	411
South/Southeastern Mexico	0.51	0.50	0	1	411

Qualitative Work in Altar: Assessing Risks and Dangers

The aim of the qualitative research conducted by Prescott Vandervoet was to understand how individuals preparing to cross the Sonora–Arizona border without authorization envisioned the crossing experience, namely the risks and dangers involved. The research took place during the summer of 2007 in the city of Altar, Sonora, which is one of the primary staging areas for unauthorized migrants in the Arizona–Sonora border region. The rise of Altar as an important geographical location in the unauthorized migration process is directly related to increased border enforcement efforts, which have funneled people into rural terrain of the borderlands. The Altar research took place at the Centro Comunitario de Atención al Migrante y Necesitado (CCAMyN), a community- and parish-supported shelter, and in the main plaza in the town. Vandervoet lived at the shelter for eight weeks, which allowed him to build considerable rapport with people who stayed at the shelter.

Respondents (N = 43) included a mix of people who had previously crossed the border, with varying degrees of success, on different trips, as well as individuals who had never tried to cross. The only requirement for participation was considering a future border-crossing attempt. Similar to the MBCS, eligible respondents also needed to be at least 18 years of age, speak Spanish competently, and be willing to voluntarily participate. Participants were not entirely randomly sampled, although a degree of randomness did occur when a new cohort of migrants entered the shelter where research occurred. At times, a snowball sampling technique was incorporated into the participant selection process, but over time the researcher became embedded within the migrant community at the shelter, and trusting relationships were developed prior to respondents being asked to participate in the project. It became clear during initial stages of the research that respondents were not forthcoming with answers, and as an adaptation the researcher attempted to earn their confidence over a matter of days prior to asking them to participate in the formal mixed-methods data collection process. This flexibility is one advantage a qualitative research design has over a systematic quantitative approach that is carried out over the course of several months with numerous cohorts of participants. Never did the researcher disguise his motive for being at the shelter, and in fact nearly all participants were familiar with the topic of research prior to their participation, as they observed others participate in the research and perhaps discussed it among each other. The fact that migrants in Altar often attempted to disguise their ultimate motives or destination for an upcoming border-crossing attempt is not surprising given their marginalized status within the town and their heightened vulnerability as a result of being far from their homes.

Shelters as Research Sites When Working with Migrants

In the case of the two research projects previously described, vulnerability and marginalization take on very immediate definitions, primarily as a result of the effects and consequences of an unsuccessful crossing attempt. Thus, both projects adapted to better work with individuals who may have been experiencing heightened levels of either marginalization or vulnerability, or in many cases, an intersection of both.

Many of the people we talked to during the course of our research in Sonora, Mexico, found themselves in very vulnerable positions at the time of the survey or interview. For instance, in the case of the quantitative surveys administered in Nogales, most eligible respondents had been repatriated to Mexico after being apprehended and temporarily held by U.S. authorities the same day they participated in the study. Many had struggled for days in the desert and were still feeling the ill effects of exhaustion and dehydration. In addition, they may have experienced or witnessed horrible acts of abuse during their border-crossing process. The combination of these physiological and psychological conditions resulting from the crossing experience creates a heightened state of vulnerability on the part of the migrant. In Altar, migrants are in a similar condition as often, resources permitting, migrants who are repatriated to Nogales will make their way back to Altar as soon as possible to attempt another border crossing.

One way our research in Nogales and Altar attempted to acknowledge and account for participants' vulnerability and marginalization was with chosen locales of the research sites. The Altar project relied on both a shelter and a public space as research sites. There was a marked difference between the two. The shelter provided a sense of security to participants, as they did not have to worry about people eavesdropping on the conversation, which was common for conversations occurring in the plaza where coyotes (guides) are constantly on the lookout for clientele (migrants). Listening in on their conversations provides coyotes with reliable information regarding migrants' current situation and needs. This information is used by coyotes to manipulate business transactions or agreements with migrants. However, shelters provide a buffer against these situations, as there is a vetting process for admission to both shelters, with staff being highly knowledgeable about the true intentions of people when they ask to be admitted. In the case of the Nogales research site, the owners of the shelter require proof of repatriation to stay at the shelter, typically in the form of an official document given to migrants upon repatriation by the Mexican Instituto Nacional de Migración. Therefore, as far as we know, rarely are coyotes or recruiters able to enter the shelter grounds in either research site. Migrants thus are provided a sense of tranquility that does not exist in other parts of Altar or Nogales.

Having the support of the research site as well as the support of shelter workers was of the utmost importance to both research projects. The Altar project tried to embed the research within the setting of the site, with the researcher assuming volunteer duties at the shelter. This connection not only allowed the researcher to give back to the shelter (in the form of cleaning, repairs, and food supplies) but it also provided what may have been seen as a legitimizing presence for the researcher within the shelter by some migrants, who may have harbored a degree of suspicion as to the actual motives of the researcher for being in Altar.

Conducting research within a shelter that is recognized and trusted by the community helps ensure the safety not only of participants but also the security of researchers. In fact, it is important to note that the security of researchers was also a decisive factor in our decision to utilize shelters as research sites. There are a variety of safety concerns when working on migration issues along the border. The Arizona–Sonora border region has seen unprecedented levels of violence in the last several years, and migrants have frequently become caught up in the issue as human and drug smuggling have become interlinked. The shelters are highly controlled by an external group (i.e., private owners or a church), and thus it is less likely that smugglers or bandits will attempt any high profile actions to reveal their identities and attract attention from law enforcement. Moreover, while we were collecting data at the Nogales shelter, police would often come to check documents and search for weapons. More recently, the city of Nogales has stationed a police officer at the shelter on a daily basis during the locale's hours of operation. While we believe that this is necessary for everyone's safety, it may add to any distrust that migrants have of people asking questions.

Migrants are frequently marginalized and made more vulnerable within Mexican border communities, as they are often seen as outsiders and local residents may feel resentment towards migrants congregating in their public spaces. Similarly, a variety of racist and classist attitudes exist within Mexico and these can frequently be fomented by the unique characteristics (e.g., language use, phenotype, manner of dress) that migrants from southern Mexico and Central America possess. Our aim is not to glorify the setting of the migrant shelter within northern Mexico, as shelters definitely can be contested spaces, but the shelters do protect against some of the attitudes present towards migrants in northern Mexico.

Participation Recruitment and Survey Methodology

Relying on shelters as research sites may have helped to minimize the consequences resulting from the intersection of migrants' marginalization and vulnerability related to resource depletion and breakup of social contact and networks during the unauthorized crossing experience. However, migrants' vulnerability, resulting from physiological and psychological trauma from the migration experience, proved to be a challenge in itself, especially when it came to participant recruitment.

One important understanding was agreed upon by team members before beginning our survey work in Nogales: we are humanitarians first, and researchers second. We felt that we had to be respectful of, and sensitive to, the immediate needs of migrants once they arrived at the shelter. This included ensuring that eligible respondents ate before researchers attempted to recruit them and ensuring that their beds would not be taken while they were with us by other people arriving at the shelter later in the evening. The survey itself was an intense one-hour experience with many different sections and complicated and repetitive questions. Therefore we ensured that participants were allowed take breaks from the survey if they needed to eat or drink, and that they could end the survey if they were too exhausted to continue.

The sensitivity to the needs of migrants also impacted our recruitment of participants and sampling procedure in the Nogales study. While we made sure to utilize a systematic random spatial sampling procedure, there were times when people who were randomly selected were too ill, exhausted, or injured to participate in the survey. In these instances we trusted our instinct and moved on to the next respondent in the sampling frame. However, it must be noted, seldom were people too tired, ill, or hurt to participate and therefore we would not expect our sampling method to be biased.

Our heightened awareness of the immediate needs of migrants, as well as their reservations regarding the sensitive nature of the questions, impacted the manner in which the survey instrument was administered. Previous researchers who have conducted similar work with this population in sending and receiving communities are well aware of the difficulties of administering conventional structured surveys (Massey 1987; Massey and Zenteno 2000; Cornelius and Lewis 2007). For example, in the Mexican Migration Project (MMP) (Massey 1987), researchers opted not to use a structured survey, instead relying on the development of the "ethno-survey" (Massey 1987). This alternative instrument was designed to capture the migration history of a respondent by allowing for a flexible interview schedule (Massey 1987; Massey and Zenteno 2000). While this approach has garnered some criticism from strict survey methodologists, it is important to note that they are trying to address the need for sensitivity in the examination of migration issues. We chose to use a more traditional approach with the administration of the MBCS survey in Nogales, but we also allowed for a more flexible protocol when reading respondents the survey questions, letting researchers make judgment calls about how to deliver questions and how to probe for more specific responses. Furthermore, we were open to deviating from the survey instrument if the respondent felt like he or she had other questions or concerns, or wanted to discuss another matter with us regarding his or her migration experience. Providing ample time for people to tell their stories helped us establish rapport with respondents in a short amount of time and allowed us to proceed with the rest of the survey.

One obvious factor that comes to mind when conducting research with any population is the issue of participant recruitment and whether or not to provide an incentive to participate or to compensate respondents for their time. Occasionally, phone cards were given as a sign of appreciation and compensation for people who participated in the research in Altar, although no compensation was offered as an enticement for participation. The researcher also contributed food donations and provided labor services to the shelter as a demonstration of his appreciation and gratitude for allowing him to conduct his research there. However, issues of incentives and compensation were not as easily sorted out when it came to our work in Nogales, primarily due to the high turnover rate, the sheer number of people at the shelter (50–150 per night), and the sampling procedure utilized in the project. In fact, this was a long-debated issue within our MBCS research team. In the end, rather than compensate individual respondents, we opted to make weekly donations to the shelter.

The MBCS research team seriously debated whether or not to offer respondents an incentive or compensation for participating in the study. Again, safety was a concern, as was equality. Given the systematic random sampling procedure utilized in the study, not all of the people who were present at the shelter were selected to participate, nor were those selected necessarily eligible to participate. Rather, only individuals who had been randomly selected *and* had attempted a crossing, been apprehended, and repatriated (all within the last six months) were eligible. An unnecessary and awkward situation could have occurred had we offered compensation to only those who completed the survey, and not to those who were ineligible or who wanted to participate but were not randomly chosen. In fact, we experienced similar situations when people wanted to participate in the study but were not randomly selected. We had to explain to these individuals that we were required to randomly choose people, but that we would be happy to informally talk with them before we left for the night. We are certain that the situation would have been much more difficult to manage had word gotten around that we were providing an incentive to participate.

We were also concerned about placing people at higher risk for being robbed or abused at the shelter or upon leaving the shelter in the morning, as it is not all that uncommon for people to have their possessions stolen while at the shelter. One must keep in mind that the intersection of, and heightened levels of, marginalization and vulnerability many migrants experience after or during a crossing attempt may place them in a situation of survival while near the border. Unfortunately, in some cases, people are forced to engage in activities that they would have otherwise never imagined doing, including stealing from others, out of desperation. By providing some people compensation (e.g., money, food, or phone cards) for their participation and not others, would we unknowingly be placing people at risk for having altercations or arguments with fellow migrants? As mentioned, given the sheer number of people present at the shelter on a given night, as well as the turnover rate of cohorts coming in and out of the shelter on a weekly basis, it would have been economically unfeasible to compensate those who participated, those who were not eligible to participate, those who refused to participate, and those who wanted to participate but were not randomly selected. In the end we decided to bring donations to the shelter on a nightly basis, including cleaning supplies, garbage bags, coffee, food, and clothes that would be managed and distributed by the shelter workers in a manner and time as they saw fit.

Overall, our research at these two sites has given us an awareness of the marginalization and vulnerability migrants experience that could have only come through firsthand accounts of working with the population. Ultimately, we had to adapt our methodologies and project goals to ensure that the immediate needs of participants were a top priority. We hope that our experiences and the knowledge gained throughout the research process can serve as a reference point for future studies.

Conclusion

Our research in both locations was carried out with the rights and safety of migrants in mind. The MBCS was essentially created with the help of migrants' testimonies and could have not been completed without their assistance. The six months of rigorous pre-testing in the shelter prior to the administration of the survey was crucial to the creation of the instrument and largely shaped the direction of the project. Most importantly, as we progressed with our research, we moved into a mixed-methods approach to gather narratives as well as closed-ended survey responses. As stated previously, we allowed for extensive conversation and researcher flexibility, but we did not systematically document these narratives. In the future, by combining both qualitative and quantitative approaches, we hope to maintain the rigor and possibilities for quantitative analysis without missing the opportunity for the nuanced understanding brought about by qualitative research.

We are constantly looking for new ways to limit the impact of research on our participants. While it is easy to make statements about how we sample or about allowing for participants to refuse or stop the process at any time, there is a lot of pressure on us as academics to maintain the highest, most rigorous methodological standards. This necessity is a result of the expectations of our peers in the academic world. Formulating a wider discussion between disciplines and topics will help to create a more realistic vision of acceptable and appropriate research methods when working with vulnerable and marginalized populations.

All too often seamless descriptions of methodologies prevail when attempting to publish research findings. The reality is, when it comes to executing a research design, one does the best one can with what the situation allows. This is especially true when working with a population whose immediate needs must be tended to. Moreover, for us, priorities need to shift from the researchers as experts, extracting "data" from "subjects," to working collaboratively to produce relevant and applicable scholarship that conveys the urgent needs related to the issues at hand. Only in this way will we generate truly powerful scholarship that not only has a wider impact, but also creates a scenario that does not contribute to the marginalization or the vulnerability of research participants. We need to be clear that our principal responsibility is to the generous people willing to share their experiences with us, and not just to the academic world.

Notes

Address correspondence to Daniel E. Martínez at the Department of Sociology, The George Washington University, 801 22nd Street, NW, Suite 409, Washington, D.C., 20052 (e-mail: mada0102@email.arizona.edu).

1. A significant portion (21 percent) of our sample spoke an indigenous language, although some preferred to speak English as well.

References

Andreas, Peter. 1998. The U.S. Immigration Control Offensive: Constructing an Image of Order on the Southwest Border. In Marcelo M. Suárez-Orozco, ed. *Crossings: Mexican Immigration in Interdisciplinary Perspectives.* Pp. 341–356. Cambridge, MA: Harvard University Press.

Anzaldo, Carlos, and Minerva Prado. 2005. *Indicie de marginación urbana, 2005.* Mexico, D.F.: Consejo Nacional de Población.

Bustamante, Jorge A. 2002. Immigrants' Vulnerability as Subjects of Human Rights. *International Migration Review* 36: 333–354.

Collins, Patricia Hill. 2000. Gender, Black Feminism, and Black Political Economy. *Annals of the American Academy of Political and Social Science* 568: 41–53.

———. 1998. It's All in the Family: Intersections of Gender, Race, and Nation. *Hypatia* 13: 62–82.

Cornelius, Wayne A. 2005. Controlling "Unwanted" Immigration: Lessons from the United States, 1993–2004. *Journal of Ethnic and Migration Studies* 31: 775–794.

———. 2001. Death at the Border: Efficacy and Unintended Consequences of U.S. Immigration Control Policy. *Population and Development Review* 27: 661–685.

Cornelius, Wayne A., and Jessa M. Lewis. 2007. *Impacts of Border Enforcement on Mexican Migration: The View from Sending Communities.* San Diego: Center for Comparative Immigration Studies.

Dávila, Alberto, José A. Pagán, and Gökçe Soydemir. 2002. The Short-term and Long-term Deterrence Effects of INS Border and Interior Enforcement on Undocumented Immigration. *Journal of Economic Behavior and Organization* 49: 459–472.

Eschbach, Karl, Jacqueline Hagan, Nestor Rodriguez, Rubén Hernández-León, and Stanley Bailey. 1999. Death at the Border. *International Migration Review* 33: 430–454.

Lindstrom, David P., and Nathanael Lauster. 2001. Local Economic Opportunity and the Competing Risks of Internal and U.S. Migration in Zacatecas, Mexico. *International Migration Review* 35: 1232–1256.

López-Córdova, Ernesto, Andrea R. Tokman, and Eric A. Verhoogen. 2005. Globalization, Migration, and Development: The Role of Mexican Migrant Remittances. *Economía* 6: 217–256.

Martínez, Daniel E. Forthcoming. Migrant Deaths in the Sonora Desert: Evidence of Unsuccessful Border Militarization Efforts from Southern Arizona. In Raquel Rubio Goldsmith, Celestino Fernández, Maribel Álvarez, and Araceli Masterson, eds. *¿No Vale Nada la Vida? La Vida No Vale Nada: Political Intersections of Migration and Death in the U.S. Mexico–Border*. Tucson: University of Arizona Press.

Massey, Douglas S. 1987. The Ethnosurvey in Theory and Practice. *International Migration Review* 21: 1498–1522.

Massey, Douglas S., and Rene Zenteno. 2000. A Validation of the Ethnosurvey: The Case of Mexico–U.S. Migration. *International Migration Review* 34: 766–793.

Rubio Goldsmith, Raquel, M. Melissa McCormick, Daniel Martínez, and Inez Magdalena Duarte. 2006. *The "Funnel Effect" and Recovered Bodies of Unauthorized Migrants Processed by the Pima County Office of the Medical Examiner, 1990–2005*. Tucson: Binational Migration Institute, Mexican American Studies and Research Center, University of Arizona.

STRATFOR. 2008. *Mexican Drug Cartels: Government Progress and Growing Violence*. Available at http://www.stratfor.com/sample/analysis/mexican-drug-cartels-government-progress-and-growing-violence

United Nations. 2007. *Human Development Report 2007/2008*. New York: United Nations Development Programme. http://hdr.undp.org/en/media/HDR_20072008_EN_Complete.pdf.

U.S. Citizenship and Immigration Services. 2010. Personal Communication.

CHAPTER SIX

Entre Los Mafiosos y La Chota

Ethnography, Drug Trafficking, and Policing in the South Texas–Mexico Borderlands

Santiago Ivan Guerra

Anthropologists have relied on ethnography as the foundational method-ology for learning about other cultural worlds. But what of anthropologists who study and write about their own communities? How does the ethno-graphic enterprise function for these so-called native anthropologists? In this chapter, I provide an analysis and description of the methodological tools employed in my ethnography of drug trafficking in the South Texas–Mexico borderlands, and I explore the varied effects of drug trafficking, drug abuse, incarceration, poverty, and violence through examples from my family history and my own life history.

An Anthropologist's Craft: The Ethnographic Enterprise

An anthropologist's mission is to document the social and cultural lives of people throughout the world. As part of this mission, anthropologists rely on ethnography as a methodological tool to gather information on a particular culture, and in the process produce a written ethnography that describes the cultural lives of these people: "The ethnographer's goal is to describe the way of life of a particular group from within, that is, by under-standing and communicating not only what happens but how the mem-bers of the group interpret and understand what happens" (Smith and

Kornblum 1996: 2). Anthropologists have, in the process, emphasized and aggrandized their ability to understand these cultures and relate them to others. What many anthropologists strive for is to "authentically" represent native informants' voices. These native voices are the firsthand accounts of different and often exoticized peoples distinct from the anthropologist's own cultural group. Within the American Boasian school of anthropology, the emphasis on native voices was part of an effort to legitimize ethnography, and by extension the field of American anthropology: "[B]y representing the 'native point of view' as text, Boas won modern ethnography the scientific authority to objectively present an unspoiled past uncontaminated by outsiders" (Lassiter 2005: 28).

However, critiques of both American and British anthropology stemmed from the anthropologists' objectification of their informants. Anthropologists studied at a distance from their native informants, observing by looking over their shoulders rather than engaging with the culture alongside their informants. In the early phases of ethnography, anthropologists were more accurately observers, watching, documenting, and studying the village from the safety of their tents. The critique of disengaged, observant anthropologists resulted in the "argument that individual experience should be more firmly situated at the center of ethnographic inquiry . . . an extremely significant turning point in ethnography itself, mainly because it demanded a more sustained and long-term focus on collaboration with native interlocutors" (Lassiter 2005: 39).

As a result of this critique, anthropologists more firmly established the methodological practice of participant observation, pushing anthropologists not just to observe other cultures, but also to participate in cultural practices alongside their native informants. The practice of participant observation, however, came with stipulations and warnings for anthropologists. As Ruth Behar eloquently notes, "Our intellectual mission is deeply paradoxical: get the 'native point of view' *pero por favor* without actually going native" (Behar 1997: 5). Moreover, the move towards participant observation put anthropologists in more direct contact with their native informants. Behar states: "We now stand on the same plane with our subjects; indeed, they will only tolerate us if we are willing to confront them face to face" (Behar 1997: 28).

As anthropologists came face to face with their native informants, they discovered that the natives could indeed "talk back." It was now possible for natives to contest the representation of their communities and eventually some of these natives even became anthropologists themselves, able to represent their communities and talk back to other anthropologists:

"Beginning with Americo Paredes, it was Chicano and Chicana critics—not the Nuer—who turned the anthropological mirror, questioning the way they had been represented by outsiders and offering their own, more complex and more lacerating representations, which made salient the question of who was the authority to speak for whom" (Behar 1997: 162). It was these so-called native anthropologists who challenged the notions of what it meant to do ethnography, and what it meant to be an anthropologist, a producer of cultural knowledge.

From Native to Anthropologist:
The Native Anthropologist Dilemma

Ordinarily, exceptional natives serve as the anthropologist's reliable key informants. The key informant served as a go-between who could aid the anthropologist in the understanding of the native population's cultural milieu. The key informant served as "a knowledgeable insider willing to serve as an informant on informants" (Weiss 1995: 20). The key informant is also a vital resource in helping the anthropologist build rapport with members of the native community. Establishing rapport is a critical part of the ethnographic process. As Robert P. McNamara makes clear,

> Gaining entry into hard-to-reach populations presents a host of problems for researchers. Often, the researcher must rely on informants to provide key information about the population as well as providing introduction to its members. Early on in my research, shopkeepers pointed out areas where a good deal of hustling takes place, offered opinions on the nature of the problem, and, in a few cases, introduced me to hustler. (1996: 52)

However, building rapport among native informants becomes even more difficult when researching clandestine activities. Such is the case with Claire Sterk, who states of the research endeavor:

> A researcher—a stranger—cannot simply walk up to a potential informant and start chatting with him or her, especially if the informant is involved in illegal activities. When initiating a conversation, the researcher must justify his or her presence and indicate the desire for interaction, usually without knowing whether the other person can be trusted. Gaining trust is very important. (1996: 89)

For many anthropologists, gaining entrée into their research community and establishing rapport are critical processes that consume most of the time dedicated to fieldwork. As a native anthropologist working in my own community, I rely on lifelong relationships as key resources for conducting my research. My connection to my community and my position as a native bring forth many questions in terms of the long-held anthropological debate regarding the effectiveness of insider or outsider status in conducting research. As Ruth Behar states of native anthropology:

> The last decade of meditation on the meaning of "native anthropology"—in which scholars claim a personal connection to the places in which they work—has opened up an important debate on what it means to be an insider in a culture. The importance of this "native anthropology" has helped to bring about a fundamental shift—the shift toward viewing identification, rather than difference, as the key defining image of anthropological theory and practice. (1997: 28)

The insider debate has had a significant impact on native anthropologists, who are criticized by mainstream anthropologists for being too intimately connected to the culture and the community and therefore taking for granted the significance of many social and cultural processes. On the other hand, natives and native anthropologists have critiqued mainstream anthropologists for often misinterpreting and misrepresenting their cultures and communities. As anthropologists, however, our status as insiders and/or outsiders is often a more complicated issue. As Nancy Naples argues regarding this debate: "'[O]utsiderness' and 'insiderness' are not fixed or static positions but ever-shifting and permeable social locations. Thus, when conducting ethnographic research in their country of origin, social scientists are simultaneously insiders and outsiders" (Naples 1996: 139).

As a native anthropologist, I recognize the limitations of doing fieldwork in my own community, but I also recognize the advantages. As a native with friendly and familial relationships with many of my informants, I have access to a large pool of research informants. As Doug Foley mentions in his study of race relations in his hometown in Iowa: "Since I already knew many people, I was able to talk to hundreds of people during my stay in Tama" (Foley 1995: viii). Established rapport and entrée is one of the most important advantages of being a native anthropologist and/or conducting research in your home community. For myself, the ability to speak to informants about taboo subjects and the ability to quickly identify important informants helped me to make the most of my fieldwork. In the case of research on drug trafficking, having to ask around town about what drug traffickers to talk to, or even about who is a drug trafficker, could pose a risk to the safety of the social scientist. Furthermore, gaining entrée and establishing rapport within this insular group presents great difficulty for many social scientists.

Yet for native anthropologists, including myself, the research experience is not simply "a walk in the park," or a simpler and easier endeavor. Rather, the research experience for native anthropologists is just as emotionally and mentally taxing as it is for mainstream anthropologists. As Edmundo Morales makes clear regarding his experience researching coca production in the Andes: "Becoming an ethnographer of the Andes, native though I was, was a long process, for learning from or observing other people whose culture and society is the same as one's own roots I found very difficult and possible only when a disciplined approach was incorporated into my everyday routine" (Morales 1996: 120). What is often not considered about the native anthropologist critique is that these individuals are, after all, trained anthropologists. They receive the same theoretical and methodological training as any other anthropologist in their field. They often follow similarly rigorous research routines as their mainstream anthropologist counterparts. However, for native anthropologists their emotional connectedness to the community presents a host of difficult problems associated with returning home. For Doug Foley, returning home to Iowa is both emotionally rewarding and difficult at the same time. He states:

> In many ways studying race relations in my hometown is terribly difficult for me. My memories of growing up on an Iowa farm are very positive. I still tell stories about haymaking that extoll my noble heartland origins. My urban, academic friends chastise me for romanticizing rural life. They say I have consumed too much foreign food and films to ever return. Yet, for all my travels and fancy education, I still feel these Iowa roots. (Foley 1995: viii)

For myself, returning home to conduct research on the impact of drug trafficking and policing was a rewarding and taxing experience bound up with feelings of pain, guilt remorse, nostalgia, excitement, and happiness. As a native significantly affected by drug trafficking and policing in this community, my experience and my knowledge are just as important as those of my other informants. I rely on this experience as a source of ethnographic knowledge through a related practice of native anthropology—the method and practice of auto/ethnography.

On Reflexivity: Auto/ethnography and the Vulnerable Participant

Due to the nature of my study, I employ auto/ethnography methodology because I am both a "native" of the group that I am studying, but also because I was raised in this community and as a result I myself was significantly impacted by the policing and drug trafficking taking place in this community. According to Deborah E. Reed-Danahay (1997), "[A]utoethnography is defined as a form of self-narrative that places the self within in a social context. It is both a method and a text in the case of ethnography" (1997: 9). Moreover, the "term has a double sense—referring either to the ethnography of one's own group or to autobiographical writing that has ethnographic interest" (1997: 2). Therefore, my own research applies to both senses of the term because I am writing about my own group, as well as incorporating parts of my own autobiography, to understand the effects of drug trafficking in Starr County.

As a native ethnographer, I must maneuver through my different roles in the community (brother, uncle, cousin, friend, nephew, son, etc.) at the same time that I am attempting to establish my new role as anthropologist. I also employ auto/ethnography as a research tool by interrogating my own life history and that of my family in this community as well as the people who were present during my adolescence. As Ruth Behar states, "The genres of life history and life story are merging with the *testimonio*, which speaks to the role of witnessing in our time as a key form of approaching and transforming reality" (Behar 1997: 27). Problems, however, arise in conducting critical, self-reflexive ethnographic research on my own community, and my own life history. In bearing witness and attempting to write about my community, I become what I like to think of as a vulnerable participant, expanded from Ruth Behar's conception of the vulnerable observer. Interrogating something as sensitive as the history of drug trafficking in a rural border community becomes an exercise in vulnerability.

Reflexivity has become an integral part of contemporary ethnographic practice. However, social scientists have been critical of anthropologists' implementation of reflexivity. Speaking in defense of the value of personal reflection, Ruth Behar argues that "[e]fforts at self-revelation flop not because the personal voice has been used, but because it has been poorly used, leaving unscrutinized the connection, intellectual and emotional, between the observer and the observed" (Behar 1997: 13–14). Behar continues: "To assert that one is a 'white middle-class woman' or a 'black gay man' or a 'working-class Latina' within one's study of Shakespeare or Santeria is only interesting if one is able to draw deeper connections between one's personal experience and the subject under study" (Behar 1997: 13). Therefore, reflexivity is not in itself an important or useful methodological practice. Rather, it is a practice that must be critically employed with the purpose of providing a perspective that supports and enhances the ethnographic data.

For this study, the significance of my own life history, and my reflection on it, stems from the impact of the drug trade on my family members and myself. My testimonio serves as a situated base of knowledge about the drug trade and drug abuse and its impact on individuals and families in Starr County. Other social scientists conducting research on clandestine activities have attempted to situate themselves within their communities and get close enough to "feel" and reflect upon the complexities of their informants' lives. Terry Williams, an influential sociologist, conducted ethnographic research among cocaine dealers and crack users in New York City during the 1980s and 1990s:

> A guiding principle of Williams's research is the desire to take the insider's point of view, rather than approaching his subject with the preconceived ideas of an outsider. In order to see the world through the eyes of the insider he must become intimate with the people he is observing. In fact, he becomes part of their life; they are no longer "subjects" or informants but friends and associates. (Smith and Kornblum 1996: 27)

As a native ethnographer, I am already intimately involved with many of my research informants. These intimate relationships allow for access to taboo and guarded information. But maneuvering through these relationships is also part of the auto/ethnographic method and practice, and forms part of a specialized type of auto/ethnography termed *intimate ethnography*.

Entre Familia: Intimate Ethnography and the Family

Due to the nature of studying such a taboo and "dangerous" subject and practice, I also employ a type of auto/ethnography described by Alisse

Waterston and Barbara Rylko-Bauer (2006) as intimate ethnography, where one engages in ethnography with interlocutors who are intimately connected to the ethnographer. Now, in the case of studying the drug trade, intimate ethnography is important because it allows the ethnographer to "probe at a very deep level of intimacy" (Waterston and Rylko-Bauer 2006: 397). Furthermore, the method allows for deep access, and it "offers a way to expose the multiple layers of consciousness, connecting the personal to the cultural" (Waterston and Rylko-Bauer 2006: 397).

In defending the use of intimate ethnography as an important practice of anthropology, Waterston and Rylko-Bauer argue that:

> Anthropology leads us to examine the multiple connections between individuals and larger histories, and we use the discipline as our guide to understanding how social forces become embodied as individual experience. Our positionality as anthropologists allows us to explore intimate domains without obscuring the role of cultural, historical, and social-structural factors in causality. In this way, anthropology rescues our projects from falling into solipsism, from psychological reductionism as well as the distortions of disembodied abstractions. (2006: 409)

Waterston and Rylko-Bauer's goal involves "talking to and interviewing a respective parent with the goal of writing a life history that is embedded in broader frames of political economy and a sociohistorical context" with the purpose of exploring the "implications of their experiences for understanding the aftermaths of history as well as the world we live in today" (Waterston and Rylko-Bauer 2006: 397). Due to their familial relationship with their research informants, Waterston and Rylko-Bauer are positioned as daughters within the research endeavor, but "the anthropologist in each of us is ever present, posing broader questions and looking beyond the personal story" (Waterston and Rylko-Bauer 2006: 397). For me, my familial relationship to drug traffickers and policing agents prompted and facilitated my research endeavor. The incarceration of my *primo* Jay and the kidnapping of my *primo* Joker inspired me to critically understand the impact of drug trafficking and border policing on our community and our family.

Waterston and Rylko-Bauer recognize that there are those who might critique research with family members and about intimate subjects. As they state: "We are aware that we stretch the methodological boundaries in taking the deeply personal and emotional as our anthropological subject" (Waterston and Rylko-Bauer 2006: 398). However, they defend their approach to intimate ethnography, arguing, "A long tradition exists within anthropology of using personal experience as impetus for studying a particular subject or of actually incorporating those experiences into the process of research and analysis" (Waterston and Rylko-Bauer 2006: 405). Ultimately, they argue that innovative approaches to ethnography, such as intimate ethnography and auto/ethnography, "enrich ethnography while challenging anthropologists to represent ourselves and those from whom we are privileged to learn in ways that honor and do justice to the reality of our informants' lives and history" (Waterston and Rylko-Bauer 2006: 405). Throughout my research, I have used auto/ethnography and intimate ethnography as a mechanism to highlight the impact of drug trafficking and policing on Starr County. In the ethnographic descriptions that follow I paint an intimate picture of the effects of drug trafficking, drug abuse, violence, and policing on my family, through examples from my family history and my own life history.

El Armadillo: Law Enforcement Officers in the Line of Fire

The best-known casualty of the drug war is the Mexican American Drug Enforcement Agent Enrique "Kiki" Camarena, who was murdered while serving undercover in Guadalajara, Mexico. Camarena was a naturalized U.S. citizen, and joined the Drug Enforcement Administration in 1974 after serving in the U.S. Marine Corps for two years. For the first few years of his career, Camarena served as an agent in the Calexico and Fresno, California, district offices. Eventually Camarena was promoted to the rank of DEA special agent, and he was transferred to the Guadalajara resident office in July 1981. At the time, Guadalajara had become an important drug trafficking site and home base for the Guadalajara cartel led by Rafael Caro Quintero and Miguel Angel Felix Gallardo. While the Guadalajara cartel was initially involved in marijuana and heroin smuggling, in the 1980s they also became involved in large scale cocaine trafficking through their partnership with Colombian cartels. When Camarena joined the DEA's Guadalajara office, he began serving as an undercover agent attempting to infiltrate the area's drug trafficking organizations. He was able to help disrupt and even break up some of the organizations working out of Guadalajara. However, on February 7, 1985, Camarena was kidnapped by members of a drug trafficking organization presumably under the direction of the Guadalajara cartel. Nearly a month later, Camarena's body was discovered. It was later discovered that he had been tortured before finally being killed (United States Drug Enforcement Administration, "Biographies of DEA Agents and Employees Killed in Action").

After Camarena's death the United States launched an intense investigation to bring Camarena's killers to justice. The government was eventually able to capture some of the individuals suspected in Camarena's kidnapping and death, and after an eight-week trial they were found guilty of the murder (Malone 1989). After his death Camarena became a symbol of the U.S. government's war on drugs. He was incorporated into popular culture as well, through a television docudrama mini-series titled *Drug Wars: the Camarena Story*, which detailed his death and the investigation that followed. After his death, the Drug Enforcement Agency also used Camerena as a symbol for their drug-free Red Ribbon Week Campaign (United States Drug Enforcement Administration, "Red Ribbon Week Factsheet"). The Red Ribbon Week Campaign was launched in 1988 to urge young people throughout the United States to live a drug-free life: "By wearing red ribbons and participating in community anti-drug events, young people pledge to live a drug-free life and pay tribute to DEA special agent Enrique 'Kiki' Camarena" (United States Drug Enforcement Administration, "Red Ribbon Week Factsheet").

At the time of the launching of the Red Ribbon Campaign in 1988, the drug trade in South Texas was rapidly transforming Starr County. In 1989 a group of Starr County Sheriff's deputies were involved in a gunfight with alleged drug traffickers in northern Starr County. My uncle Xavier Lopez was one of the deputies involved in the gunfight. One night in April 1989, a group of men stormed a home in Roma, Texas, and began opening fire on people inside the home. The violent scene was part of escalating violence in the Starr County region attributed to conflict between drug trafficking organizations. Shortly after shots rang out in the Roma neighborhood, sheriff's deputies were called out to respond. My *tio* Xavier was on duty that night serving in the Starr County Sheriff's Department's Roma substation. In the late 1980s only two deputies were on duty for the Roma area overnight. By the time Xavier responded, the shooting suspects had already fled the scene, and a high-speed chase ensued down Highway 83 in Starr County. So Xavier sped southeast on Highway 83, in close pursuit of the suspects. After a short chase through Starr County, the suspects lost control of their vehicle, and it came to a screeching halt. Xavier stopped close behind the suspects' disabled vehicle, and he exited the police cruiser. As Xavier exited his vehicle, a gunfight ensued between him and the suspects. Shortly after the gunfight began, another Starr County Sheriff's deputy responded to the scene as Xavier's backup. During the exchange of gunfire, Xavier and the other deputy were wounded. Even though they were both down, the deputies continued to exchange gunfire with the suspects. Eventually, more law enforcement units arrived at the scene, and authorities were able to arrest the suspects. The damage, however, had already been done.

My tio Xavier had been shot a total of six times during the entire exchange. At the time I was six years old, and my mother and I were staying at my great-grandmother's home. That night the local evening news covered the story. Images flashed on the screen of a man on a gurney being wheeled into the emergency room; he was covered in blood and a breathing mask covered his face. After the reporter delivered the news, we knew that the man on the gurney was Xavier. My great-grandmother began crying at the sight of her youngest son, close to death, being wheeled across the screen; she had already lost two sons. My mother, also in tears, walked over to my great-grandmother and attempted to comfort her.

After doctors were able to stop the bleeding, Xavier eventually recovered from the gunshot wounds. He continued to serve as a Starr County Sheriff's deputy for a few more years, and today he works as a jailer for the Starr County Sheriff's Department. Now everyone knows him by his nickname, "El Armadillo." I have asked family members about why my uncle is nicknamed El Armadillo. Most of them typically respond: *"Pues quien sabe?"* [Who knows?] I then suggest, *"No crees que le llaman el Armadillo, porque se lo tirotiaron y como quiera vivio,* you know *como si fuera* bulletproof like an armadillo?" [You don't think they call him the Armadillo because they shot him up and he survived, you know like if he was bullet proof like an armadillo?] When I told my mom and some other relatives this, they replied *"Ah . . . pues a lo mejor"* [Ah . . . well maybe so]. And since the shooting, my uncle's reputation has grown and he's become a larger-than-life figure known by most law enforcement officers and criminal justice personnel as El Armadillo. His reputation grew even more in the late 1990s, when a *conjunto* musician composed a *corrido* in his honor about the shooting of El Armadillo. In 1999, Mingo Saldivar released his album *El Chicano Alegre*, with a track entitled *El Corrido del Armadillo*. In the corrido Saldivar, a close friend and *compadre* of Xavier's, describes the shooting that almost took El Armadillo's life, but he also portrays Xavier as a larger-than-life hero who would not go down even after being hit by six rounds of ammunition. Saldivar constructs a counter-narcocorrido, in which the Mexican American lawman is celebrated, singing *"que vivan los judiciales, guardenlos en su memoria"* [long live the law officers, keep them in your thoughts/memories]. The corrido celebrates El Armadillo's heroic actions, but it silences the fact that Xavier almost lost his life in the process and he came very close to becoming another fallen officer of the drug war.

In late 2007 a group of us, including my mother, my aunt, and my fiancée, visited El Armadillo at his home. He welcomed us in and after a few minutes of "hellos" and "como ha estado" [how have you been], we all sat around to watch the Dallas Cowboys game. We all sat down to watch the game, but El Armadillo, always a jokester and showman, took advantage of the captive audience before him. He quickly retreated to his room to fetch the x-rays from his recent motorcycle accident. Then he gathered everyone around to give us all a comical account of how his accident unfolded. Everyone burst into laughter at the lighthearted retelling of the accident and El Armadillo's carefree mood. He even told everyone about how he fought with the doctors during rehabilitation, hit on the pretty nurses, and complained about the food. He showed us all the x-rays of the pins that they had used to resent his bones. The accident inevitably led to questions about his other near death experience, and my aunts (El Armadillo's sisters) responded by saying *"Es como dicen, hierba mala no se muere"* [It's like they say, a bad weed never dies]. El Armadillo even lifted his shirt to show everyone his scars from the shooting, a series of long marks that ran across his chest and waist. But then he became more serious, an uncommon occurrence for him, and he was nearly in tears reflecting on the fact that he could have died. He recalled that when the shooting took place he was not afraid; he was young and invincible. But now at the age of 57, he can see how close to death he really was.

His serious moment quickly faded, and El Armadillo returned to being the fun-loving, attention-grabbing individual he has been for as long as I can remember. He quickly turned our attention to the armadillo memorabilia all over the living room. He tells us, *"Mira todos los regalos que le traen al Armadillo"* [Look at all the gifts they bring the Armadillo]. El Armadillo was lucky to have not died that night in April 1989. He could have been another casualty in the drug war, like Enrique Camarena or the number of other law enforcement officers who have fallen in the 40-year duration of the drug war.

Mis Primos, Los Mafiosos:
South Texas Drug Traffickers

Of the five *primos-hermanos* I was raised with, three have worked as drug traffickers in South Texas. Two of them served extensive jail time for serious drug convictions, and I am the only one of the six who pursued a college degree. These are not optimistic numbers for young Mexican American men growing up along the South Texas border. Increasingly, many of these young men are funneled into the drug trade, to work as mules, marijuana packers, and in some cases as drug trafficking hit men. As historian Ramon Ruiz attests, "If smugglers need a 'mule,' they find a teenager who wants to earn a buck driving a truck from the river to Rio Grande City, one of Starr County's towns. After a while, the unemployed young man begins wearing fancy cowboy boots and driving a new pickup" (Ruiz 1998: 191). The stories that follow are of two young men who formerly participated in the drug trade as low-level drug workers. I collected these stories through informal interviews with these young men, as well as through my own recollections of the events described.

Jay: A Drug Mule

When I was in high school my cousin Jay began working as one of these drug mules. At the time he had dropped out of high school, after being held back for three years. Jay's position in the drug trade entailed driving a 4x4 pickup loaded with marijuana from the river to a stash house a couple of miles away. He had worked in the drug trade for a few years without incident, but in the process he had developed a cocaine habit that would later develop into addiction. Consequently, most of Jay's earnings were spent on supporting his drug habit. Jay's addiction to cocaine made him want to continue participating in the drug trade simply to facilitate his own access to drugs. Then, in late 2000, he was busted transporting 2,000 pounds of marijuana. One unlucky night Border Patrol agents intercepted radio conversations that discussed the shipment that Jay was transporting. He told me that when they were at the river loading the truck, they were suspicious of some people talking on their radio frequency. However, the boss decided that they would continue to complete the transaction, and Jay got in the truck and started driving. After a while the Border Patrol's Expedition, a type of vehicle that is ubiquitous in Starr County, was already close behind him. He sped up and drove through fences and finally jumped out of the truck to run—but not before he grabbed a few bales of marijuana and threw them into the brush to hide them. As he was running, he said that a helicopter was overhead and they started shooting at him from above. He said that he eventually got tired of running and he knew that they were going to catch him either way, so he just kneeled on the ground and put his hands on his head. A few moments later, a Border Patrol officer kicked him in the back and proceeded to handcuff him. When I ask him about what he was feeling during all of this, if he was scared at all, he tells me, "*Yo ya sabia que no me iban a matar, que nomas me estaban tirando pa'sustarme. Pero el chingazo que me dio el Border Patrol si me dolio chingos.*" [I already knew that they were not going to kill me, that they were just shooting to scare me. But when the Border Patrol hit me it hurt like hell.]

Jay was eventually convicted in federal court of drug possession with intent to distribute and was sentenced to three and a half years in prison. He told me that at his trial, he knew that if he said anything, like pointed fingers at any of the other people involved—what is referred to on the border as *poniendo el dedo*—he would be as good as dead. He said he remembered knowing that there were people in the courtroom working for his boss, observing what he was saying. This is the case with many low-level drug traffickers; if you get caught, your boss will help you with an attorney and even send you money for the commissary when you are in jail, but you have to keep your mouth shut. Jay began serving his sentence in 2001, or as many Mexican Americans from the Valley call it, "*Se fue al colegio*"—he went off to college. At the time I was myself in "college" and Jay was transferred to the Bastrop Federal Correction Center. Since I was the relative living closest to Jay, I began visiting him on the weekends and I became one of his primary visitors since our family was unable to make the trip to visit him very often. On Saturday mornings, while other college students were nursing hangovers or recovering from late nights of partying, I was up early driving to the prison so I could see my primo. I always had to remind myself to pack quarters in a Ziploc bag in case my cousin wanted a snack from the vending machines.

Of the men in U.S. prisons, a majority are men of color serving time for drug convictions, mostly charges of conspiracy and possession. In Texas a large contingency of these men are Mexican American, giving rise to prison gangs such as the Mexican Mafia, Texas Syndicate, and the Chicano Brotherhood (TCB). Since the 1980s an increasing number of these Mexican American inmates are from the Rio Grande Valley. As a result, within many federal and state prisons across Texas, a new Mexican

American gang is now present, *Vallucos*, composed of men from the Rio Grande Valley. Prison gangs, including Vallucos, are based on the same structural organization as the hierarchy of the military and policing agencies. During his time in prison, Jay became a member of the Vallucos, primarily because of the protection that the gang provided. Before he became a member of Vallucos, Jay was not guaranteed protection from other prisoners. As a result, he ended up getting into conflicts with various prisoners and most probably was in danger of losing his life. El Mesteno, a cousin of ours from El Canton, came to Jay's rescue. As a high-ranking member of Vallucos, El Mesteno was able to recruit Jay and provide him with the necessary protection he needed to survive his prison experience.

Jay has often recounted stories of the violence he experienced within the prisons he was held in. The different gangs often settled disputes between one another with violent actions such as stabbings and hand-to-hand combat. But prison gangs often settle disputes within their own ranks by using physical violence, and often *brincan* (jump) other members to discipline them. The engagement in physical violence by gang members in the prison system reproduces fear and violence. Once released from prison, Jay still had to attempt to distance himself from the practice of drug trafficking, which previously was an integral part of his life, for fear of returning to prison. In doing so, he had to overcome his addiction to cocaine, so as not to be enticed to return to the drug lifestyle that had landed him in jail in the first place. Although his participation in drug rehab programs allowed for him to slowly overcome the desire to partake in the drug lifestyle, Jay still faces the problem of being unable to secure a good job due to his felony conviction, making his reentry into society and abandonment of the drug trade a complicated and daunting task. Today, Jay works as a roughneck on some oilfields in Louisiana. Most of his crew of roughnecks are former drug smugglers from the Rio Grande Valley. He has a three-year-old daughter now, and though she's given him a new lease on life he continues to struggle with drug addiction.

Joker: A Marijuana Packer

Jay's younger brother Joker also began working in the drug trade as a teenager. Joker is just a week older than I am. He has worked for many years in the drug trade as a marijuana packer and a transporter driving drugs up to *conectas* in Houston, Texas. However, the majority of his work in the drug trade centered around being a marijuana packer. At the time, he lived in a small one-room cinderblock building behind my uncle's house, where he compressed marijuana into blocks of various sizes. The purpose of Joker's worker was to repackage large 100-pound marijuana bundles into smaller, strategically packaged blocks that could be hidden in *clavos*, or concealed compartments in automobiles. Joker and some of his associates also tried to devise new ways to package drugs to ship past the Border Patrol check-points located within 100 miles of the South Texas border, in order to reach their conectas up north.

Joker had been involved in the drug trade since the age of 17. Like Jay, his brother, he dropped out of high school because severe dyslexia made it impossible for him to continue to the next grade level. Since dropping out of high school, Joker has attempted to support himself in a variety of ways ranging from construction work to oil drilling. However, between the late 1990s and 2005, he primarily worked as marijuana packer. However, on January 1, 2004, Joker's life took a tragic turn when he entered a system of debt bondage with his bosses. On New Year's Eve, Joker went out and partied with his friends and girlfriend, leaving a large load of marijuana unattended in his *cuartito*. When he returned in the early morning, he found that someone had broken in and taken the marijuana. Later, that afternoon, Joker's bosses picked him up and took him to a secluded ranch. They tortured him and beat him for several hours, expecting that he would own up to the fact that he himself stole the marijuana or at least turn in whoever he suspected of the theft. His bosses also accused Joker's brother Jay of having stolen the shipment, to which Joker replied: "*Trayte a es culero pa' ca y si se las robo el, yo mismo me trueno al bastardo*," which translates to, "Bring that asshole here and if he did steal the pot I'll kill him myself. The bosses did eventually bring Jay to the ranch, and tortured him as well. However, they could not prove that either Joker or Jay had stolen the pot. The bosses eventually released both Joker and Jay, telling them, "*Si no hubiera sido tan buen amigo del difunto Blas, aqui me trueno a los dos*"—essentially, that if it was not for his friendship with our deceased grandfather, he would have killed them both. Joker, however, was charged with the responsibility of packing marijuana for most of 2004 without pay in order to make up for the "lost" shipment. It was eventually revealed that Joker's own bosses had taken the shipment to teach him a lesson. This unfortunate incident served to keep Joker entangled in the complicated web of the drug trade, and furthermore to keep him in a state of constant fear and distrust.

Conclusion

The complexities of drug trafficking in the borderlands require a critical social analysis that situates the experiences of borderlands communities within the larger networks of international drug distribution. My research on drug trafficking in the South Texas–Mexico borderlands reveals the complex social relationships that emerge in border communities as a result of the escalation of the drug trade and the related practice of border policing. The drug trade and border policing affect not just drug traffickers and drug enforcement agents, but also their family, friends, and other members of border communities.

Ethnography as the foundational method of anthropology has transformed throughout the history of the discipline. Within anthropology, debates have raged about who can adequately represent the cultural lives of people around the world. While some mainstream anthropologists have argued that native anthropologists cannot adequately represent their own culture, native anthropologists have critiqued mainstream anthropologists for misrepresentations of various cultures. My goal in this chapter has not been to privilege native anthropologists over mainstream anthropologists, but rather to recognize my positionality as a native anthropologist and to elaborate on my use of auto/ethnography and intimate ethnography as important methodological tools for critically exploring social and cultural phenomena in Starr County.

My own personal history, as well as my family's history, has been shaped by both the escalation of drug trafficking and the related practices of border policing and border militarization. In the process of becoming an anthropologist, I have come to recognize the ethnographic value of our stories. Growing up as a borderlander within kinship networks of both drug traffickers and drug-policing agents has provided me with insight into the nuances of both social worlds. It has also shown me where the lines of distinction between these two worlds blur to form a borderlands of legality and illegality, of good guys and bad guys, of us and them, that has proven difficult for others to interpret and decipher.

The personal experience of growing up within this social, cultural, and legal borderlands has proved profound in shaping my professional practice as an anthropologist. Employing auto/ethnography and intimate ethnography has been vital to my research endeavors. For many of us, our bordered experiences, or our experiences in the borderlands, have informed the initiation of our research projects. My own research on drug trafficking did not develop until my cousin Jay was imprisoned on drug trafficking charges. It was the visits to a federal prison with Jay and our weekly conversations that sparked in me the intellectual curiosity to investigate the social phenomena of drug trafficking, border policing, and border militarization. Until then, drug trafficking was just another unwelcome part of growing up along the border.

More than a methodological advantage and decision, my research efforts also emerged from an ethical decision informed by my growing activist spirit and social justice mission. I was initially drawn to anthropology with the goal of participating in a knowledge-building project that could shape social justice projects along the border. Having witnessed injustices and the transformation of my borderlands home into a militarized zone where Mexicans on both sides of the border have become the victims and executioners of the international drug war, I was driven by the need to understand the conflict. Moreover, the ethical decision to embark on this research project was also spurred by the growing body of literature on the border drug war. The drug war literature that exploded was empty of stories like those I had experienced and witnessed along the South Texas–Mexico border, and it was also absent of any invested connection to the many borderlands communities affected by drug trafficking and drug policing. I have since found it necessary to expand the drug war policy conversation through the knowledge of the border interlocutors who have shaped my research. It is through this research and this situated knowledge that a new avenue of drug policy might open up—one that might minimize human rights abuses throughout the Americas, incarceration rates of people of color in the United States, and deaths throughout Latin America.

This research project, however, has also posed significant dilemmas for me both personally and professionally. Having embraced auto/ethnography and intimate ethnography, my research has occasionally been subject to criticisms of bias and lack of objectivity. Moreover, I am cognizant of the fact that conducting research in my hometown and within my own kinship networks poses possible risks for my research informants. I constantly struggle with new research efforts and writing strategies to protect the identities of my research informants. Coincidently, the ethical dilemmas that I have faced throughout this research process have proven beneficial in shaping new, refined methodological practices. For most current and future border researchers, myself included, engaged study of border policing, border militarization, drug trafficking, undocumented migration, and criminal enterprise requires a sustained reflexivity that will continue to shape and refine research methods and ethics in our current and future research projects.

References

Behar, Ruth. 1997. *The Vulnerable Observer: Anthropology That Breaks Your Heart*. Boston: Beacon Press.

Foley, Douglas. 1995. *The Heartland Chronicles*. Philadelphia: University of Pennsylvania Press.

Lassiter, Luke E. 2005. *The Chicago Guide to Collaborative Ethnography*. Chicago: University of Chicago Press.

Malone, Michael P. 1989. *The Enrique Camarena Case: A Forensic Nightmare*. Report by the Federal Bureau of Investigation: Washington, D.C.

McNamara, Robert P. 1996. Earning a Place in the Hustler's World. In Carolyn D. Smith and William Kornblum, eds. *In the Field: Readings on the Field Research Experience*. Pp. 51–58. Westport, CT: Praeger Publishers.

Morales, Edmundo. 1996. Researching Peasants and Drug Producers. In Carolyn D. Smith and William Kornblum, eds. *In the Field: Readings on the Field Research Experience*. Pp. 119–127. Westport, CT: Praeger Publishers.

Naples, Nancy A. 1996. The Outsider Phenomenon. In Carolyn D. Smith and William Kornblum, eds. *In the Field: Readings on the Field Research Experience*. Pp. 139–149. Westport, CT: Praeger Publishers.

Reed-Danahay, Deborah E. 1997 *Auto/Ethnography: Rewriting the Self and the Social*. New York: Berg.

Ruiz, Ramon Eduardo. 1998. *On the Rim of Mexico: Encounters of the Rich and Poor*. Boulder, CO: Westview Press.

Smith, Carolyn D. and William Kornblum, eds. 1996. *In the Field: Readings on the Field Research Experience*. Westport, CT: Praeger Publishers.

Sterk, Claire. 1996. Prostitution, Drug Use and Aids. In Carolyn D. Smith and William Kornblum, eds. *In the Field: Readings on the Field Research Experience*. Pp. 87–95. Westport, CT: Praeger Publishers.

United States Drug Enforcement Administration. N.d. Biographies of DEA Agents and Employees Killed in Action. http://www.justice.gov/dea/agency/10bios.htm, accessed January 7, 2010.

———. N.d. Red Ribbon Week Factsheet. http://www.justice.gov/dea/ongoing/redribbon_factsheet.html, accessed January 7, 2010.

Waterston, Alisse, and Barbara Rylko-Bauer. 2006. Out of the Shadows of History and Memory: Personal Family Narratives in Ethnographies of Rediscovery. *American Ethnologist* (33)3: 397–412.

Weiss, Robert Stuart. 1995. *Learning from Strangers: The Art and Method of Qualitative Interview Studies*. New York: Free Press.

CHAPTER SEVEN

Shaping Public Opinion on Migration in Mexico

The Challenges of Gathering and Proving Information for the National News Media

Manuel Chavez, Scott Whiteford,
and Silvia Nuñez Garcia

Introduction

Mexicans learn about the perils and opportunities of the trip north to the United States, crossing the border, and migrant life from return migrants, songs, government announcements, and the media, especially newspapers, radio, and television. Despite the importance of the media, few studies have systematically examined the context in which journalists and reporters from influential elite news media in Mexico report on migration experiences, weapons smuggling, trafficking drugs and people across the border, and violence experienced in the area. Similarly, reporters inform the public about the changing conditions of the labor markets and their impact on migration, the flows of remittances, and the migrant experiences with U.S. agents at the border. Knowing how journalists provide first reports and how the media shape information and influence public opinion is essential to understanding how citizens perceive and understand issues ranging from U.S. immigration policy to binational initiatives to address border security. The importance of media information is essential in creating public opinion, which in turn often impacts public policy.

In this chapter we use qualitative content analysis and interviews to examine how four major Mexico City–based newspapers covered and presented to their readers important issues associated with migration, border security, and international cooperation. The newspapers play a critical role in informing the public, but in so doing they also contribute to public discourse by framing the discussions on national policies and programs. Drawing on well-known columnists, academics, and political figures, Mexican newspapers' owners and editors compete for readers, audiences, and advertisers. As a result, papers significantly differ from each other politically, professionally, and in terms of style. Access to and the sharing of information with the public about organized crime activities or high-profile political issues as migration are often dangerous for reporters as well as editors, as the tragic killings of Mexican reporters between 2010–2012 demonstrate (Archibold 2012; Shirk 2011, 2010).

While this volume examines a range of research methods used by researchers studying immigration and the social/political conflicts inherent to the border itself, this chapter focuses on the journalistic practices of the Mexican news media and their methods of gathering and editing information, and how material comes together as final stories presented to the public. All of these functions raise ethical issues for both reporters and social scientists alike, which we explore in the conclusion of this chapter. Of particular importance is contextualizing the border in the structure of power of two major countries. News professionals including journalists, reporters, and editors are always subject to biases derived from their own personal perspectives. These perspectives stem from political ideologies, personal education, ethics, and professional training. Managing editors are responsible for adjusting and reducing the personal biases that journalists inevitably introduce into their stories and reports. Some news media organizations have the assistance of community councils, section editors, and professional copyeditors to ensure that the stories reflect objectively the reality they report.

A systemic problem in the Mexican news media is that Mexico City, as capital and central node of power, concentrates the most influential national news media organizations, both printed and electronic. Regionally, there are examples of excellent journalism, such as in Hermosillo, Monterrey, Nuevo Laredo, Mérida, and Guadalajara; but the Mexican national news media continues to set the public agenda through the national newspapers (*Reforma, El Universal, La Jornada, El Financiero*, and *Excelsior*). In addition, the influential syndicated radio shows are all transmitted from Mexico City to the entire country, including Radio Mil, Radio Formula, Radio XEW, and Radio Cien, with journalists, columnists, conductors, and sources all based in the national capital. TV broadcasting follows similar patterns of the radio, as the major networks (Televisa and TV Azteca) with their large newsrooms are located in Mexico City and they transmit digitally and via cable to the rest of the country. So, as the Mexican news media have a dominating capital-centric perspective, it is not surprising to see the frames, bias, and weight of Mexico City in the information that is provided to the rest of Mexico about migration to the U.S. (Guerrero 2011; Hughes 2006; Lawson 2002; Chavez 2008).

We will lay out a qualitative approach to content analysis in the context of national opinion-makers framing the debate on migration, asking, among other questions, such as how migrant voices are represented and framed by the national press. We also wanted to know how border security and violence is presented by the newspapers and which newspapers focus on binational cooperation, for example by addressing public health needs, in contrast to the intensification of the pressure to deal with human rights abuses or arms smuggling.

A second theme of inquiry examined in the chapter is the interplay between newspaper and academic research in Mexico on migration to the United States, migration policy, and the role of the press and academic publications in shaping public views in Mexico. There is a clear national dimension of research and writing by newspapers and academic scholars. As stated before, this chapter focuses on the Mexican side, and it is part of our binational examination of immigration, making sure that the voices and perspectives from both sides of the border are examined.

The Two Sides of Mexican Migration to the United States

Mexican immigration to the United States is a point of tension between the two countries and an ambivalent concept for both societies. The two governments see the same process from different perspectives. For the United States, immigration is an issue of sovereignty, border security, and cheap labor, as well as maintaining a working relationship with a critical trading partner. In Mexico, on the other hand, migration is viewed in multiple ways, including citizens' human rights, regional revenues in the form of remittances, territorial security, and as an escape valve during economic downturns (Nuñez and Chavez 2008). In this chapter we use the term *migration* in reference to Mexico and *immigration* in reference to the United States, where migration reflects the movement between places and immigration reflects settlement in the destination country.

In the United States, the arrival of Mexican immigrants has been perceived with ambivalence. On the one hand, Mexican immigrants are seen as families and individuals who integrate well socially, are highly productive and law abiding, and have a high level of entrepreneurial spirit. On the other hand, Mexican immigrants are seen as reluctant to assimilate, as law violators, and as abusers of the social welfare system. The larger the concentration of Mexican immigrants in cities and metropolitan areas in the United States, the more polarized these perspectives are (Levine 2005).

Similarly, in Mexico, immigrants (such as Central Americans) may also be judged using a double standard. Residents in rural communities and impoverished regions of Mexico tend to empathize with newcomers, sharing conditions that offer little alternative except to migrate to improve their economic situations as well as the hope that new opportunities will enable them to save enough money to open a business or build a house. Conversely, especially in large metropolitan areas, immigrants have been seen as quitters who only seek to take advantage of the host country (Massey et al. 1991).

Both the U.S. and Mexican governments have taken action to solve issues related to immigration with particular focus on the border. The United States, which is affected directly by the influx of migrants, has resorted to intense border enforcement that includes quasi-military operations, electronic surveillance equipment, significant increases in the numbers of law enforcement agents, and the expansion of a division wall on the borderline. Also, in most of the country, regardless of its location, U.S. Homeland Security agents have conducted as common practice numerous raids and stringent audits against employers. In addition, some states have passed their own legislation to restrict access to public services and, even worse, in Arizona local and state law enforcement agents can request anyone they suspect to be of illegal status to provide documents proving they are not illegal (Senate of the State of Arizona 2010). This last action has been traditionally reserved for federal law enforcement.

Traditionally, the Mexican government focuses most of its efforts on safety, the protection of human rights, and assistance with deportation or repatriation, remittances, family reunification, and other legal issues. The *Secretaria de Relaciónes Exteriores* (Ministry of Foreign Affairs) throughout its 51 consular offices serves thousands of Mexican citizens regardless of their legal status in the United States and the majority of their activities take place close to the border (Chavez 2009). These protective functions are perceived by many Americans as a direct foreign intervention and encouragement of illegal immigration.

Historically, Mexican immigration to the United States had some peak periods during the twentieth century, as during the Mexican Revolution, when many fled violence; after World War II, when many Mexican workers who entered legally through the Farm Worker Program decided to stay; and during and after the border industrialization program that took place from the end of the 1960s to the mid-1980s. The 2010 census shows the remarkable impacts of a combination of fecundity and immigration as roughly close to 33 million of the 50 million Hispanics are of Mexican origin (Pew 2011).

However, the migration process has created a point of tension that requires political action, especially in the United States. This is due to the fact that political forces have used immigration in the United States in very unusual ways. Conservative, nativist, and right-wing political groups have discussed it using incendiary rhetoric all over the country. Restrictions in state budgets have provoked a constant political mobilization of conservative groups that attempt to restrict public services to undocumented migrants, including failed proposals to deny constitutional birthright citizenship to those born in the United States. According to a 2013 report published by Pew Research Center, 75 percent of Americans feel the immigration laws need major revisions and 35 percent want it completely changed (Pew Research Center 2013). As this volume goes to press, a massive immigration reform bill is being debated in the U.S. Congress with members from both parties deeply engaged in the debates from multiple angles including paths to citizenship to enhanced border security.

Migration as a Domestic Issue in Mexico

While immigration to the United States was reported by Mexican journalists through observation and interviews, academics provided in-depth information and shed more light on the migrants, their families and communities, and their experiences. Academics writing columns, editorials, and invited opinion editorials ("op-eds") for the major national newspapers started a process to educate Mexicans about their own migration.

Significant scholarship has been written about Mexicans' migration to the United States dating back to the 1930s, scholarship that grew rapidly in the 1960s and 1970s. Most of the research presented the border implicitly but with no direct link to the migration process. By the 1970s, Mexican scholars and analysts had begun to note that migration from rural areas to the United States accelerated very rapidly. Scholars including Jorge Bustamante started in the mid-1970s, first in the Colegio de México and later in the Colegio de la Frontera Norte (founded in the border city of Tijuana), to document the patterns, mechanisms, and actors behind the flows of immigrants arriving in the United States. With a privileged location on the border, Bustamante studied the duality of migrant labor in the service and agricultural sectors of the United States, especially in areas where these sectors required a constant and productive labor force. Bustamante also documented the factors involved in the migration process on both sides of the border, with some of them pushing and others pulling the migrants. He first documented and published in academic journals and the newspapers *Excelsior* and *El Universal* (Bustamante 1975, 1977; Cornelius and Bustamante 1989).

New scholarship followed as small towns in central and southern Mexico, especially in Jalisco, Michoacán, Guanajuato, Puebla, and Oaxaca, experienced a drastic increase of male migration to the United States (García y Griego and Verea Campos 1988). Before the mid-1980s, migration was not seen as a permanent exodus of Mexican citizens, but rather as a temporary back-and-forth process (Massey et al. 1987). Monica Verea Campos placed immigration in the context of foreign policy and international relationships between the two countries without losing view of the forces behind immigration. She also paid close attention to the role of Mexico's Secretariat of Foreign Affairs in dealing with the issue as part of the binational agenda of the two countries (Verea Campos 1982). Two Colegio de Michoacán scholars, Jorge Durand and Rafael Alarcon, worked with Douglas Massey in developing surveys, in-depth interviews, and demographic studies with families and migrants themselves in the area with the highest rates of migration in Mexico. Their studies are longitudinal and provide a clear picture of the local conditions of towns in the Bajío region and the characteristics of the families, the impacts of migration on family structures, and the consequences of male-absent households, as well as the first studies of local economic impacts of migrant remittances (Massey et al. 1987, 2006).

The economic importance of remittances gained national attention through articles in newspapers and scholarly journals, which attracted renewed government attention and new policies to help communities take advantage of the inflow of remittances (Fajnzylber and Lopez 2008; Taylor et al. 2005; Hernandez-Coss 2005). As remittances from Mexican immigrants maintain their level of almost $25 billion dollars annually (2008), this economic flow constitutes the second largest source of Mexico's foreign revenue after oil (Millman 2009).

In addition to Bustamente, scholars such as Sergio Aguayo and Jesus Tamayo used their academic credentials to write editorials, op-eds, and columns for major national newspapers in Mexico. They wrote on migration using their research and investigative skills to report on the migrants' journey across the borderlands and often back home to Mexico. Yet most of the articles were based on the origins of migration in Mexico and its consequences for family and community, and focusing on the interconnection between economics and politics of migration. Agrarian policy and its impact on the peasantry were highlighted in a growing number of newspaper articles especially after the signing of the North American Free Trade Agreement. Both journalists and academics examined the processes and impacts of this reform. Migration became a major topic of academic research at the border-located Colegio de la Frontera Norte (COLEF), which started to track the number of immigrants attempting to cross to California. Researchers at the Centro de Investigaciónes sobre América del Norte (CISAN), Universidad Nacional Autónoma de México, placed immigration in the context of international affairs and the binational relationship between the two governments. In other words, the increasing presence of Mexicans in the United States provoked policy attention by the two governments. As migration research scholars wrote articles and editorials for newspapers during the 1990s, an increasing number of journalists also began to report on migration.

Nevertheless, studies showing how migration is reported by the news media in Mexico, which consequently shapes public opinion and influences policy, are scarce. Understanding how the Mexican news media present migration to the public is important because it does impact the nature of the public discourse on migration, U.S. laws/policy, and migrant experiences, thus shaping public opinion.

The Importance of the News Media in Mexico

Despite the popularity and ratings of radio and TV in Mexico, newspapers continue to be the most important sources of information and have the most influence on the public agenda (Lawson 2002; Hughes 2006; Chavez 2009). Every morning in the daily broadcasts anchors present to their audiences what the newspapers reported in their editions. This is a normal trend used to show two things: first that their radio or TV stations are open to other editorial perspectives, and second, to seize the "main" stories and use them to show a continuity of the important topics by their own newsrooms.

Large newspapers complain frequently that small radio and TV stations in Mexico steal their stories by reading the content to their public, yet the main national or international stories that the newspapers publish turn into topics that shape public opinion in most of the country. The leading stories of the large newspapers—*Reforma, El Universal, El Financiero*, and *La Jornada*—are placed in front of the public to be shared and discussed by readers and other media. This type of reporting by the newspaper's newsrooms became hot topics for public debate (Hughes 2006).

TV shows and radio programs are without a doubt influential in the formation of collective opinion in Mexico, but newspapers continue to be the leading source of reporting on migration. While electronic media have the advantage of speed and immediacy, the newspapers have the advantage of analysis, discussion, comparison, diversity, and scrutiny. In the large markets of Mexico City, Guadalajara, and Monterrey, the numerous stations can clutter and saturate news to the point of irrelevance. A consequence is national newspapers still dominate the market with four or five major newspapers (Orme 1997).

Another reason for the relevance of newspapers is that except for the national broadcasting networks Televisa and TV Azteca, which have large newsrooms, the majority of stations have minimal journalistic support to cover nonlocal news. Large news organizations in Mexico have a sizable newsroom staff with between 500 to 1,000 members supporting the coverage of national, regional, local, and international news (Hughes 2006; Chavez et al. 2010). And despite economic and political problems in the newspaper industry, some newspapers have been able to survive and thrive, such as *El Universal, La Jornada, El Financiero*, and *Reforma*. These four newspapers are influential and have the largest circulation in the country.

While exact numbers are difficult to find, the numbers reported tend to be higher than the actual circulation. Only *Reforma* and *El Universal* use audits regularly to demonstrate their circulation. The circulation numbers in table 7.1 show that the most influential newspapers in Mexico have a daily circulation barely above 500,000. For a country of 110 million people, this circulation is rather small and weak.

The newspapers publish articles and stories reflecting the political or ideological perspective of the owners, publishers, and/or editors—which is consistent all over the world where there is a free press. For instance, *El Universal* reporting tends to hover around the center with oscillations

Table 7.1. Circulation of Largest Mexican National Newspapers

Newspaper	Circulation (daily)	Audited
El Universal	175,000	Yes
Reforma	155,000	Yes
La Jornada	107,924	No
El Financiero	147,000	No

Source: Bacon Newspaper Directory, 2011.

to the right or the left depending on the issues and the decisions of the managing editors. *Reforma* tends to be in the center with movements toward the right, despite the fact that the newspaper does not publish written editorials advocating any particular ideology. The publisher prefers to use op-eds that are commissioned from academics, intellectuals, or leaders of opinion from any ideological perspective. *La Jornada* tends to be to the left of ideological perspectives and has maintained a hard line against the government and the private sector—regardless of what political party is in charge. *El Financiero* is a financial newspaper, which also reports on social, political, and environmental issues with heavy national, international, and local (Mexico City) news content. This newspaper tends to be to the right of center (Hughes 2006).

Ethical and Methodological Issues in Reporting Mexican Migration to the United States

Journalists traditionally have used qualitative research methods to report their stories. In their profession, they rely heavily on direct interviews with migrants, border patrol agents, migration officers, judges, lawyers, and "official governmental sources." Reporters engage in significant oral history practices to document the voices of families and friends left behind or who share the experience of living in the shadows in the United States. American journalists are also trained as observers, and sometimes as participants, to gain real access to the conditions and processes that individuals being reported on experience. In addition, journalists conduct qualitative document research that includes texts, graphs, photos, and other materials to better understand the topics they report on and the human nature involved in the process.

Journalists as the first social reporters, who document events happening every day, face ethical and methodological problems. These are the same problems that any other social scientist faces in interviewing and researching human subjects. Some pressing ethical issues relate to the use of real names and identities when referencing interviewed subjects and identifying real locations, places, paths, or processes used by the immigrants, as well as to the identification of confidential sources and the related issue of protecting immigrants in Mexico or in the United States. In addition, some governmental sources, including members of the Department of Homeland Security and border patrol, may choose to provide information but ask to remain as a confidential source. Methodological issues relate to the best journalistic techniques available to reporters to prepare their stories accurately, objectively, and without bias. These techniques include in-depth interviewing, visual and text analysis, content analysis, focus groups, participant observation, simple observation, and oral history (Lindlof and Taylor 2010).

Ethical and methodological issues in journalism are paramount during the professional training in American schools and departments of journalism. Ethics courses are required as part of the journalism curriculum since the mid-1980s to provide students with the required techniques to ensure ethical behaviors to avoid plagiarism; fabrication; staging; and misrepresentation of facts, events, and human actions. These are issues that few social science programs have in their curricula (Christians 2008). As journalism students advance to graduate training, many accredited schools and programs require their students to take media law courses. These courses focus on the legal consequences of errors, mistakes, libel, and defamation not only of the news media organizations but of the journalists themselves. In some cases, reporters have faced incarceration as judges forced them to reveal their sources or real names reported in their stories or articles (Bowers 2008).

Despite Mexico's advance in the professional training of journalists in the last 20 years, journalism schools and departments teach ethics as part of other courses but not as an individual required course. The slow inclusion of this type of course is the result of new federal and state laws granting access to information and regulating libel and slander (Guerrero 2011).[1] Methodologically, both American and Mexican journalism students learn the same techniques and methods to report events.

Despite this training, migration in Mexico generates heated debate reflecting ideological perspectives, assumptions, and stereotypes, due to how information is disseminated and received. Increasingly attention has focused on Central American migrants crossing Mexico on their way to the United States and the large complex relationships between cartels, migrants, and security efforts on both sides of the border. In the United States, as the process continues to evolve, most of the academic attention is on the impacts of U.S. federal measures and new state laws targeting immigrants and their families, communities, and economies. And yet little attention is given to the format of reporting given by the news media to this process (Chavez et al. 2010).

In both Mexico and the United States, some coverage and reporting of immigration is still biased by the ideological frames of journalists and editors. These frames are similar to the frames that any empirical social researcher has to choose when studying and reporting an issue where legal status is central to the safety of research participants. This may create an personal ethical tension for the journalist who seeks to represent social events in the most accurate way possible while protecting the confidentiality of their sources, which is a top priority for journalists. And while the results of academic research face peer review where the results of their works are critically examined on methodological and analytical grounds, journalists face the same scrutiny and challenges, from editors, copyeditors, and ultimately the public. Objective, unbiased, and impartial reporting is intended to be a fundamental element of good journalism and it is part of the mission and goals of professional news media organizations. Editorials most often are different as they see their role as one of directly influencing public opinion.

Migration to the United States as Represented in the Leading Mexican Newspapers

Migration in Mexico and immigration in the United States are embedded in the public mind by the frames used by the elite, media, and other sources. Framing is a byproduct of the way in which information is presented to the public by the news media, political communicators, and elite sources. As a sociological and psychological process, framing is the repeated use of themes, topics, and concepts by the media that influence the public. Framing is not used purposely by the press, but many times is a byproduct of the ideological biases of editors and reporters. Studies of framing demonstrate the influence it has on shaping the thinking of the public on a particular issue (Entman et al. 2009; see also Gans, this volume).

In Mexico, migration to the United States is widely studied by academics and reported systematically by the media. However, as in the United States, few Mexican academics study the country's news media and how it is used to present information to the general public about the process of migration. Some of the exceptions of news media studies conducted in Mexico focusing on migration include the works of Jose Lozano (1991) and Gonzalo Meza (2006). Lozano's research on radio and identity focuses on how broadcasting, no matter how rudimentary, has profound consequences for migrant communities; it is an effort to understand the particularities of the culture, identity, and resilience of migrants, commuters, and those who live across the U.S.–Mexico border (Lozano 1991).

The writing of Gonzalo Meza, focused on the printed media and Mexico's foreign policy, is pioneering. Although he studies the bilateral relationship between Mexico and the United States viewed from the point of view of the Mexican press, he includes migration as part of his agenda. And yet he takes some examples of the U.S. congressional initiatives viewed by the Mexican press, such as the Border Security and Immigration Improvement H.R. 2899; the Immigration Reform Act of 1986; the H.R. 4437; and the Border Protection, Antiterrorism, and Illegal Immigration Control Act of 2005. He also examines how the press reports on the Mexican governmental agenda with regards to the United States related to migration as well as border security and its link to national security, terrorism, migrants, and narcotics (Meza 2006).

The Mexican newspapers have reported on migration from a wide range of perspectives, ranging from short reports to in-depth investigative reporting. As migration increased and represented a national phenomenon rather than a local/regional trend, the coverage become more frequent and added more angles. Generally, the four newspapers in this chapter tend to cover it from their different perspectives. Some focus on national policies, others focus on U.S. actions, others on migrants' perspectives, and others on the economic issues.

As mentioned in the previous section, Mexican newspapers during the 1970s reported on migration sporadically and tended to view is as a regional trend spurred by the Bajio in central Mexico. But by the mid-1980s, Jorge Bustamante, who actively conducted academic research at the COLEF, started writing for *Excelsior*, *La Jornada*, *El Universal*, and now for *Reforma*, first as a columnist and later as an editorialist focusing on migration, the border, and the binational relationship of the United States and Mexico. His work called the attention of policy-makers as well as public opinion to the growing trend of migration to the United States and its perils. Magazines published weekly, such as *El Cotidiano, Nexos,* and *Vuelta,* started also to run stories with in-depth investigative reporting or with journalistic versions of academic research on immigration and the border (Meza 2006).

As Mexican migration to the United States increased during the 1990s and 2000s, newspapers and other news media started to report it regularly. During this time, the Mexican press began to segment its coverage into three major topics: immigration, the border, and the binational relationship. The coverage usually increased when the U.S. Congress or the White House had a particular position on immigration or on border policies. For instance, when IRCA was passed in 1986, the press reported on U.S. immigration reform and its potential impacts on Mexican migrants and on the changing pattern where migrants stay longer in their new locations. The news media, especially the printed media, covered the process from the time the bill was introduced to the debates and perspectives taken by the Democrats and Republicans (Meza 2006).

The press in Mexico during the beginning of 2000 started to align with the Mexican government under the belief that the two governments were close to arriving at an agreement to regulate immigration across the U.S. border. In fact, the visit of President Vicente Fox to Washington, D.C., in September 2001 was viewed officially as the first formal step to regularize immigration (Meza 2006). However, the events of September 11, 2001, changed the American attitudes about security and "the other." As part of the change the perceived lack of border security and immigrants were seen as threats to the United States. Since most of the migration was still Mexican, the impacts on the agenda to be negotiated were strong enough to make it disappear rapidly.

The reporting in the rest of the 2000s focused on border security and on the efforts to restrict immigration. By 2006, as violence increased on the U.S.–Mexico border, migrants were victims of two forces: human trafficking associated with organized crime, and U.S. law enforcement (Slack and Whiteford 2010). The Mexican media reported on border security and violence, but in a fashion very different from most U.S. papers, which emphasized U.S. security as highlighted by political debates in the U.S. Congress. The articles in the Mexican paper emphasized Mexican security issues, which included migrants, citizens, and the growing violence of the drug trade driven by Americans' seemingly insatiable appetite for drugs. In 2008, the downturn in the U.S. economy brought with it high unemployment and massive layoffs that soon worsened conditions for immigrants and their families living there. How the Mexican press captured the complex international and border dynamics and presented them to their readers and the public has had a major impact on how Mexicans see and understand the United States and its policies.

It is relevant to point out that according to the Pew Global Attitudes Project in 2012, the Mexican public's views of the United States remain positive, at 56 percent, close to the European approval rate of 60 percent. Yet Mexican approval of Obama's international policies has fallen to 39 percent, as in other countries, and while the survey does not ask specific questions about immigration policy, enforcement, border security, or drug interdiction, it can safely be assumed that how these topics are framed in the news and the historic understanding of the public underlie these perceptions (Pew 2012).

Methodology

The research for this chapter emerged as a binational collaboration between academic institutions in Mexico and the United States. Scholars from UNAM (National Autonomous University of Mexico), the University of Arizona, and Michigan State University worked together to develop the research questions, data capture, and analysis of the data, and to formulate the next steps in the research. The research team worked fluidly via email and phone conference calls, and only on a few occasions were there problems related to the understanding and meaning of colloquial expressions used in the articles or stories.

While the study uses quantitative methods to perform content analysis of the formats and frames used by the press to cover and report on Mexican migration, qualitative methods were used to fully explore the stories found in the research. Content analysis (CA) is a powerful method for systematically doing comparative study of texts using statistical techniques to empirically measure length, dispersion, location, content, frames, and style used. Qualitative content analysis provides an additional tool to examine in depth the entire published stories to find categories and themes used by the news media. Analyzing qualitative data offers an opportunity for the researchers to explore multiple angles, perspectives, and topics that pure numerical explorations do not offer. Because this is the first time that Mexican newspaper stories have been studied in this way it is important to use a methodology that allows full exploration of the content (Lindlof and Taylor 2010; Bernard and Ryan 2010; Saldana 2009; Silverman 2006).

Content analysis allows a researcher to examine closely how any texts are conceptualized, written, prepared, formatted, organized, and finally published. While quantitative content analysis pays close attention to measures that describe most characteristics of a report, article, story, or text, qualitative content analysis concentrates on the characteristics of what is written and the likely impact of its content. Each method has its own limitations; for instance, quantitative CA requires a large number of stories, randomness, and reliability codes that require more time, as well as multiple coders and the use of computers and statistical programs. The method provides a good level of measurement with high reliability but is limited to examining intention, bias, ideology, and writer perspectives (Riffe et al. 2005). Qualitative CA limitations relate to the level of generalization that is possible from a small number of specific stories, and with reduced reliability scores (Schreier 2012). The limitations of both quantitative and qualitative content analysis are reduced when the researcher opts to combine both methods. Most researchers in communication and journalism use one or the other, but recently scholars have started using both methods to ensure more reliability and validity (Lindlof and Taylor 2010).

The following research questions guided this study:

RQ 1. What are the major themes used by the Mexican news media to report on Mexican migration to the United States?

RQ 2. What frames are used by the Mexican press to report on its citizens' migration to the United States?

RQ 3. Are there positions or sides taken by the Mexican press when reporting on migration to the United States?

The study selected the four major national newspapers published in Mexico, *Reforma*, *El Universal*, *El Financiero*, and *La Jornada*. While the newspapers are published in their entirety in Mexico City and the newsrooms and most of their reporters are based in Mexico City, each newspaper has a group of national correspondents working on different regions of Mexico. However, these newspapers are the national leaders in opinion and influence in Mexico.

This research surveyed all the papers selected for a period of one year from June 2008 to June 2009, for a total of 13 weeks. The reason for the selection of this period was twofold: First, it coincided with the 2008 presidential election in the United States, and the expectation was that the political candidates would use immigration as one of the topics of their national campaigns. Second, the period included represents the beginning of an economic crisis that surged in the United States and rapidly expanded to Mexico and the rest of the world. The team believed that these two trends would have significant effects on the number of stories published and on the different frames used by the press. We only included the stories published in the printed version of each newspaper, so we did not include reports posted only on their websites.

We randomly selected one week from each month to ensure that selections had the same chances to be chosen. All four newspapers were surveyed for the week selected, so all newspapers were reporting on similar events or stories. We included editorials (including op-eds) and stories reported, even if they were short in length, but excluded letters to the editor. Letters to the editor were excluded because, during the first search, it was found that there was no consistency in the numbers received by each newspaper.

Findings and Analysis

In the 13 weeks researched there were a total of 314 stories or editorials published in the major newspapers of Mexico. Close to a fifth of all the stories on migration to the United States published in Mexico were located on the front pages of the four newspapers. While there is some variation in the number of front pages where migration studies were published, no significant differences were found except for *El Financiero*, which, given its thematic focus on the economic stories and somehow limited coverage on social issues, had only 14 percent of all of its stories on the front page. As seen in table 7.2, *Reforma* and *El Universal* had more migration stories published on their front pages than the other two newspapers. Since both newspapers have the largest circulation in Mexico, their influence in setting the agenda of public affairs is more evident when they publish articles on the front page.

Newspapers reported immigration from a context that included the migrants' living conditions in the United States, U.S. government policies towards immigrants and their families and Mexican policies on migration and their relationship with the U.S. government, as well as U.S. law enforcement, border security, and remittances. In table 7.3, the three most recurrent themes are listed and the frames most commonly used are included. For the most part, the national media in Mexico reports on similar topics but the frames tend to be different, as the table shows. *El Universal,*

Table 7.2. Migration Stories and Reports: June 2008–June 2009

	Total Published	%	Front Page	Pct. of Reports
El Universal	73	23.2	17	23.3
Reforma	87	27.7	19	21.8
La Jornada	90	28.7	16	17.8
El Financiero	64	20.4	9	14.1
TOTALS	314	100.0	61	19.4

for instance, focused on binational cooperation to solve the challenges of migration and on the harsh conditions migrants and their families experience in the United States. *Reforma* also reported on binational cooperation and on U.S. politics and policies related to immigration, and on the new regulations of border security targeting immigrants. While these stories examined border issues, they were framed as international issues and written mostly from newsrooms in Mexico City.

The other newspapers also exhibited differences in their frames about topics. For instance, *El Financiero* more frequently covered the impacts of remittances on the national economy and the consequences of the massive layoffs provoked by the beginning of the American recession. Likewise, *La Jornada* reported on the same issues but focused more on families and communities and how they are impacted by those conditions. In addition, *La Jornada* used frames of the risks of crossing the border including detention, harassment, and mistreatment by the border patrol and the growing number of deportations.

A clear pattern in the reporting emerged as most coverage on migration is in three major categories: U.S. government actions towards immigration (including binational cooperation), immigrants and their families' experiences in the United States, and economic conditions of the migrants on their receiving communities. This shows that newspapers in Mexico cover migration to the United States from different perspectives and angles because of their different editorial policies and ownership. A topic that was consistently reported by all newspapers was the need for examples of binational cooperation by the two governments. With this "agenda-setting" editorial policy, it seems that the elite newspapers try to foster binational cooperation to arrive at positive, effective, and long-lasting solutions to the migration "problem."

Table 7.3. Migration Stories and Reports: Main Themes and Frames

	N	*Main Themes*	*Frames*
El Universal	73	- Migrants & families - U.S. politics - Labor markets	- Binational solutions - Harsh life conditions - Economic impacts
Reforma	87	- U.S. politics & migrants - Border security & violence - Cooperation between governments	- Binational solutions - U.S. law enforcement risks - U.S. politics & policies
La Jornada	90	- Migrants & families - Remittances to relatives & families - Border security & violence	- Harsh life conditions - Remittances positive impacts family & community - U.S. law enforcement risks
El Financiero	64	- Remittances - Border security - U.S. labor and economics	- Harsh life conditions - Remittances' impacts on economy - Layoffs & economic decline

The patterns of reporting to the public are located in different areas, as seen in table 7.4. Stories were located in *El Universal* and *Reforma* in two sections that usually are considered as most read, the national and international sections. In *La Jornada* coverage was located in the politics section, which would be the equivalent of the national section of the other papers, and in the editorial pages, which include op-ed pieces. In *El Financiero* the coverage was located in the political section and in the economics section, which clearly correspond to the newspaper's orientation.

For the most part, the average length of stories published was almost 600 words. *El Financiero* had stories with an average of 430 words and *El Universal* had a high average of almost 750 words per story or editorial. Most stories were produced by the papers' own newsrooms, ranging from 62 to 91 percent. *El Universal* published more stories from wires than any other newspaper. While almost all newspapers have correspondents based in border cities, they are located in three major cities—Tijuana, Nuevo Laredo, and Ciudad Juárez—leaving the rest of the border without the proper coverage.

The research shows that Mexican newspapers consistently publish an average of seven stories or editorials on migration to the United States per week, a much higher figure than the major newspapers in the United

Table 7.4. Migration Stories and Reports: Length, Location, Reporting Sources

	N	Average Length	Location	Pct. Own reports
El Universal	73	746.5	int/nat	62.0
Reforma	87	517.4	nat/int	81.2
La Jornada	90	695.4	pol/edit	90.8
El Financiero	64	430.8	pol/bus	70.0
TOTALS	314	597.5		62–91

Table 7.5. Migration Stories and Reports: Weekly Publication

	N	%	Average per week	Range
El Universal	73	23.2	5.6	3–12
Reforma	87	27.7	6.7	3–16
La Jornada	90	28.7	6.9	3–15
El Financiero	64	20.4	4.9	2–10
TOTALS	314	100.0	24.2	2–16

States. Clearly, the news media in Mexico considers migration an important topic for the public and for the national policy agenda. The variations in number of stories were relatively insignificant, averaging five stories or editorials per week. As seen in table 7.5, the last column indicates the range of published stories, from 2 to 16.

Three months prior to the U.S. presidential elections in 2008, not unexpectedly, the newspapers had the most frequent number of stories published. Beginning in July and ending in October more stories were published that related to how the U.S. candidates would manage immigration. As it happened, neither Obama nor McCain included major proposals during their campaigns. According to U.S. political analysts, the topic was too controversial to be debated. And yet the news media in Mexico reported when either candidate was attracting Latino voters, especially in the Southwest. At least 20 percent of all the stories were related to how the candidates cultivated Latino voters.

No newspaper had a story that addressed the constant U.S. assumption that the Mexican government promoted or stimulated migration to the United States. Indeed, to the contrary, our findings indicate that the

Table 7.6. Migration Stories and Reports: Editorials and Stories

	N	Editorials & Op-Eds	Pct.	Stories & Reports
El Universal	73	15	20.5	58
Reforma	87	13	14.9	74
La Jornada	90	25	27.8	65
El Financiero	64	7	10.9	57
TOTALS	314	60	19.1	254

Mexican press pounded the government for its incapacity to provide sufficient economic opportunities to avert the exodus. The press has not only described the lack of regional economic development but also the absence of local investments to incentivize undecided migrants. Also, little was found related to the Mexican government programs that assist migrants and their families, such as retirement plans, health insurance, and remittances insurance.

Newspaper stories we researched showed a tendency to frame or to induce "agenda setting." For instance, *La Jornada* used more editorial pages than any of the other newspapers. As seen in table 7.6, *La Jornada* had almost double the numbers of editorials compared with *Reforma* and almost three times as many as *El Financiero*. This reflects the tendency of the newspaper to attempt to influence the government with its editorials and op-eds, leaving the rest (almost 70 percent) to stories and reports. Other newspapers preferred to use in-depth reporting or long Sunday articles to underline their perspectives on migration. As mentioned in the beginning, most of the stories originated in Mexico City with little input from correspondents located on the border or from sources based in the area. However, most of the stories relied heavily on interviews with migrants and their families. Governmental sources through interviews and documentary research were also part of the methods used by Mexican reporters.

Conclusions

The newspapers examined in this chapter placed a high priority on reporting to the public stories on Mexican migration to the United States, but took very different tacks in their framing of topics to be covered by articles reflecting the different readership and ownership of the papers. While border security and violence are themes reported, most articles covered broader topics such as remittances, human rights, travel experiences, and migrant living conditions in the United States.

Despite the presence of of some national newspapers' correspondents in the border area, their reporting has focused most recently on regional topics especially organized crime, violence and local politics and then migration. The absence of specialized reporters working for the four Mexico City newspapers on the border reflects the continuing centralization of the media. At the same time, the growing hostility to migrants, particularly Mexican migrants, in the United States, and evidenced especially in the Arizona legislation (SB1070) that was enacted after our study finished, drew tremendous readership interest and required reporters traveling to the border to report on the legislation and it impacts on migrants. As documented by Guerrero and Campo, the Mexican newspapers have been informing the Mexican public on the impacts of the Arizona bill under two different migrant perspectives—as victims and as heroes. Likewise, Guerrero and Campo show that the Mexican media is advising migrants to avoid Arizona as a destination (2012).

As the news media introduces different dimensions of migrating to the United States, it creates a frame that shapes public opinion. To understand the social construction of migration, this research concentrated on the major national newspapers of Mexico that set the public agenda by being the source of information of policy-makers and the huge audience of readers in Mexico City. The results provide an understanding that despite ideological differences, all newspapers reported on similar issues and used frames that were closely comparable.

All four major newspapers covered migration from a socially sensitive perspective. This means that the coverage tried to present to the public the difficulties of the migrants' journeys to the United States from their local communities, the experience of crossing the border, and migrants' experiences in the United States. The Mexican news media highlighted the importance of migration's health impact and its impact on education and on the well-being of families, especially children. These topics are of great concern to Mexicans with family members who have migrated or are considering migrating. Writing from one of the two centers of power in the country, Mexico City, journalists did examine the macro politics of cooperation on the border and migration. A few touched on the challenge facing the U.S. government in grappling with a very large number of un-documented people, and the challenges especially for states and local communities. Similarly, few articles reported on voices asking to close the border to further migration and the worst-case scenario of converting the border into a military zone like the borderlines separating Israel from its Arab neighbors.

In the code of ethics included at the end of this volume, there is a call for greater collaboration between Mexican and U.S. scholars writing on border issues. The same could be said for reporters writing on border issues, migration, and binational affairs. While informally editors and columnists may have felt a need for binational reporting, collaborative reporting was minimal in all papers, both in the United States and in Mexico. Mexicans wanted to read reports and analysis by Mexicans, as Americans want to read a U.S. perspective in their news. While balanced reporting is valued and practiced, it requires resisting the temptations of sensationalism. At the same time, complex border issues need to be understood in the context of the struggle between powerful interests on both sides of the border, and usually located thousands of miles away from the border. Writers usually attempt to include the complexity in their writing, but because of limitations of space or understanding, this is often not included in their articles.

With newspaper reporters, especially those working on binational issues (e.g., the drug trade, the movement of firearms from the United States to Mexico, and border officials' corruption), fair and balanced reporting in a dangerous environment is increasingly risky and challenging. The efforts by the United States to stop migration in the name of national security have proven to be unsuccessful, and this has been extensively reported in the Mexican press and even in the U.S. press.

At the same time, Mexicans eager for a reduction of the violence, while suspicious of greater U.S engagement in the fight against the cartels, increasingly see the need for some form of U.S. role in the fight against the cartels—at least on the U.S. side—while blaming the U.S. for the market. A greater emphasis on protecting the human rights of migrants is needed in both countries. This has been called for by editorials in both countries. More investigative reporting of experiences of the vulnerable and economic contributions of migrants is needed to counter the growing social and cultural gulf dividing not only the two countries but social classes within each country. Without it, the gulf between Mexico and the United States will continue to grow.

Notes

The authors thank the research collaboration of Jennifer Hoewe, Carmen Flores, and especially Argentino Mendoza Chan for gathering information on the Mexican press.

1. Dr. Manuel Guerrero, Department of Communication, IBERO. Interview with Manuel Chavez in Universidad Iberoamericana, Santa Fe, D.F., Mexico, May 20, 2011.

References

Archibold, Randal. 2012. Attacks on Mexico Papers Underline Peril to Journalists. *The New York Times*, July 12, A4.

Bernard, Russell, and Gary Ryan. 2010. *Analyzing Qualitative Data. Systematic Approaches*. Los Angeles: Sage Publications.

Bowers, Peggy. 2008. Between the Summits: Teaching Media Ethics. In Thomas W. Cooper, Clifford G. Christians, and Anantha S. Babbili, eds. *An Ethics Trajectory: Visions of Media Past, Present and Yet to Come*. Urbana, IL: University of Illinois Press.

Bustamante, Jorge. 1975. *Espaldas Mojadas: Materia Prima para la Expansión del Capital Norteamericano*. Mexico, D.F.: El Colegio de México Press.

———. 1977. Undocumented Immigration from Mexico: Research Report. *International Migration Review* 11(2): 149–177.

Chavez, Manuel. 2008. Information, News Media and Diplomacy under the Security and Prosperity Partnership of North America: Increasing Cooperation in Turbulent Times. In Silvia Nuñez Garcia and Manuel Chavez, eds. *Critical Issues in the U.S.–Mexican Relations: Stumbling Blocks and Constructive Paths*. Pp. 57–72. Ciudad Universitaria, Mexico: Universidad Nacional Autónoma de México.

Chavez, Manuel, Scott Whiteford, and Jenifer Hoewe. 2010. Reporting on Immigration: A Content Analysis of Major U.S. Newspapers' Coverage of Mexican Immigration. *NorteAmérica* 5(2): 111–125.

Christians, Clifford G. 2008. "Between the Summits: Media Ethics Theory, Education, and Literature." In Thomas W. Cooper, Clifford G. Christians, and Anantha S. Babbili, eds. *An Ethics Trajectory: Visions of Media Past, Present and Yet to Come*. Urbana: University of Illinois Press.

Cornelius, Wayne A., and Jorge A. Bustamante. 1989. *Mexican Migration to the United States: Origins, Consequences, and Policy Options*. Bilateral Commission on the Future of United States–Mexican Relations. Center for U.S.–Mexican Studies. San Diego: University of California Press.

Entman, Robert, Jorg Matthes, and Lynn Pellicano. 2009. Nature, Sources, and Effects of News Framing. In Karin Wahl-Jorgensen and Thomas Anitzsch, eds. *Handbook of Journalism Studies*. New York: Routledge.

Fajnzylber Pablo, and J. Humberto Lopez. 2008. *Remittances and Development: Lessons from Latin America*. Washington, D.C.: World Bank.

García y Griego, Manuel, and Monica Verea Campo. 1988. *México y Estados Unidos Frente a la Migración de Indocumentados*. Mexico, D.F.: Miguel Ángel Porrúa Publishers.

Guerrero, Manuel, and Maria E. Campo. 2012. Between Victims or Heroes: Mexican Newspapers Framing Immigration to the U.S. In Otto Santa Ana and Celeste Gonzalez de Bustamante, eds. *Arizona Firestorm: Global Immigration Realities, National Media, and Provincial Politics*. Lanham, MD: Rowman & Littlefield.

Hernandez-Coss, Raul. 2005. The U.S.–Mexico Remittance Corridor. The World Bank Working Paper No. 47. Washington, D.C.

Hughes, Sallie. 2006. *Newsrooms in Conflict: Journalism and the Democratization of Mexico*. Pittsburgh, PA: University of Pittsburgh Press.

Lawson, Chappell. 2002. *Building the Fourth Estate: Democratization and the Rise of a Free Press in Mexico*. Berkeley: University of California Press.

Lindolf, Thomas, and Bryan Taylor. 2010. *Qualitative Communication Research Methods*, 3rd ed. London: Sage Publications.

Levine, Elaine. 2005. Mexican Immigrants' Incorporation into Life and Work in Los Angeles. *Journal of International Migration* 9(2): 108–136.

Lozano, José Carlos. 1991. *Prensa, radiodifusión e identidad cultural en la frontera norte*. Tijuana: El Colef.

Massey, Douglas, Rafael Alarcon, and Jorge Durand. 1991. *Los Ausentes: El Proceso Social de la Migración Internacional en el Occidente de México*. Mexico: Alianza CONACULTA.

Massey, Douglas, Rafael Alarcon, Jorge Durand, and Humberto Gonzalez. 1987. *Return to Aztlan: The Social Process of International Migration from Western Mexico*. Berkeley: University of California Press.

Massey, Douglas, Jorge Durand, and Fernando Riosmena. 2006. "Capital Social, Política Social y Migración desde Comunidades Tradicionales y Nuevas Comunidades de Origen en México." *Revista Española de Investigaciones Sociológicas* 116: 97–121.

Meza Razo, Gonzálo E. 2006. *Medios impresos mexicanos y política exterior de Estados Unidos*. Tesis de maestría en estudios México-Estados Unidos. FES-Acatlán, UNAM, Acatlán, Edo. de México.

Millman, Joel. 2009. Remittances from Mexico Fall More Than Forecast. *The Wall Street Journal*, January 28, 9.

Nuñez Garcia, Silvia, and Manuel Chávez. 2008. *Critical Issues in U.S.–Mexican Relations: Stumbling Blocks and Constructive Paths*. Ciudad Universitaria, Mexico: Universidad Nacional Autónoma de Mexico.

Orme, William, ed. 1997. *The Culture of Collusion: An Inside Look at the Mexican Press*. Miami: North-South Center Press, University of Miami.

Pew Hispanic Center. 2012. *Census 2010: 50 Million Latinos Hispanics Account for More Than Half of Nation's Growth in Past Decade*. Washington, D.C. 2011.

Pew Research Center. 2012 *Global Opinion of Obama Slips, International Policies Falter*. www.pewglobal.org/2012.

Pew Research Center. 2013 Most Say Immigration Policy Needs Changes But Little Agreement on Specific Approaches. www.pewglobal.org/2013.

Riffe, Daniel, Stephen Lacy, and Frederick G. Fico. 2005. *Analyzing Media Messages: Using Quantitative Content Analysis in Research*, 2nd ed. Mahwah, NJ: Lawrence Erlbaum.

Saldana, Johnny. 2009. *The Coding Manual for Qualitative Researchers*. Los Angeles: Sage Publications.

Schreier, Margrit. 2012. *Qualitative Content Analysis in Practice*. London: Sage Publications.

Senate of the State of Arizona. 2010. Arizona Senate Bill (SB1070). http://www.azleg .gov/legtext/49leg/2r/summary/s.1070pshs.doc.htm.

Shirk, David. Drug Violence in Mexico: Data and Analysis from 2001–2009. *Trends in Organized Crime* 13(2–3): 167–174.

Silverman, David. 2006. *Interpreting Qualitative Data*, 3rd ed. Los Angeles: Sage Publications.

Slack, Jeremy, and Scott Whiteford. 2010. Viajes Violentos: La Transformación de la Migración Clandestina hacia Sonora y Arizona. *NorteAmérica* 5(2): 79–107.

Verea Campos, Monica. 1982. *Entre México y Estados Unidos: Los Indocumentados*. Mexico, D.F.: Ediciones El Caballito.

PART THREE

Fieldwork among Entrapped Communities

Researching Women's Vulnerability and Agency with Regard to Sexually Transmitted Diseases during Migration through Altar, Sonora

Methodological and Ethical Reflections

Katherine Careaga

Introduction

In January 2005, I began doctoral studies as a foreign (American) student and Fulbright recipient at El Colegio de Sonora in Mexico. I embarked on this academic adventure after having earned my bachelors and masters degrees from the University of Arizona in Tucson, where I had continued to work in border public health at the university, county, and state health departments for several years after graduation from the masters of public health (MPH) program in 1998. During my time as a research specialist at the University of Arizona, I developed close working relationships with my binational counterparts at El Colegio de Sonora while researching binational collaboration at the U.S.–Mexico border. Although my roles and organizations changed, I continued to work with the same colleagues in Tucson and Sonora. In 2004, the University of Arizona College of Public Health received a USAID TIES grant to implement a binational MPH program that would first provide scholarships to a cadre of Sonoran public health personnel to pursue an MPH in Tucson, and would later establish an MPH program in Sonora. Inspired by the proposal and with the newly established doctorate of social science program with a sociocultural epidemiology focus at El Colegio de Sonora, I decided to do the opposite, complementary exchange, by electing to study in Mexico.

The seeds of the reflexivity I was able to achieve were planted by the aforementioned cumulative experiences leading up to the doctorate, along with their sometimes stark contrast with this new reality. They were misleading: after working with my counterparts at El Colegio de Sonora for over five years, the fact that I had to deal with severe culture shock was, well, shocking to me. The professors, in seeming collusion with the cultural immersion experience itself, called into question so many of my assumptions regarding definitions of higher education, theory, and legitimate academic research, in particular conceptualizations of methodology and ethics. I spent about a year struggling, unable to understand what was expected of me as a doctoral student and researcher. Specifically, there was no systematic protocol to ensure the ethical treatment of human subjects, nor was there an explicit definition of ethical requirements. From my previous educational and research experience, ethics was at the fore of my considerations while planning my methodology. The importance I place on ethics, in combination with the lack of direction on the matter, demanded continual reflection on my part.

Things finally clicked when I was given the assignment of presenting Nancy Scheper Hughes's "Three Propositions for a Critically Applied Medical Anthropology,"[1] jolting me back into the anthropological perspective and onto a path of ongoing paradigmatic relativism. They clicked because this article was personally relevant for me and it illustrated a fundamental contradiction in my past academic and professional experiences: I remembered that I was an anthropologist (trained in part by Hans Baer, who is caricatured in the article), who had always practiced within public health and therefore possibly co-opted to a certain degree by this other discipline often criticized as overly biomedical, positivist, and interventionist by critical medical anthropologists.

The intensity and deeply challenging nature of my entire academic experience is reflected in the formative planning process of my doctoral dissertation research protocol, in which I focused on deconstructing the idea of vulnerability and how it was being applied in public health promotion. Here I focus on my admittedly subjective reflections before, during, and after conducting dissertation research on women's vulnerability and agency to sexually transmitted diseases during the migration process of Altar, Sonora. I performed this research in three separate fieldwork trips from fall 2006 to spring 2007. Such reflections were produced by comparing and contrasting my previous academic research experiences on either side of the U.S.–Mexico border. Reflections will be discussed along a three-stage continuum of the research process: design, fieldwork, and data analysis/write-up.

Research Design

Coming from a public health perspective, I started my studies interested in highlighting the vulnerability of migrant women, which could eventually serve as justification of need for funding of some kind public health intervention at the local level. I was interested in doing applied research; frankly, I had little interest in broader social theory and felt that purely theoretical work was, in a sense, unethical in that it did not directly satisfy the needs of the study subjects. I was interested in tying together my vestment in and knowledge of public health on both sides of Mexico's northern border with the United States and its southern border with Guatemala. This led me to select Altar, Sonora, as my study site, and migrant women in transit to the United States as the study population. Later, through the literature review process and my doctoral coursework on social science theory, I came to realize that I could not talk about vulnerability without recognizing the other side of the coin: agency.

Assumptions

The decision to focus on migrant women in transit was in and of itself a difficult ethical decision, made only after exploratory research, and even then, with much reflection and some reservations. In practicing applied anthropology at the border through community-based public health, I and my colleagues at the University of Arizona have always tried to serve border "communities" whose resources are extremely taxed by the constant passing through of (undocumented) immigrants, affecting the social fabric and creating divisions over how to handle the phenomenon. At the same time, as an anthropologist, I struggled to incorporate the idea of "giving voice" to the most marginalized of populations—in this case, the outsiders, the gypsies, the wanderers, the migrants. Although theoretically justifiable, this choice reflected some of my own assumptions about and stereotypes of power relations in Altar.

As an American student studying in a Sonoran doctoral program, I came to realize that I had learned to apply anthropology in public health within a certain context and a certain paradigm that was perhaps not as relevant in this new political and social context. This paradigm was policy focused, using anthropology to "give voice" to the little guy, the common citizen but citizen nonetheless, de facto perhaps—if not able to vote, at least able to demonstrate, resist, organize—and to small border communities that were historically as politically marginalized as they were marginalized geographically. Through this process, we were continuing to ignore a large component of these border communities. Since they couldn't vote and couldn't organize, and after all were only sojourners, we assumed that they had no interest in "the community." From this perspective, at least at the local level, this group met with the strictest definition of "vulnerable population"—they were represented as mere victims of policies, unprotected by a tangible legal framework, open to any and every violation of their human rights.

I chose to work with migrant women in transit through Altar because, at the beginning, they seemed like the most vulnerable of the vulnerable. During this time, Altar had been serving as the primary hub and waiting room for people from all over Mexico, Central America, and other parts of the world embarking on a journey by foot through the Sonoran desert of Arizona and into the United States as undocumented migrants. While a certain sector of Altar had uniquely embraced the arrival of undocumented migrants, particularly the local Catholic Church, by proselytizing the migrant's journey as similar to Jesus's, the image of Altar promoted in the Mexican media was that of a dangerous, lawless place; primarily, the local residents were demonized as opportunistic.

Migrants were represented (often accurately) as vulnerable to a multitude of abuses from locals and authorities. Being in Altar was the beginning of a particularly vulnerable point of the migration process and Altar as a community has been described as the periphery of the border region, removed from the political line, rural, and economically depressed. It does not receive attention or adequate government funding, nor has it been the destination of border development efforts implemented in the sister cities. Altareños lament being passed over as a place to develop the *maquiladora* industry.

Since Altar was known almost exclusively as an unimportant transitory place for impoverished people desperate to find work and enter illegally into the United States, at the same time with money (often borrowed from family members) in hand to pay for the journey and smuggling services, many residents and outsiders did come to take advantage of their situation,

so that Altar became known throughout Mexico also as a lawless, dangerous place of thieves, thugs, rapists, and *polleros* (people smugglers, not
usually highly regarded in mainstream Mexican society or in their communities). As a community, Altar sees itself as being vulnerable and unprotected from illicit activities, while Mexicans see Altar as preying on the
individuals who pass through it.

Finally, women migrants were continuing on a trajectory of gender-
specific vulnerability that began in their sending communities. In the public health literature, both migrants' and women's vulnerability to STDs
was particularly recognized, but separately: representations of migrant's
vulnerability were androcentric, while representations of women's vulnerability were stereotypical. When women were discussed within the topic
of migration, they were consistently painted as either "those who stayed
behind," literarily imprisoning them in the sending community and in a
role of faithfully waiting for their migrant husbands to return home, or as
immigrant women residents living in the United States, usually as married
women (e.g., Galindo 2005; Hirsch et al. 2002; Hirsch 2003; Hirsch et al.
2007; Salgado de Snyder et al. 1996). In her review of Hirsch´s work, Binford points out that it fails to adequately take into account the changing
nature of gender relationships from within Mexico; likewise, Organista et
al. state that more research is needed on "female partners of migrant men,
including *amantes*" (S231). Studies on vulnerability to STDs among Mexican women in the United States consistently looked at married women,
validating the self-fulfilling prophecy of vulnerability and painting them
as innocent victims of gender ideals and the sexual improprieties of their
macho husbands. Finally, during migration and in migrant passing points,
women were primarily portrayed either as sex workers presumably ser-
vicing male migrants who were away from their wives, and as trafficked
women (though that is seen as more distant from the Mexican reality).

The aforementioned assumptions were not only in the literature; I
shared them, and this was reflected in the initial planning of my methodology. I initially saw women migrants as virtually helpless "sitting ducks"
for rape and sexual coercion; I believed they were at a high risk for sexually transmitted diseases (STDs), and that they knew this, felt it, and could
do nothing about it other than travel with male family members. I also
believed my study subjects would be shy and difficult to talk with about
such taboo topics. While I took into account certain assumptions about
my own participation and gender interactions when planning the methodology, such as that it would be easier for me as a female researcher

to research women, I neglected to anticipate certain related difficulties when I proposed to implement the PLACE methodology, which had been implemented by a mixed-gendered research team on STDs in migrant populations in transit at Mexico's southern border (Negroni-Belén et al. 2003).

I firmly believe that one of the most ethical first steps of my research was to recognize and question all these assumptions, and integrate this process into the study design. This allowed me to carefully and conscientiously identify my study population based on anthropological criteria, as well as a complementary internal logic of studying vulnerability through the voices and subjective experiences of the vulnerable themselves. Other assumptions would not become evident until confronted by contradictions in the field.

Researcher Responsibility

One day, in my qualitative methods course, I participated in a spirited discussion of ethics that clarified some of the confusion I was experiencing. In my doctoral program, the concept of ethics was being presented as the responsibility (*compromiso*) of the researcher to "do his/her job," and as a student in a doctorate of social sciences program, my job, according to faculty, was to contribute to the development of social theory.

Prior to this conversation, I had been barraged with comments to the effect that "Americans don't understand theory," and "American research tends to be empirical, not theoretical." These stereotypes always befuddled me; in response, I would cite behavior change models, acculturation scales, etc. Professors would respond that there are different levels of theories, and that they were referring to broader social science theories rooted in the historical development of the discipline. Eventually, I came to understand their point of view. Although I certainly do not discount the legitimacy and need for applied research, I now recognize that research focusing exclusively on the development of social theory and critically examining the application of key concepts (such as "vulnerability") offers social benefits in its own right by creating a deeper understanding of the social underpinnings of human behavior, including health-related behaviors and potentially revolutionizing previously unquestioned paradigms, while exclusively applying (or only funding the application of) unquestioned social theory to public health problems threatens to stagnate that continually evolving understanding.

However, I am not totally convinced this is entirely a matter of cultural differences between Mexico and the United States; rather, it also reflects a difference between institutional and disciplinary orientations. Keep in mind that I was the only anthropologist in the group; most others had training in sociology or economics, but as a *gringa* anthropologist working in public health, my idea of ethics has always been the taking into account of how my research impacts the research subjects, planning for and avoiding collateral effects, as reflected in our human subjects review boards and the Hippocratic Oath of medicine—do no harm. I, at least, concluded that the relationship I established with my study subjects (I hate that word, but as Walker points out, it's better than "objects") was an integral part of "doing my job." At the same time, I understand more and more every day that *cumplimiento de deber*, in terms of completing basic functions and not allowing oneself to be distracted by other interests, continues to be a key challenge for professionals in the Mexican context. However, in order to achieve this, I believe that it is important to go beyond having ethics as a goal to be completed; rather, the idea of ethics should be grounded within the process, integrated within methodology.

In retrospect, I believe that the institutionalization of human subjects review boards would have been counterproductive to this reflexive process, and is certainly no substitute for it. My Mexican colleagues expressed a decidedly negative evaluation of this form of handling ethical matters, perceived as very American and inappropriate for doing research in Mexico. Along with distracting and consuming researchers' energy with a bureaucratized ethics process, consent forms run the risk of creating distrust among research subjects, especially when they are asked to sign something that they may not be able to read or fully understand. Written consent forms are symbolically invoked in hegemonic power relationships, while the most marginalized may not even know how to sign his or her name.

Though these conclusions may seem to merely echo that which is already well established in the anthropological literature, my educational exchange experience stimulated in me a constructivist, reflexive learning process that allowed me to appropriate such knowledge. Deciding on what ethics was, what it meant to me as an anthropologist, as a researcher, and how I would incorporate it in my research was only the beginning. I would continue this critical mental practice throughout my literature review, project design, fieldwork, data management, analysis, and write-up. During fieldwork, I explicitly recorded it as subjective field notes that went beyond mere empirical observations.

Summary of Research Planning and Protocol

Reflecting back on the moment I began to question my epistemological assumptions as a researcher, I believe my reflexive attitude was a key factor that later, in the field, enabled me to establish trust with potential interviewees and actually do my research. First, it allowed me to question my own assumptions about vulnerable populations as a public health practitioner and come to an understanding of how the limitations of these people are so disproportionately emphasized by public health literature so as to render invisible their agency. Of course, the development of the concept of vulnerability contextualized historically is a laudable reaction of resistance to the extreme overemphasis on personal agency traditionally conceptualized in public health as risk behaviors based on individualistic and rationalist assumptions. The challenge is to maintain the balance between the two in order to approach such populations with compassion and at the same time with noncondescending, nonpatronizing *respect* of in-group diversity and possibilities for successful power negotiations, both in our interactions with them and in our representations of them.

Throughout the intellectual process, I had selected and justified the study topic, site, and population. However, many were not convinced of the accessibility of the information I proposed to collect. I constantly received critical comments from professors, administrators, colleagues, and friends—"It can't be done." "The Colegio receives funding from the State of Sonora and we have an obligation to the Sonorans." "How do you think you (as a gringa) can go into Altar and get women who are migrating clandestinely to talk to you about sexually transmitted diseases?" "We're concerned about/feel responsible for your safety." I was considered naïve, with an overactive imagination perhaps, and unserious about doing academic research, instead suspected of just wanting to take a few pictures and sensationalize the "problems" in a journalistic way.

Leaving the Ivory Tower: In the Field

Frustrated with my stubbornness, my review committee said I just needed to get on with it and start my fieldwork, thinking, I believe, that it would be a reality check. Indeed, it was, but beyond revealing the need for some methodological adjustments, it ironically proved to me that what I was endeavoring to do was possible, important, and worthy of academic research.

My fieldwork consisted of four visits to Altar within the course of one year from May 2006 to April 2007:

- May 2006: Exploratory visit with a group of public health practitioners in a binational certification program that was part of the TIES project
- October–November 2006: Key informant and pilot interviews
- December 2006–January 2007: In-depth interviews
- April 2007: In-depth interviews

From the constructivist perspective, I began to reflect on the (culturally relative) meaning of being "in the field." This term is often used unpolemically in anthropological research, reflecting a history of researching marginalized places from the center. In this model, anthropologists leave their central academic bases to (traditionally) spend extensive periods of time "in the field." In my case, although I spent a total of approximately 10 weeks in Altar, I had also been living and studying in my state of research, Sonora, Mexico, for a year and a half, in the country (Mexico) for many years as in the U.S.–Mexico border region, and in one of the primary Mexican sending states of my study subjects (Chiapas). During fieldwork in Altar, I frequently was able to establish trust quickly with migrants by talking about landmarks and personalities from Chiapas of which we both shared knowledge. There is a growing debate on the practicality, relevance, and necessity of anthropologists' traditional extended time in the field given the changing conditions and actors of globalization (Lewellen 2002); a similar debate is necessary over the ambiguous and constantly fluctuating borders of "the field."

Initial Visits

Personal Safety and Team Research

Armed with my humbled, reflexive attitude, I took the critiques as learning opportunities. I used them to anticipate and plan for ways to deal with challenges, without accepting the impossibility of the research. Preparing for personal safety considerations was particularly important in keeping with our previously negotiated definition of ethics—to complete the job, and open the door for others to enter into "risky" situations to conduct

much-needed research, especially female researchers. As one precaution-
ary measure, I made my first field visits with a group of students from
another research project. As my research progressed, I noticed that people
within the community started to watch out for me and take care of me as
well.

Along with piloting the in-depth interviews, I used my first field visits
to pilot the Priorities for Local AIDS Control Efforts (PLACE) method,
which combines contextual, epidemiological, and demographic information and techniques to identify high transmission areas, as well as specific sites, where STD prevention programs should be implemented. As
in Ciudad Hidalgo, where the method had previously been implemented,
in Altar, I would identify interviewees within these "new partner meeting places." However, in Altar this translated to interviewing sex workers,
where I was interfering with transactional negotiations. I quickly understood that this was not going to work for me, as a female researcher seeking to talk with sex workers who were also female. At the meeting places,
only men would talk with me, and the female sex workers wanted me
to go away. The lack of exploration and discussion of how gender had
influenced previous implementation of PLACE under the pretense of objectivity, as valued in public health, limited its applicability as a viable
research model. A similar revelation took place in terms of implementing
team-based/Rapid Assessment Process (RAP) research, as described in the
next section.

Pilot Interviews

A consideration of ethics, with a deep respect for the research subjects;
a humble, curious, self-questioning attitude; and being conscious of the
challenging nature of what I was undertaking, all facilitated the establishment of trust with my interviewees. My first pilot interview with a migrant
woman was astounding even to me. I approached her in the plaza while
she was eating breakfast with a few companions. I explained the project
and invited her to do the interview if she wanted, once she finished eating. As I started to explain, she immediately gestured "no," but then her
companion intervened, saying that "yes," she would do the interview. I
walked away, pointing to where she could find me if she decided to do the
interview.

A few minutes later she found me and said she would do it, though she
did not want to be recorded. She told me that the man she was with, who
insisted that she do the interview, was acting as her husband in order to

cross the desert. He had been verbally and physically abusive to her since they had met in Chiapas, currently threatening to "leave her to die in the desert" if she did not do as he said. She explained that his ordering her to do the interview was an effort to demonstrate his power over her, and that he believed that she would not say anything to me out of fear. We were just out of earshot of her impromptu "husband," but within sight of him.

With a tone of defiance she recounted the details of her story, and when she got to how she had had to leave her children behind with her abusive ex, tears welled up in her eyes, but she stopped herself, explaining that if her companion saw her crying, he would know that she was telling me everything. Before this interview, I was conscious in a very abstract way of the need to find a relatively private space so that interviewees would feel more comfortable and could be more forthcoming with their information. During the interview, I became acutely aware of the need to not only be where we could not be heard, but also unseen, and how serious the consequences could be of not doing so. I also became aware of how much vulnerable women felt the need to talk, both in terms of processing what they were going through, and in order to reach out. I began to understand that getting them to talk would not be the problem; rather, keeping them safe when speaking out was the risk and my primary concern, which I addressed by seeking places to conduct interviews in more private settings, away from the center stage of the main plaza.

In-Depth Interviews with Migrant Women in Transit

Introductions and Researcher Representations

Interviewees' candidness continued throughout the in-depth interviews. One woman described an incestuous rape, stating that she had never told anyone about it before. Another interviewee, Elvira, confided in me about her first sexual encounter, which had taken place in a guest house in Altar several days prior to our interview, and how "low" she felt afterward.

I began to wonder about what motivated the women to share such personal information with me. Was there an expectation that I could somehow provide them with therapy? Did they feel safe with me, trusting that it was indeed a confidential and nonjudgmental interaction? If so, why? Though I haven't entirely answered these questions, I believe there were various factors involved, among them the very nature of this migration process. One theory proposes that globalization is changing the very nature of anthropological subjects (Lewellen 2002); globalized actors and migrants in particular are more accustomed to change and need to be able to quickly establish trusting relationships.

Sometimes, global relations may provide more space for trust than local ones. Most of the women I interviewed were from rural communities where everyone knew each other. Negotiations in these communities were intimate and complex, entangling multiple interests that were constantly in play. Now in Altar, and particularly with me, there was total anonymity. We shared no past and no future. They had no reputation to uphold in Altar. I also believe that being an American woman helped in some respects, as I was perceived to be more open minded and liberal, and symbolically represented what they aspired to achieve from migration.

I also believe perceptions of me as a professional played a role in interview dynamics. I was constantly asked, "What are you doing here? Why are you here?" Since the ethnographic field methods course that I had taken in Ensenada while doing my master's degree, I had learned to identify myself as a student, a title considered worthy of respect in Mexico. However, upon talking about health and sexually transmitted diseases in the interview, many of the interviewees seemed to assume that I was a "public health authority" (as they are known in Mexico) and interacted with me as such. Some would cite epidemiological data and information they had learned through health promotion activities in their home communities, or would fret about not remembering everything about a particular disease, as if I were giving them an exam. I would repeat that I was not a public health authority, much less a doctor, and that this was not an exam, trying to curb the hegemonic dynamic.

As my work continued in Altar, certain gatekeepers developed their own interpretations of who I was and what I was doing. One was the manager of one of the guesthouses that allowed me to enter and interview female guests. Elvira had mentioned that he was making unwelcome sexual advances, and as I returned to other interviews and found her still there, eventually told me there were rumors that he was going to rape her to charge her unpaid stay. Nevertheless, the possibility of me finding out about these incidents did not seem to worry him; on the contrary, he helped convince women to talk with me, stating, "It will help you. She's like a psychologist."

Indeed, it may have been more helpful for me to have had some kind of training in psychology, both in order to deal with my own emotions while taking in such serious information about rape, incest, abuse, and kidnapping, and to feel more empowered to help these women who were so generously sharing their time and experiences with me. I resigned myself to the fact that my witnessing, companionship, listening, and encouragement may have been helpful to my research subjects, even if it were only momentary. After Elvira confided in me about the rape threat, I came to understand that my presence and gaze were also potentially protective and I tried to return to the guesthouse as much as possible to "follow up" with her. After so many misinterpretations, I continue to believe that introducing myself as a student (or anthropologist or sociologist) continues to be preferable, and more accurate, than public health authority, doctor, or psychologist. However, as a result of my interviews, I am conscious of the fact that this title can also be alienating, since one of the principal ways that these women had of interpreting their vulnerability was in terms of lack of access to education, rather than along the lines of gender.

Confidentiality

Once I had introduced myself and the project, I explained that interviews were confidential, but that I was using first names to identify the information from the interview. I gave women the choice of using their real names or a pseudonym. I was surprised when I observed that most of the women chose to give me their real first names, and when they did select a pseudonym, the process was very transparent—they used their nickname or a backward spelling of their first name. This led me to believe that beyond having something to say and wanting to be listened to, vulnerable subjects wanted their voice to be identified with them, even if it meant assuming certain risks. I got the distinct sense that my interviewees felt they were doing something important and were proud to contribute to the recognition and better understanding of women in migration.

I think it is important to build in these kinds of choices into methodology so that research "subjects" feel more a part of the process, rather than like objects of study. In other words, it is possible to design research that empowers those participating in it. It is especially conducive to the participation of change agents. Convenience sampling and self-selection used in my research may not be representative, but it is another method that brings to the fore bolder change agents, since they are usually not timid or content with staying quiet. Similarly, the context of migration is optimal for identifying women agents.

Data Collection, Reporting, and Representation of Study Subjects

A final note about the priority of giving interviewees options over a rigid methodological structure has to do with data collection. In my research, I typically chose to record interviews, but also gave interviewees the choice of opting out if they did not want to be recorded, taking careful notes instead. I also made the choice not to take photos of people in Altar. The focus of my research was not to provide a visual image of women migrants, but rather to gain a deeper understanding of how they interpreted their own vulnerability, and this subjective reality is something to which a photograph cannot do justice. When I was conducting that first pilot interview, I was traveling with a crew of photographers. They started setting up their cameras near us, and since the woman had already declined to be recorded, I also assumed she did not want to be photographed, so we got up and went to a more private place. The photographers then followed us and took her picture, at which point I confirmed with her that she did not want to be photographed and requested that they respect her wishes and eliminate the photo they had just taken. This experience confirmed my conviction that photographing women migrants not only did not fit within the parameters of my project, but it could potentially damage the interviewer-interviewee relationship if used coercively. It also made me reconsider the risks of team-based research, which of course can be minimized if all team members share similar training and commitment to ethical considerations. The development of and group participation in a guided reflexive process on ethics modeled after something like my individual one could be another strategy for ensuring ethical treatment of research subjects during team research.

Field Notes and Reflexivity

Along with detailed notes of the interviews, I kept field notes of my research experience on a daily basis. I recorded process and contextual information based on my own observations and subjective reactions (feelings). This practice was a useful method for me to handle the intensity of the context and the interviews themselves, to work out on paper the connections between the women and their changing context, and to document my own experience as participant-observer, thus moving beyond mere empirical observations.

Beyond the field notes, the field diary also became a repository for relevant contextual materials; for example, while walking through the streets of Altar, I found an insert from a package of emergency contraception. Though I did not take pictures of my interviewees, I did take pictures to document public health campaigns/messages that targeted my study population, including an HIV/AIDS prevention campaign targeting migrants in Altar and another that targeted women in sending communities in Chiapas.

Analysis, Write-Up, and Beyond

The decision not to take photographs presents several dilemmas. It flies in the face of an anthropology directed towards influencing policy-makers, who tend to respond better when data are presented in visual and abbreviated format. In general, it makes the presentation of results, especially qualitative data, more challenging. I have opted to portray the information I collected through direct quotations from the interviews; however, I do at times become overwhelmed with the sheer complexity of summarizing this kind of research in a clear, visual manner without losing the diversity (agency) and dynamic nature of it, without oversimplifying and falling into stereotypes.

Another limitation is the inability to follow up directly with the study subjects, since after the interview, for the most part, they can no longer be systematically located. This limits research options, including the possibility of doing long-term research with the study population, be it epidemiological longitudinal studies or qualitative case studies. It also makes applying research methods to interventions that would directly help study participants impossible. Interventions applied in places with high proportions of transient populations could help the population as a whole, although it may not reach the same individuals involved in the study.

At the same time, the results of qualitative studies such as these are not generalizable to the population as a whole, as it is not possible to obtain a representative sample. Nor is this the objective of such research; qualitative research is designed to deepen understandings of culturally constructed meanings. In this sense, this research makes an important contribution to our understanding of the dynamic process of negotiation of women's vulnerability and agency during migration by women migrants themselves, other actors in the migration process, and the public health actors. This understanding can help public health actors to support women's efforts to

exercise and expand on their agency, and to reflect upon their own participation in reinforcing existing power structures that contribute to women's
vulnerability or in truly empowering them through their interactions.

Conclusion

Despite all of the methodological limitations that doing research among
vulnerable populations and in vulnerable places implies, my research has
proven that it is possible, and indispensable if we want to truly understand
vulnerability. What is also indispensable is a careful and ongoing reflection on ethics in order for it to be successful and to avoid reinforcing the
same power relationships that produce vulnerability. Integrating such reflection as an ongoing part of the process of methodological design and
implementation; considering researcher assumptions in the selection of
place and study subjects; thoroughly grasping the ethical pros and cons
of both theoretical and applied research; and with attainable objectives
and expectations of what one's responsibilities are to the academic field,
to "the field," and to research subjects are all important elements of such
a process.

When conducting research binationally and/or in multicultural teams,
it is important to keep in mind that ethical methodology is culturally relative and contextually informed, and that it cannot conform to a singular
dogma. Given the importance of context, research protocols may never be
ethically irreproachable until they are tested in the field, indicating the in-
dispensability of linking theoretically informed methodology with praxis.
For these reasons, formulaic methodological prescriptions and inflexible,
bureaucratically preapproved protocols are unadvisable. Although it is
highly unlikely that U.S. universities will do away with human subjects
reviews in the near future, U.S. researchers must take into account that
demands for ethical reflection and adjustments extend far beyond this process, especially when doing research in the U.S.–Mexico border region,
among vulnerable populations, and binationally. Where mechanisms of
legal accountability may not be as strong, conditions necessitate that researchers carry an ideology of ethics with them into the field and are capable of self-monitoring/reflection.

While the ethical challenges faced on the Mexican side of the border
may be greater, including less accountability, the way of dealing with the
issues and teaching ethicality through ongoing dialogue and questions
that provoke reflection (in small classroom settings and periodic public

"colloquia" presentations of the research) may indeed be superior, at least based on my experience at El Colegio de Sonora. A written manual modeled after this pedagogical method and specific to border and binational research that researchers could take into the field would be a useful instrument to systematize the teaching of ethics in institutions of higher education on either side of the border.

Note

1. This essay was originally published in 1990 in *Social Science and Medicine* 30(2): 189–97.

References

Binford, Leigh. 2005. Review of *A Courtship after Marriage: Sexuality and Love in Mexican Transnational Families*. *American Anthropologist* 107(1): 151–152.

Galindo, Blanca Patricia. 2005. El Sida Crece en Poblados Expulsores de Migrantes [AIDS Spreads in Migrant-Emitting Towns]. *El Universal*, October 3.

Hirsch, Jennifer S. 2003. *A Courtship after Marriage: Sexuality and Love in Mexican Transnational Families*. Berkeley: University of California Press.

Hirsch, Jennifer, Jennifer Higgins, Margaret Bentley, and Constance Nathanson. 2002. The Social Constructions of Sexuality: Marital Infidelity and Sexually Transmitted Disease–HIV Risk in a Mexican Migrant Community. *American Journal of Public Health* 92(8): 1227–1237.

Hirsch, Jennifer S., Sergio Meneses, Brenda Thompson, Mirka Negroni, Blanca Pelcastre, and Carlos del Rio. 2007. Inevitability of Infidelity: Sexual Reputation, Social Geographies, and Marital HIV Risk in Rural Mexico. *American Journal of Public Health* 97(6): 986–996.

Lewellen, Ted C. 2002. *The Anthropology of Globalization Cultural Anthropology Enters the 21st Century*. Westport, CT: Bergin & Garvey.

Negroni-Belén, Mirka, Galileo Vargas-Guadarrama, Celina Magally Rueda-Neria, Sarah Basset-Hileman, Sharon Weir, and Mario Bronfman. 2003. Identificación de Sitios de Encuentro de Parejas Sexuales en Dos Ciudades de la Frontera Sur de México, Mediante el Método PLACE [Identification of Sexual Partner Meeting Places en Two Southern Mexican Border Cities Using the PLACE Method]. *Salud Pública de México* 45(5): 647–656.

Organista, Kurt, Hector Carrillo, and George Ayala. 2004. HIV Prevention with Mexican Migrants. *Journal of Acquired Immune Deficiency Syndrome* 37(4): S227–239.

Salgado de Snyder, V. Nelly, M. J. Diaz-Perez, and M. Maldonado. 1996. AIDS: Risk Behaviors among Rural Mexican Women Married to Migrant Workers in the United States. *AIDS Education and Prevention* 8: 134–142.

Walker, S. 1998. Health Interventions: A Focus for Applied Medical Anthropology. *NEXUS* 13: 74–88.

CHAPTER NINE

Reflections on Methodological Challenges in a Study of Immigrant Women and Reproductive Health in the U.S.–Mexico Border Region

Anna Ochoa O'Leary, Gloria Ciria Valdez-Gardea, and Azucena Sánchez

Introduction

In this chapter, we reflect on the methodological challenges arising from research conducted in the U.S.–Mexico border region in 2008–2009.[1] In particular, these emerge from the increased vulnerability of both migrant and immigrant women whose limited access to health care in transit and settlement communities subject them to numerous risks. Such trends force researchers to be ever more cognizant of the relationship between social scientists and vulnerable research participants (Bilger and Van Liempt 2009). This is especially true when gathering data about sensitive topics that may include legal status, clandestine activity, intimate partner relations, and sexually transmitted diseases (see also Careaga, this volume). To be sure, within the research process even a routine or in-depth analysis of the methodological issues—let alone a robust reflection of methodology—often remains peripheral and outside our "field of vision" (Sprague 2005). Perhaps, as Sprague suggests, critical reflection on the methods we use is uninspiring, or worse yet, intimidating. It goes without saying that a reflection on this process should be considered along with the analyses of the data and the formal presentation of results. In the case of our research, we address several issues emerging from context rife with apprehension among migrant and immigrant populations due to environments that are notably antagonistic towards immigrants. The shift in migration patterns dominated by migrants from nontraditional sending states in an almost perpetual state of flux also complicates our ability to accurately identify the contours of researched populations (O'Leary 2012).

This project was a binational study where teams of researchers addressed related questions on both the U.S. and Mexican sides of the border. Gloria Ciria Valdéz-Gardea (Colegio de Sonora, Mexico) was the co-principal investigator responsible for the research in Altar, Sonora, and Anna Ochoa O'Leary (University of Arizona) was the co-principal investigator responsible for the research in Tucson, Arizona. For the research in Altar, our discussion concentrates on the unequal distribution of resources, which contributes to the vulnerability of immigrants who find themselves insufficiently supported. In Tucson, our discussion concentrates on the challenges of participant recruitment in a state increasingly vexed by anti-immigrant measures, making migrants more fearful (O'Leary and Sanchez 2011, 2012; O'Leary 2009a). After a brief summary of the research, we will proceed to discuss the following eight methodological issues that were resolved for completing research:

Recruitment in Altar
Tucson Recruitment Procedures
Fieldwork Challenges
Contending with the Political Climate in Arizona
Ascertaining Immigration Status
Mitigating Sample Bias
Locating Participants
"Safe Place" Bias versus Improved Respondent Response Rates

Brief Summary of the Research

The research project, "A Multidisciplinary Binational Study of Migrant Women in the Context of a U.S.–Mexico Border Reproductive Health Care Continuum," was designed to document and analyze the reproductive health care strategies of im/migrant women, and their access to reproductive health care services.[2] The reproductive health-care strategies that im/migrant women adopt are analyzed in the context of increased exposure to various types of risks that come with the migratory process, including the risk of death (Cornelius 2001; O'Leary 2008; Goldsmith et al. 2006); sexual assault (Falcon 2001); and illness when health care services in settlement communities are restricted, denied, or underutilized (see for example Fuentes-Afflick, Korenbrot, and Greene 1995; Guendelman, Thornton, Gould, and Hosang 2005; Ojeda 2006). Such services are critical to women's health and safety in the course of migration, and ultimately, for settlement in destination communities. In this way, the research reflects the use of a feminist methodology and approach as gender is central to our attempt to critically understand how social, economic, and political systems intersect with inequality (Sprague 2005).

In line with this analytical approach, a theoretical concept, the "reproductive health care continuum," was developed for the research. The "continuum" is conceived as the repertoire of reproductive health-care strategies and the associated knowledge that immigrant women draw upon in the context of their plans to migrate northward. The continuum develops in response to conditions in destination communities where other problems may arise, such as scarce resources, social hostilities, and/or restrictive policies (Wilson and McQuiston 2006; Wilson 2008). For example, Valdez-Gardea (2007) shows that the emergent concentration of migrants 120 miles south of the U.S.–Mexico border in Altar, Sonora—a major staging area for migration north—has produced a strain on services that support migrants. Sixty miles north of the border and along the migrant corridor, in Tucson, Arizona, there has been a curtailment of supportive services, largely driven by a highly politicized anti-immigrant sentiment and the implementation of anti-immigrant legislation like Proposition 200 in 2004, which requires that state and local governments verify the legal status of all applicants for certain state and local public benefits (Ferreira-Pinto 2005; O'Leary 2009a; O'Leary and Sanchez 2011). Known as "policies of attrition" (Vaughn 2006; O'Leary and Sanchez 2011), much of this legislation designed to discourage immigrants from settling or remaining in their destination communities places disparate burdens on women immigrants (Wilson 2008; Marchevsky and Theoharis 2008). Therefore, locations on both sides of the border were selected to gather data by binational research teams in 2008–2009, using both quantitative and qualitative methods. This binational approach is also consistent with Hannerz's (1998) suggestion for organizing transnational research, where instead of the conventional community study of migrants at the end or beginning of their migration journey, migrants are viewed as somewhere in between (Hannerz 1998).

Approach, Methods, and Procedures Used
in the Research

Approach

For the research, binational research teams shared responsibility for gathering and analyzing the data, and training and supervising research assistants involved in the study. In Sonora, the researchers from the Colegio de Sonora (COLSON) brought to the project extensive experience in conducting research in Altar, Sonora, which is about 120 miles from the Arizona–Mexico border. The research in Altar focused on the reproductive health care continuum based on the migrant women who had settled there or were en route to the north. Here, the research focused on reproductive health-care strategies that migrant women used, including seeking reproductive health-care services such as contraceptives, medical attention for sexually transmitted diseases (STDs), or medical care for pregnant or nursing mothers. This information was seen as crucial for understanding the impact of migration on the immediate safety and health of migrant women in Altar as well as for understanding and comparing the structural determinants of reproductive health care in places where migrants settle, such as Tucson, Arizona (O'Leary and Sanchez 2012; O'Leary and Valdez 2013).

Parallel to the research in Altar, the research in Tucson, Arizona, was essential for providing a balanced and truly binational exchange of timely information between neighboring states. In Tucson, the work concentrated on the nature of the reproductive health care strategies and resources that were available to migrant women who had settled there, some of whom are undocumented. The term *undocumented* is saturated with ambiguity and its variety of meanings have both real and symbolic consequences for immigrants that have been difficult to identify and measure (Plascencia 2009). In the United States, where this is an issue, there are different ways for individuals to fall into an immigration category that prevents most from legally working and residing in the United States. We relied on Cornelius (1982: 378) to help us formulate a description of "undocumented" as that individual who enters the United States without inspection and without official authorization, who may have entered legally but has subsequently overstayed the term limit of their visa, or who may have entered legally and is legally present but is not a legal *resident* (and therefore not entitled to public benefits). As immigrants and as women, the participants in our study were doubly marginalized, first, because as females they face inequality in most realms of social and integration when compared to men; and second, because as immigrants, they face greater risk of being racially profiled and detained and questioned by law enforcement officials, and potentially deported (Goldsmith, Romero, Goldsmith, Escobedo, and Khoury 2009).

Methods

In Altar, the research team used mixed research methods in three phases, with rapid appraisal techniques (RATs) used at different phases of research.[3] These techniques are historically rooted in anthropological research, having emerged initially from development research (Carruthers and Chambers 1981). However, with greater frequency they have been used in the design and assessment of public health interventions. These techniques were deemed suitable and appropriate for the research in Altar as it involved trips to the area to gather data by the research team from the Colegio de Sonora. The choice of method is also consistent with theoretical approaches that help researchers identify the contours of the field site when populations are no longer bounded but rather in a state of flux (O'Leary 2008, 2009b). This approach also follows Hannerz's (1998) suggestion for organizing transnational research. Instead of the conventional community study of migrants at the end or beginning of their migration journey, migrants are viewed as somewhere in between two points, temporarily suspended between systems that simultaneously regulate and impede their mobility. Cunningham and Heyman (2004) argue that national borders are particularly well suited to empirically examining the diametrically opposed processes that characterize borders and mobility: "horizontal" processes that enclose the state and impede mobility, and "vertical" processes that facilitate the movement of people, jobs, trade, goods, information, culture, and language. Both processes intersect at the border, and help conceive of a field site for unbounded populations under study (O'Leary 2008, 2009b).

In Altar, the first phase of the research included short visits to the field site to identify important variables and the population segments that were required for the study. This helped set up the "triangulation" necessary to effectively carry out planned RATs (Beebe 2001). Key informants were identified, including those working in shelters, boarding houses (*casas de huespedes*), a mobile clinic, and private medical facilities. These also provided an inventory of the public health infrastructure that was available to migrants coming into the areas. Altar's commercial infrastructure has been well adapted to meet the dramatic rise in populations in transit, with dozens of hotels, casas de huespedes, taxis, vans, and an array of fast-food stands with regional variety to accommodate a population of migrants from various parts of Mexico. Other commercial ventures are attuned to the needs of migrants planning to journey into the United States on foot, selling caps, gloves, jackets, backpacks, and boots. It was calculated that 75 percent of the residents in Altar subsist on the sale of migration-related goods and services.

The first visits were organized around finding women at the migrant shelter in Altar, migrant assistance agencies, hostels, and medical professionals. Informal, fact-finding interviews were conducted with shelter volunteers and employees, as well as with migrant women. The initial phase was followed by the second, in which various ethnographic techniques such as participant observation, in-depth interviews, and focused interviews were used to gather data from the selected populations. Qualitative data were gathered from 12 in-depth interviews through which women provided accounts of their reproductive health-care strategies and the obstacles that they have encountered to receiving health care. This latter phase was seen as important not only for revealing the reproductive health-care continuum in concrete terms but also for understanding how different variables interact. For example, a study of contraceptive use by Mexican women by Romero-Gutiérrez, Garcia-Vazquez, Huerta-Vargas, and Ponce-Ponce de Leon (2003) used 12 different variables (such as experience with previous birth control methods, level of education, and number of completed pregnancies) to study how women determined contraceptive use. However, migration experiences contribute to the formation of other reproductive health care variables that may be material (Organista, Organista, and Soloff 1998) or attitudinal in nature (Wilson and McQuiston 2006). The information gathered in the second phase of the research was the basis for the third phase of the research. In the third phase, a survey questionnaire administered to 66 respondents was used to collect basic demographic information (age, origin, education level, and reproductive health history). The short demographic survey data were entered in the software tool SPSS (Statistical Package for the Social Sciences) and the qualitative interviews with women migrants were recorded and transcribed.

Like their COLSON counterpart, the Tucson research team used mixed methods that entailed a similar demographic and health indicators survey and in-depth interviews with immigrant women. The Tucson team partnered with the Mexican Consulate's health referral program, *Ventanilla de Salud*, to identify 40 respondents who solicited reproductive health-care services or resources for "Sample C." It was hoped that a snow-ball sampling process would produce another 40 women who were responsible for the health care needs of at least one undocumented individual and therefore not eligible to receive services for "Sample D." This anticipated outcome failed and is one of the issues discussed below. The closed-ended questions were also entered in SPSS for quantitative analysis and the open-ended, qualitative interviews were tape-recorded and transcribed for later content analysis. Binational sets of data were thus gathered to help us determine a transnational reproductive health-care continuum and to draw comparisons in terms of the reproductive health care of women who are migrating, and of immigrant women who have settled in their respective communities.

Methodological Issues

Recruitment in Altar

In Altar, migrants were recruited from the casas de huespedes, dining rooms, hotels, and the migrant shelter, Centro Comunitario de Asunción al Migrante y Necesitado (CCAMYN). These sites also served as places for conducting interviews. However, a disadvantage of conducting interviews at these sites was that we were frequently interrupted by migration-related activity in these areas. Very often, we had to abruptly terminate the interview because the person being interviewed was called away or because of the need to attend to a pending matter such as work responsibilities, family matters, or the care of children. If such was the case, we returned the next day to finish the interview.

Another issue that complicated the data gathering process was that the women migrants we interviewed for the survey expressed insecurity in the community. Many preferred to omit some information because they felt it would take too much time and they were in a hurry. This predicament was also found to be true in Tucson when women were initially recruited at the El Rio Community Health Center.

In spite of a thriving commerce dedicated to meeting the demands of migrants coming into Altar, the environment is hostile to migrants (see also Careaga, this volume). The insecurity migrants sensed is an important aspect to consider as tensions logically negatively impact the goal of establishing trust and rapport with interviewees and informants. This is especially true when interviewing migrants who are in a vulnerable situation, not knowing the area and the people who surround them. The scarcity of basic services due to the exorbitant demand placed by a growing population in transit has promulgated the creation of informal and clandestine industries and black-market commerce where *"[n]adie controla, nadie gobierna, y nadie ordena"* [nobody controls, nobody governs, and nobody orders] (Santibáñez 2004: 5; see also Magaña, this volume)

Tucson Recruitment Procedures

In Tucson, the research team partnered with the Mexican Consulate's office, through its program Ventanilla de Salud, where the immigration status of potential clients does not preclude them from accessing services. This program provides its clients with referrals to social service and health-care agencies. Reliance on the Mexican Consulate was key to the proposal for research, and its design. Foremost in considering the research design were the possible insecurities and fear that potential respondents might experience when a member of the household is unlawfully residing in the state. Given the current social and political climate, it was reasonable to expect that respondents would be hesitant to divulge information to strangers that might jeopardize their well being or that of their families. However, the research also contemplated identifying 40 respondents who had solicited reproductive health-care services or resources and who may have been or had in their households a member who was not eligible to receive health-care services of any kind due to his or her irregular immigration status. At the same time and due to the political climate in Arizona, we were reluctant to follow procedures such as the one described by Granberry and Marcelli (2008) where a series of questions about residency status led indirectly to the conclusion that a respondent was undocumented. Therefore, we decided to partner with the Ventanilla de Salud, which collaborates with the El Rio Community Health Center to organize binational health fairs held in October of every year. The Ventanilla is thus well known and has earned the trust of the immigrant community living in Tucson. The proposed procedure was to approach recruiting potential subjects, female clients of the Ventanilla de Salud program. The procedure was initiated by approaching women who came to the consulate's office. They were handed a flyer that summarized the project in Spanish and asked if they were interested in participating in the project or having the project explained in more detail. Permission was requested for the researchers to conduct the survey and interview. The original plan was to ask potential participants provided they agreed to provide a convenient time for them to meet the researchers for the survey and interview.

The consulate also initially provided the researchers with a space to conduct the interview. The interviews were all conducted orally in Spanish. Permission to waive an informed consent document was requested from the university's institutional review board (IRB) for the protection of human subjects. Given the political climate in Arizona, we suspected that subjects would be wary of persons inquiring about access to health service agencies since they may be members of "mixed immigration status" families, i.e., families with members with varied legal status, including "undocumented." The rationale for requesting and receiving a waiver of the standard requirement for informed consent from potential research subjects was that omitting a document in which a respondent's signature was required would put subjects at ease. Because of this, a disclaimer document was considered appropriate and received approval by the university's IRB.

Once respondents agreed to be interviewed, researchers entered the information on the survey instrument. If participants agreed (and very few did not), their interviews were audio-taped for more accurate data entry and transcription. After the survey and interview, respondents were asked if they could refer the researcher to someone they knew who was responsible for the health-care needs of at least one undocumented individual and therefore not eligible to receive services (for Sample D). This procedure did not work out for recruiting participants for Sample D. Although researchers were told by many respondents that they would call with information, no call was ever received. This left researchers with the problem of recruiting a subsample of women who were, or were responsible for, someone in their household who was ineligible for health-care services while remaining faithful to the proposed research plan.

Fieldwork Challenges

The greatest challenge in implementing fieldwork in Altar was that researchers quickly became aware of the need to adjust their planned techniques to accommodate the constraints on migrants' time. Thus, in addition to finding women to interview who were at some stage of movement through Altar, information was gathered from a range of related key informants who were identified during phase one of the research. These actors within the migration process were shelter owners, personnel working at the mobile clinic and private medical facilities, hotel managers, taxi drivers, van operators, and those involved in an array of fast-food stands. Fortunately, it turned out that many of these were former migrants from various parts of Mexico who were now engaged in the booming commerce of the migration industry. However, again, it was not uncommon for commerce to take priority during these interviews, resulting in numerous interruptions. Often, these interviews could not be completed.

Researchers also quickly came to the conclusion that the design of the questionnaire was based on an outdated and traditional concept of the border in which analysis is premised on the geographical delineation of state boundaries, known as "methodological nationalism" (Wimmer and Schiller 2003). In this regard, the research parallels trends toward newer conceptualizations of state boundaries as fluid and nonconforming to territorial limitations and constructs. Consequently, researchers in Altar reconsidered the research design to include the realities of migrant movement, primarily the fact that women migrants often cross the border in experimental or repeated fashion. The borders they overcome are not necessarily those that define states but rather include those boundaries demarcated by ethnicity and culture, in Mexico and in the United States. In this way, their mobility revealed more about migrant agency and social organization than it did about borders.

With this reassessment, the questionnaire was reformulated and applied to 66 women who had resided in Altar for a minimum of five years. It included topics related to family unity and family separation, the migration process, their time in Altar in relation to their point of departure to the United States, and their general state of health.

In addition, 21 women in transit to the north were interviewed in depth about their plans to cross into the United States. One of the findings from these interviews was that women in general perceived their vulnerability in light of scarce resources and the lack of public health infrastructure. They were unable to find needed medications at their pharmacies and increasingly opted for home remedies for their medical needs.

Meanwhile, the research efforts in Tucson, Arizona, concentrated on identifying participants for two purposeful subsamples of immigrant women to appreciate changes in the reproductive health-care continuum as women move northward. The first subsample of immigrant women (C) was composed of those eligible for health services. The second subsample (D) was composed of immigrant women whose legal status (or that of someone in their care) might pose problems for accessing health care. What follows is a discussion of related methodological and ethical issues that emerged from the research conducted in Tucson.

Contending with the Political Climate in Arizona

Issues of recruiting participants for the study are largely blamed on the contemporary social and political climate that became codified with a series of legislated measures in Arizona since 2004 (O'Leary 2009a). In this way Arizona provides an appropriate context for understanding the threat to immigrant integration into destination communities. For example, in Arizona alone, about 37 immigration-related bills flooded the second regular session of the Arizona State Legislature in spring 2006 (O'Leary 2007, Appendix). These were but a fraction of the more than 500 anti-immigrant state-level bills introduced that year across the United States, many of which replicated established federal immigration enforcement responsibilities (Harnet 2008). Harnet (2008) reports that in 2007, the number of bills nationwide dealing with immigrants tripled to 1,562, as every state in the union considered some form of immigration regulation. Kohout (2012) reports that from 2005 to 2010, over 6,600 immigration-related measures were considered throughout the nation.

The research, conducted in 2008–2009, tested the proposed procedures for subject recruitment in this environment. The assumptions that informed the design had considered the insecurities that potential respondents might feel about questions regarding health-care access. We also considered the apprehension that those harboring others whose immigration status might be questioned might feel. They, too, might be hesitant to participate in the research, fearing that any information would jeopardize their well being or that of others. The state's recent history informed these assumptions. Similar to California's debates over Proposition 187 in 1994, nativist responses in Arizona since 2004 have coalesced around immigrants' use of public resources. In Arizona, as in other states, the widespread myths about immigrants' use of publicly funded programs, especially health care, has been blamed for the underutilization of services by even those who are entitled to them (King 2007). Arizona House Bill 2030, passed in 2006, was premised on the misrepresentation of Latinos as welfare-seeking intruders, and it focused the electorate's attention on immigrants' access to public programs. This bill made it a requirement for Arizona state government employees to verify an applicant's immigration status with the Department of Homeland Security's Secure America with Verification and Enforcement (SAVE) program before providing services.

Media attention on propositions, anti-immigrant rhetoric, and fear of being discriminated against and humiliated have all converged to erect barriers to health care, in particular for women (O'Leary and Sanchez 2011; Wilson 2008). In 2006, section 36-2903.03 of the Arizona Revised Statutes related to the indigent health-care system, known as the Arizona Health Care Cost Containment System (AHCCCS), was amended to obligate its employees to verify the immigration status and eligibility of applicants through the alien verification system administered by the U.S. Department of Homeland Security. The bill replicated the provisions already contained in the federal 1996 Personal Responsibility and Work Opportunity Reconciliation Act, which among other things imposes a five-year ban before recent legal immigrants become eligible for federally funded public benefits programs. Arizona HB 2030 impacted Department of Economic Security (DES) public assistance programs through he Department of Education (DOE), and Arizona Health Care Costs Containment System (AHCCCS) (its Medicaid system). Inda (2006) argues that placing entitlements at the center of public debate allows discriminatory tendencies to proliferate by making immigrants increasingly visible and increasingly singling them out for additional scrutiny (see also Michelson 2001). Indeed, ethnographic research by Marchevsky and Theoharis (2008) shows that immigrants, based on their appearance, language use, and facial characteristics, may be more likely to be more scrutinized by welfare officials charged with implementing policies. Moreover, they argue that because officials are influenced by the public discourse and public prejudices, their decisions result in eligible applicants being denied much-needed public benefits. A prevailing assumption that informed the research and its design, therefore, was that respondents would be fearful of divulging information that might jeopardize their access to and participation in health-care programs and potentially endanger their well being or that of their families.

Moreover, in November 2009, after the conclusion of the data gathering portion of the research, changes to Arizona Revised Statues A.R.S. 1-501 and A.R.S. 1-1502 governing DES polices were implemented as the result of Arizona HB 2008. Section One of A.R.S. § 1-501(E) now states:

> Failure to report discovered violations of federal immigration law by an employee of an agency of this state or a political subdivision of this state that administers any federal public benefit is a class 2 misdemeanor. If that employee's supervisor knew of the failure to report and failed to direct the employee to make the report, the supervisor is guilty of a class 2 misdemeanor.

Section Two of A.R.S. § 1-502(E) was also amended to include the same penalties for those administering any state or local public benefits. Like the provisions made under proposition 200 in 2004, this bill mandated electronic reporting to Immigration and Customs Enforcement when a violation of the law was discovered. We considered the timing of this law with the conclusion of our research as a fortunate coincidence as these types of developments have been known to further suppress the daily activity of immigrant community residents out of fear (see also Montoya Zavala, this volume).

Ascertaining Immigration Status

The issue of how fear influences research has been little studied, but Cornelius in 1982 addressed some of the "trade-offs" in research design where fear of reporting self-incriminating information is a potential factor. Cornelius pointed out some of the methodological challenges inherent in interviewing undocumented immigrants, where personal interviewing is the primary data gathering technique. In 1978 fieldwork among undocumented migrants in California, Cornelius made use of less threatening questions to ascertain the legal status of respondents. Similarly, in the current study also, no question about respondents' legal status was asked. Instead, questions correlated with expected behaviors consistent with efforts to avoid unwelcome attention. These proxy questions used to determine "undocumented status" were informed by assumptions and known behaviors that immigrant families use to compensate for not having access to health-care programs. Combining such questions became the basis for determining the multifaceted construct of "undocumented." Examples of survey questions that were combined to make this determination included:

- Example 1: What was the most recent date that member solicited services from a health or social service agency?

  In some cases, a spouse or other member of the household had never solicited services. When combined with other answers to other questions, we presumed that this member of the household was undocumented.
- Example 2: In the last 12 months, was there any time or someone in your family did not have some type of medical insurance?

  In some cases, respondents themselves or a member of their families had not solicited services, did not qualify, or did not have insurance through an employer, conditions that may be used to determine the problem produced by undocumented legal status.

- Example 3: What was the reason that [respondent] had gone without medical coverage?

  In some cases, respondents did not have the proper documents to register for services, or "earned too much" to qualify for health plans for indigent care.

In addition, and following Cornelius (1982), open-ended questions were included, which in some cases helped to obtain information that could be used to determine Subsample D (immigrant women whose immigration status—presumably undocumented—precluded them or at least one member of their family from accessing services:

Examples of some of the answers to open-ended questions and "testimonies" used to determine if a respondent (or someone in her household) was of a "mixed immigration" status (Subsample D).

- Although unsolicited, some respondents provided the information about their undocumented immigration status or that of a member of their family (e.g., spouse, child).
- Some testimonials provided information about an inability to travel to Mexico for services or prescriptions because of the difficulty in returning to the United States.
- Some testimonials provided information that someone in the family would go to Mexico for medical services or products, suggesting (a) that the respondent herself could not go, or (b) the respondent or family member had a tourist visa that allowed him or her to cross the border, which did not necessarily mean that he or she was a legal resident and therefore entitled to apply for health-care benefits.
- Some provided information that they were "no longer" eligible for prenatal care, or emergency care. Women, regardless of legal status, are eligible to receive prenatal care and delivery. However, once the child is born, the mothers are no longer eligible for health-care services.
- Some provided information of some children being born in the United States while sharing that other children did not have access to health-care programs, (presumably due to their immigration status).

The narratives from the open-ended questions were analyzed with the information provided in the closed-ended survey instrument to support our suppositions about legal status. Upon inspection of the responses, certain patterns emerged to allow the research team to discuss, and later claim with reasonable certainty, that we had met our goal of interviewing at least 40 respondents in which at least one member of the household was undocumented. Forty-one households were determined with reasonable certainty to belong to Subsample D, "mixed immigration status" category. Nine were cases that no such determination could be made using the information that was provided. The remaining 39 cases (Subsample C) were households in which eligibility for health-care programs was not an issue, presumably because all members were in status. However, in adopting such a method, the research assumed certain limitations in terms of its resulting data, and consequently, its conclusions.

Mitigating Sample Bias

According to Cornelius, fear introduces systematic bias into the research results in two ways. The first is that fear produces "extremely high" nonresponse rates. In response to this first issue, researchers must often accept smaller samples that can improve response rates. However, in doing so, the ability to generalize to a larger population is weakened. The conventions of science are largely dominated by assumptions about the desirability of the ability to generalize. Researchers must weigh this convention against the goals of their research. According to Cornelius, to achieve a better response rate (and more generalizability), researchers must work harder to locate and engage participants *and* build trust at the same time. This usually involves more complex, time-consuming approaches designed to locate undocumented populations who reside in the shadows and wish to remain undetected. Thus, given time and financial constraints, researchers may need to accept smaller samples. Such compromises are necessary "if [researchers] want to find answers to many of the empirical questions that are at the heart of the debate over undocumented immigration" (Cornelius 1982: 381).

The second way that fear introduces systematic bias is when research participants are reluctant to truthfully answer questions that may incriminate. With trends towards greater criminalization and harsher penalties for crossing the border without documentation, research participants may be understandably less inclined to state that they are in the country unlawfully. This is a problem if the goal of the research is to document the reality of undocumented immigrants. If immigrants have accessed public programs under a false identification, they may also be unwilling to share this information with anyone. In either of these cases, a disincentive to answer questions truthfully weakens what we know about those present in the country without documents if ascertaining their status is not possible without creating more anxiety among research participants. As noted above, for undocumented immigrants, fear of intense scrutiny stems from the increased pressures placed on service agencies to ascertain applicants' legal status. While not much can be done about respondents' desire not to truthfully answer questions, researchers need to incorporate more trust-building methods and more sensitivity to the political climate as an alternative to the more direct questioning about legal status and certain behaviors in an effort to enlarge sample size (Granberry and Marcelli 2007).

The bias that a fearful population may introduce in terms of the answers they give may be reduced in yet another way. In our study, we enlisted the help of highly motivated community health workers, *promotores de salud*, from El Rio Community Health Center. The promotores were already actively engaged in the community by organizing and conducting diabetes prevention and education workshops. The networks they actively sought to expand for their own work became essential for participant recruitment. The reliability of the data collection process was thus improved by reducing the refusal rate of potential participants. The promotores were already well-trained interviewers with human research subjects protection training from previous collaborative research experiences. Coming from the same cultural background as many of their respondents within the research subject population, they were sensitive to and knowledgeable about the cultural and political contexts of their clients. They had extended personal contacts within the community from the many years that they had worked in the diabetes prevention and outreach program at El Rio and they subscribed to an ethic of respect for respondents who, because of the proliferation of anti-immigrant rhetoric and media, were suffering from a low-level but constant assault on their dignity and understandably may have been reluctant to participate.

Locating Participants

Cornelius (1982: 385) argues that the most difficult part of research among undocumented populations is locating and accessing interviewees. Historically, social service agencies, community organizations, and leaders with far-reaching personal networks have been key to persuading potential research subjects to participate in studies. A "snowball" sample technique is an example of how earlier successful interviews may lead to other referrals. As Cornelius (1982: 392) explains, as the trust between the researcher and a network of acquaintances grows, so does the number of possible respondents:

> Among the Mexican immigrant population, this approach to data collection enables the researcher to take advantage of a natural sociological phenomenon—the fact that the vast majority of Mexican migrants, both legal and illegal, temporary and permanent, who are now working in the United States, are tied to extensive kinship/friendship networks.

Snowball sampling has proven to be highly successful in keeping the refusal rate low, and in ameliorating the fear that can distort the data. In the initial phase of our research, we attempted to employ a snowball technique such as the one described by Cornelius, but with considerably less success. This changed significantly with the incorporation of the El Rio promotores de salud, as they were well versed in the snowball technique as part of their strategies for recruiting participants for their diabetes education workshops. Due to their years of service and commitment to the program, they had access to a broad base of potential study participants. Although this work resulted in our achieving a desired subsample of mixed immigration status households, it also favored a resultant sample in which individuals had already taken an interest in improving their knowledge about health. In this way, the study's dependence on community agents for recruiting participants introduced bias into the resulting sample in several ways. First, it favored members of the community already engaged in health-education programs, and more likely to be conscious of the need to adopt health-care and health-seeking behaviors. Secondly, it favored individuals who are long-term residents (as opposed to temporary or recent immigrants); and as such, women who were more likely to be more assertive and self-confident (as opposed to those who might be more fearful).

"Safe Place" Bias versus Improved Respondent Response Rates

The space initially available to the Tucson research team at the Mexican Consulate's office turned out to be too small and lacking privacy. The Ventanilla collaborative relationship with El Rio provided an expansion of space by going to the El Rio facilities. However, this presented problems for meeting our goals of obtaining interviews from women who would fit the mixed immigration status category. Most all of the participants recruited at the El Rio facilities belonged to Subsample C, or were from households where eligibility for services was not contested. Moreover, our recruitment at the El Rio facility was repeatedly frustrated. As in the case of Altar, many potential respondents refused, citing busy schedules or pressing commitments elsewhere.

The research proposal had initially envisioned collaborating with El Rio personnel, so it was not inconsistent with the project proposal to adjust the procedure by engaging El Rio promotores de salud to help researchers find a solution to this problem. They resolved the problem of interviewing women who were too busy by leveraging the organization used by promotores to conduct workshops. Interviews (conducted primarily by research team members and on occasion by promotores) were thus added at the end of the time and in the same space for these diabetes education workshops. Promotores had received IRB training after working on other university research projects, so in this way conformed to IRB protocols.

Promotores thus served a dual role in this project: they provided a reliable "in" to the populations we desired to interview as part of the total sample, and they were able to provide safe [social] spaces in which to conduct research through their work in these spaces for diabetes prevention education. The high response rate (100 percent) of those invited to participate by the promotores is attributable to their years of experience in working in such settings. By comparison, without the use of promotores as recruiting agents, initial response rates experienced at the Mexican Consulate office and at the El Rio facility were extremely variable (around 15 to 50 percent).

Conclusions

A deliberate reflection on the methodological challenges arising from research conducted in the U.S.–Mexico border region in 2008–2009 reveals here a nuanced approached to border research, one that invariably requires a certain level of flexibility on the part of the researcher to accommodate rapidly changing dynamics due to increased border enforcement and parallel laws on the U.S. side of the border intended to discourage immigrants from settling in the United States (O'Leary and Sanchez 2011; Vaughn 2006). In particular, the research tactics emerged from the vulnerability of im/migrant women and issues of health-care access in transit in settlement communities where they are increasingly subjected to scrutiny, exploitation, marginalization, and victimization. Such environments have forced us as researchers to be ever more cognizant of the social and political contexts where the research takes place, and the possibility that our research may have negative unintended consequences for the subjects of inquiry (Bilger and Van Liempt 2009; Sprague 2005). In this binational research project, we encountered, experimented with, and resolved methodological issues that led to adaptation and project redesign to accommodate emerging realities in the field. We find support from feminist approaches that such creativity is exactly what social science needs. Our approach not only emphasizes a nuanced approached to gathering data, it also parallels shifting theoretical perspectives that increasingly see border regions as antithetical to the current politics of border enforcement, which emphasize cultural, state, and national boundedness, known as methodological nationalism. Our feminist approach was also in keeping with our desire to focus on gender as an important dimension for shaping social interaction in a variety of contexts, including the transnational. In this way, we advance the process through which witnessed accounts of research participants—devalued by virtue of their social and legal status—inform efforts to make the policies more equitable.

Notes

1. Support for this research came from the Programa de Investigación de Migración y Salud (PIMSA).

2. Three areas of critical reproductive health were singled out: pregnancy (prevention, counseling, termination, and prenatal care); sexually transmitted diseases (including HIV/AIDs, detection, prevention, and treatment); and postpartum care and the risks to women and infants posed by malnutrition, anemia, infection, or depression.

3. Robert Chambers might be the scholar most commonly associated with pioneering "rapid rural appraisal" techniques. Beebe (2001) provides a comprehensive history of the adoption of the method in a wide range of disciplines. Often known by different names, RATs remains consistent with the early procedures advanced by Chambers and others.

References

Beebe, James. 2001. *Rapid Assessment Process: An Introduction.* Walnut Creek, CA: AltaMira.

Bilger, Veronika, and Ilse Van Liempt. 2009. Introduction: Methodological and Ethical Concerns in Research with Vulnerable Migrants. In Ilse Van Liempt and Veronika Bilger, eds. *The Ethics of Migration Research Methodology: Dealing with Vulnerable Immigrants.* Pp. 1–24. Brighton, England: Sussex Academic Press.

Carruthers, Ian, and Robert Chambers. 1981. Rapid Appraisal for Rural Development. *Agricultural Administration* 8:407–422.

Cornelius, Wayne A. 1982. Interviewing Undocumented Immigrants: Methodological Reflections Based on Fieldwork in Mexico and the U.S. *International Migration Review* 16 (2): 378–411.

———. 2001 Death at the Border: Efficacy and Unintended Consequences of U.S. Immigration Control Policy. *Population and Development Review* 27(4): 661–685.

Cunningham, Hilary, and Josiah McC. Heyman. 2004. Introduction: Mobilities and Enclosures at Borders. *Identities: Global Studies in Culture and Power* 11: 289–302.

Falcon, Sylvanna. 2001. Rape as a Weapon of War: Advancing Human Rights for Women at the U.S.–Mexico Border. *Social Justice* 28(2): 31–51.

Ferreira-Pinto, Joáo B. 2005. *Impact of Arizona's Proposition 200: Final Report for the U.S.–Mexico Border Health Commission*. El Paso: Border Planning and Evaluation Group. Unpublished manuscript.

Fuentes-Afflick, Elena, Nancy A. Hessol, Tamar Bauer, Mary J. O'Sullivan, Veronica Gomez-Lobo, Susan Holman, Tracey E. Wilson, and Howard Minkoff. 2006. Use of Prenatal Care by Hispanic Women after Welfare Reform. *Obstetrics and Gynecology* 107(1):151–160.

Goldsmith, Pat, Mary Romero, Raquel Rubio Goldsmith, Miguel Escobedo, and Laura Khoury. 2009. Ethno-Racial Profiling and State Violence in a Southwest Barrio. *Aztlán: A Journal of Chicano Studies*, 34 (1):93–124.

Goldsmith, Raquel. R., with Melissa McCormick, Daniel Mártinez, and Inez Duarte. 2006. *The "Funnel Effect" and Recovered Bodies of Unauthorized Migrants Processed by the Pima County Office of the Medical Examiner, 1990–2005*. Washington, D.C: Immigration Policy Center brief. http://www.ailf.org/ipc/policybrief/policybrief_020607.pdf, accessed February 18.

Guendelman, Sylvia, with Dorothy Thornton, Jeffery Gould, and Nap Hosang. 2005. Social Disparities in Maternal Morbidity during Labor and Delivery between Mexican-born and U.S.-born White Californians, 1996–1998. *American Journal of Public Health* 95(12): 2218–2224.

Granberry, Phillip J., and Enrico A. Marcelli. 2007. "In the Hood and On the Job": Social Capital Accumulation among Legal and Unauthorized Mexican Migrants. *Sociological Perspectives* 50(4): 579–595.

Hannerz, Ulf. 1998. Transnational Research. In Bernard H. Russell, ed. *Handbook of Methods in Cultural Anthropology*. Pp. 235–256. London: Sage.

Harnet, Helen M. 2008. State and Local Anti-immigrant Initiatives: Can They Withstand Legal Scrutiny? *Widener Law Journal* 17: 365–382.

Inda, Johnathan Xavier. 2006. *Targeting Immigrants: Government, Technology, and Ethics*. Malden MA: Blackwell Publishing.

King, Meredith L. 2007. *Immigrants in the U.S. Health Care System: Five Myths That Misinform the American Public*. Washington, DC: Center for American Progress. http://www.americanprogress.org/issues/2007/06/immigrant_health_report.html, accessed July 21, 2008.

Kohout, Michal. 2012. Local Anti-Immigration Politics in California's Inland Empire. In Monica Verea, ed. *Anti-immigrant Sentiments, Actions and Policies in North America and the European Union*. Pp. 137–156. Mexico, D.F.: Centro de

Investigación sobre América del Norte (CISAN) de la Universidad Autónoma de México (UNAM).

Marchevsky, Alejandra, and Theoharis, Jeanne. 2008. Dropped from the Rolls: Mexican Immigrants, Race, and Rights in the Era of Welfare Reform. *Journal of Sociology and Social Welfare* 15(3): 71–96.

Michelson, Melissa R. 2001. The Effect of National Mood on Mexican American Political Opinion. *Hispanic Journal of Behavioral Sciences* 23(1): 57–70.

Ojeda, Norma. 2006. Abortion in a Transborder Context. In Doreen J. Mattingly and Ellen R. Hansen, eds. *Women and Change at the U.S.–Mexico Border.* Pp. 53–69. Tucson: University of Arizona Press.

O'Leary, Anna Ochoa. 2007. Petit Apartheid in the U.S.–Mexico Borderlands: An Analysis of Community Organization Data Documenting Workforce Abuses of the Undocumented. *Forum on Public Policy On-Line* (Winter 2007). http://www.forumonpublicpolicy.com/papersw07.html#crimjus, accessed August 8, 2008.

———. 2008. Close Encounters of the Deadly Kind: Gender, Migration, and Border (In)security. *Migration Letters* 15(2): 111–122.

———. 2009a. Arizona's Legislative-Imposed Injunctions: Implications for Immigrant Civic and Political Participation. *Mexico Institute at the Woodrow Wilson International Center for Scholars.* www.wilsoncenter.org.

———. 2009b. Mujeres en el Cruce: Remapping Border Security through Migrant Mobility. *Journal of the Southwest* 51(4): 523–542.

———. 2012. Of Coyotes, Cooperation, and Capital. In Donald. C. Wood and Ty Matejowsky, eds. *Research in Economic Anthropology* 32. Pp. 133–160. Bingley, UK: Emerald Group Publishing Ltd.

O'Leary, Anna Ochoa, and Azucena Sánchez. 2011. Anti-Immigrant Arizona: Ripple Effects and Mixed Immigration Status Households under Policies of Attrition Considered. *Journal of Borderland Studies* 26(1): 115–133.

———. 2012. Mixed Immigration Status Households in the Context of Arizona's Anti-Immigrant Policies. In M. Verea, ed. *Anti-immigrant Sentiments, Actions and Policies in North America and the European Union.* Pp. 157–174. Mexico City: Centro de Investigación sobre América del Norte (CISAN) de la Universidad Autónoma de Mexico (UNAM).

O'Leary, Anna Ochoa, and Gloria Ciria Valdéz Gardea. 2013 Neoliberalizing (Re)production: Women, Migration, and Family Planning in the Peripheries of the State. In Anne Sisson Runyan, Amy Lind, Marianne H. Marchand, and Patricia McDermott, eds. *Feminist (Im)Mobilities in Fortress North America: Identities, Citizenships, and Human Rights in Transnational Perspective.* Pp. . 75–94

Organista, Pamela Balls, Kurt C. Organista, and Pearl R. Soloff. 1998. Exploring Aids-Related Knowledge, Attitudes, and Behaviors of Female Mexican Migrant Workers. *Health and Social Work* 23(2): 96–103.

Plascencia, Luis. 2009. The "Undocumented" Mexican Migrant Question: Re-examining the Framing of Law and Illegalization in the United States. *Urban Anthropology* 38(2–4): 378–344.

Romero-Gutiérrez, Gustavo, M. G. Garcia-Vazquez, Luis Fernando Huerta-Vargas, and Ana Lilia Ponce-Ponce de Leon. 2003. Postpartum Contraceptive Acceptance in León, Mexico: A Multivariate Analysis. *European Journal of Contraception and Reproductive Health Care* 8(4): 210–216.

Santibañez, Jorge. 2004. *Migración Internacional.* Congreso de la Sociedad Sonorense de Historia, Hermosillo, Sonora.

Sprague, Joey. 2005. *Feminist Methodologies for Critical Researchers: Bridging Differences.* New York: Altamira Press.

Valdéz-Gardea, Gloria Ciria. 2007. Geografías rurales olvidadas: menores migrantes en tránsito por Altar-El Sásabe, expresión moderna del proceso globalizador. Primer acercamiento. En Arquitecturas de la globalización. Eloy Méndez, Coordinador. Hermosillo, Sonora: Mora-Cantúa Editores.

———. 2009. Revisitando la Antropología de la Migración: Frontera, Actores y Trabajo de Campo. In Gloria Ciria Valdéz-Gardea, ed. *Achicando Futuros: Actores y Lugares de la Migración.* Hermosillo, Sonora: Editorial Colegio de Sonora.

———. 2009. Crecimiento urbano en el contexto globalizador: migración en tránsito por Altar, Sonora. *Sonarida* 14(28): 26–29.

Vaughan, Jessica. 2006. Attrition through Enforcement: A Cost-Effective Strategy to Shrink the Illegal Population. Washington, D.C.: Center for Immigration Studies.

Wilson, Ellen. K., and Chris McQuiston. 2006. Motivations for Pregnancy Planning among Mexican Immigrant Women in North Carolina. *Maternal and Child Health Journal* 10(3): 311–320.

Wilson, Tamar D. 2008. Research Note: Issues of Production vs. Reproduction/Maintenance Revisited: Towards an Understanding of Arizona's Immigration Policies. *Anthropological Quarterly* 81: 713–718.

Wimmer, Andreas, and Nick G. Schiller. 2003. Methodological Nationalism, the Social Sciences, and the Study of Migration: An Essay in Historical Epistemology. *International Migration Review* 37(3): 576–610.

CHAPTER TEN

Women, Migrants, Undocumented Business Owners

Methodological Strategies in Fieldwork with Vulnerable Populations

Erika Cecilia Montoya Zavala

Introduction

In the last decade, Arizona has seen an increase in the number of immigrants moving into the state. Many of these have been undocumented immigrants from Mexico. In response, the state of Arizona has proposed a series of anti-immigration policies and laws that create barriers to economic, political, and social integration (O'Leary 2009). Mexican immigrants, representing the largest percentage of the total immigrant population in both the state and in the United States, are the most affected by these laws. Despite these adverse conditions, immigrants have been able to insert themselves into the labor market, and are even successfully developing their own businesses.

Female immigration has played an important role in starting up and developing formal and informal businesses (Hillmann 1999; Barros 2006; Hwan-Oh 2007; Oso and Ribas 2007). In this chapter, I analyze the methodology that was employed in obtaining information about undocumented Mexican women who own businesses. The research was carried out in a metropolitan area in Arizona. The study originated from a survey of Mexican homes in Phoenix, Arizona, and carried out in 2007. The research was carried out in three stages. First, a team of researchers from the Universidad Autónoma de Sinaloa located the subject population using census tract records. Secondly, survey research with the aim of understanding the conditions in which Mexican immigrants lived and their vulnerability was completed. The research continued after the survey research was completed in a third stage with a qualitative study in which 10 semi-structured interviews were carried out with women business owners and employees of beauty salons.

The Research

My research was an exploratory study aimed at discovering the business strategies used by undocumented Mexican women. In particular, I was interested in understanding those strategies used to establish and develop their businesses in the context of immigration politics that seek to limit the labor force participation and entrepreneurship of undocumented immigrants. In the process of documenting the strategies that undocumented immigrants employed to establish and develop their businesses in an environment of anti-immigrant politics, I concentrated on beauty salon owners in Arizona. For this, I designed a methodological framework to obtain information from this sector of undocumented women. It is, therefore, the aim of this chapter to describe some of the quantitative findings that formed the basis of this study, as well as the steps taken to implement qualitative research that allowed us to obtain desired information about immigrant women engaged in the beauty salon industry as owners of these businesses, or as employees within them.

Context of the Study: Policies that Limit the Business Function of Undocumented Women Immigrants

In recent years, Arizona has become the main point of entry for immigrants coming from Mexico. In 2000, 20 percent of the state population was Mexican and in 2007, their representation rose to 26.3 percent (U.S. Census Bureau 2007). Immigration in Arizona has been a contentious issue for local governments, evidenced by the intense legislative activity aimed at resolving these issues. The measures taken to resolve the so-called problems of immigration in the state have resulted in policy measures aimed at restricting the life, work, health, and education of all immigrants, particularly those who are undocumented (O'Leary 2009).

The year 2008 was characterized as a year when one of the most stringent measures against undocumented immigrants was passed. That year,

Arizona HB2779, the "Legal Arizona Worker Act," became law. This law obligates employees to verify that their employees are legally authorized to work in the United States.[1] This law imposes stronger sentences for those using the identity of another person with the intent of obtaining a job. It also imposes a license suspension for businesses of at least 10 days as well as a probationary period of five years for the employer that intentionally employs an unauthorized foreign worker.

That same year, with the modification of the HB2745 Law, it was established that in order to issue a license[2] to businesses established in Arizona, it is an indispensable requirement to prove one's legal residency in the United States. The documents that are accepted as proof of residency are an Arizona driver's license or identification issued after 1996 by the Department of Motor Vehicles (MVD), a license from a state that verifies legal residency in the United States, U.S. birth certificate, birth certificate of a U.S. citizen born abroad, U.S. passport, foreign passport with a U.S. visa, I-94 form with a photograph, work permit issued by immigration or a refugee travel document, certificate of U.S. naturalization, certificate of U.S. citizenship, or a birth certificate from the Bureau of Indian Affairs (Arizona State Legislator 2011). These are documents that in general undocumented immigrants do not possess, thus limiting their participation in the creation and development of regulated businesses.

As a result of these anti-immigrant policies in Arizona, undocumented immigrants become more vulnerable to suffering abuses and injustices in the labor market as they live in fear of being deported, excluded, limited, and subject to economic sanctions and penalties for working and carrying out business duties. These measures place undocumented immigrants at a disadvantage in society and the labor market in which they want to participate. Due to their vulnerable condition, immigrants may stop participating in certain activities or find ways to circumvent the system. They may, for example, find ways to avoid calling attention to themselves, such as electing not to report a robbery or workplace injustice out of a fear of being discovered and deported. Deportation or repatriation to Mexico would force them to leave family, material possessions, a job, and a life they've created for themselves in the United States.

Development of the Methodology: The Quantitative Section of the Study and the Beginning of Our Research

My interest in studying the participation of Mexicans in the development of businesses in Arizona stems from the Mexican household survey carried out in Phoenix in 2007, the results of which show the evident business participation of Mexican citizens in this area. The survey was carried out with a random representative sample of Mexican households in the metropolitan area of Phoenix.

The first step in carrying out the survey was to demarcate the area of study. We established a geographical area composed of 654 census tracts, distributed throughout 10 cities in Arizona. Of the 654 census tracts included in our area of study, we selected those that had a 25 percent or greater Hispanic population with respect to the total population. The result was the selection of 260 census tracts. Later, of the 260 census tracts, a representative random sample of 93 census tracts was calculated where we carried out the survey and this determined the number of questionnaires that would be applied. We determined that 561 questionnaires would be applied in order to generate the representation of the sample.

The next step was to distribute the 561 questionnaires among the 93 census tracts selected. The distribution was proportional to the number of Latino homes in each census tract and K of 98 (K was obtained by dividing the number of Latino homes estimated in the 93 census tracts by the number of questionnaires). The minimum number of questionnaires for the census area was 2 and the maximum was 15 (Valenzuela and Montoya 2012).

The questionnaire included 215 closed-ended questions and took approximately 45 minutes to administer. Some of the questions attempted to obtain information regarding all of the members of the household. The survey was comprised of 19 thematic sections, focused on obtaining information about the social demographic profile of all of the members of the household, regarding the immigration process of the head of the household, the entrance into the labor market in his or her communities of origin and destination, immigration status, social networks, level of education, business status, remittances, access to public services, perceptions of life in the United States, and political participation.

Particularly in the section regarding business, we asked if any member of the family owned his or her own business, and if the response was affirmative, we inquired about the type of business. Based on this survey, we detected 60 businesses established by Mexican citizens in different areas: commerce (11), construction (7), auto-mechanic garages (6), housecleaning (6), gardening (6), beauty salons (5), other services (5), transportation (4), restaurant work (6), alarm and stereo installation (2), etc. Additionally, through the survey we identified the immigration status and gender of the business owners. Among the findings of the survey, our attention was called to the fact that 36.65 percent of the business owners indicated that they did not have immigration documents, 28.3 percent said they had U.S. citizenship, and 35 percent said they had legal residency. Another aspect to highlight is that 70 percent of the business owners were men; in other words, 30 percent were women. This illustrates the relevance of female labor participation as business owners and in the formation of family businesses among Mexican immigrants.

The confirmation of the presence of Mexican businesses and the participation of undocumented immigrants in these activities raises a question about what strategies undocumented immigrants employ in owning a business and in order to continue operating under the context of anti-immigrant laws that demand legal residency documents in order to obtain licenses. Moreover, we were interested in the participation of women and the number of beauty salons included in this survey (5), which were entirely owned by women. It is for this reason that we decided to limit our study to Mexican women who own beauty salons.

A quantitative database of this type allows us to show a general panorama of the businesses established by Mexican immigrants in the metropolitan area in Arizona that we studied. It also provides information that allows us to demarcate our study. Consequently, our interest is to deepen the knowledge of the strategies that undocumented women have developed in the setting up and development of their beauty salons. We sought to obtain this information through qualitative research, particularly through semi-structured interviews focusing on revealing the experiences and expectations of this population.

Qualitative Methodological Strategies

We interviewed women who were willing to participate in the research; therefore it is not a representative sample. However, this approach and methodology allowed us to carry out valuable exploratory studies and to illustrate the realities of the participation of Mexican nationals in the creation of businesses. With these data, we can then analyze their perceptions regarding this phenomenon.

We used an interview guide that contained 12 topics considered important in outlining the general characteristics of the women interviewed. These topics included their immigration experiences; their work and business trajectories; the process of entering the labor market; the familial context in which they immigrated; their lives as immigrants and business owners; their perceptions of the incidental factors that occur during their foray into the labor and business market; and the economic, familial, and social changes that result from immigration. Additionally, we inquired about their economic contributions to their local communities.

The first stage of our qualitative research was carried out on the main streets of a suburban area in Arizona. Here we were able to confirm that the presence of Mexican businesses in Phoenix is overtly visible. During this stage I discovered beauty salons with names and information in Spanish; such as signs that read, "Spanish spoken" [Se habla español]. Additionally, I was able to determine the concentrations of Mexican beauty salons in various places.

I located a total of 19 beauty salons, seemingly all Mexican, and proceeded to mark them on a map and make a note of their addresses. I visited each one, introduced myself, and showed them my credentials as a professor from the Autonomous University of Sinaloa, with the intention of gaining their trust as potential interviewees. I then asked them the origin of the business owner and explained that I was searching for Mexican women who owned salons so that I could learn about their experiences as business owners in the United States. I would then make an appointment with the owner to carry out the interview, or I interviewed her on the spot if she was available. This process was somewhat difficult since interviewing these workers in their place of business meant that they would be occupied; this was the case with both stylists and business owners (see also O'Leary et al., this volume). The solution to this problem was to make appointments with them that were convenient for their schedules. The most appropriate times were during the lunch hour or on Mondays, when they didn't have customers in their businesses.

My presence in beauty salons, in general, was well received. However, the fear that I might be an official inspector, combined with the busy schedules of potential interviewees, did not help with the completion of this fieldwork. In some cases, we detected some fear caused by anti-immigration laws as well as a fear of revealing their immigrant status. On the other hand, the fact that I introduced myself as a professor from the Autonomous University of Sinaloa, showed my credentials, and explained the reason for my visit and that I was willing to return if they didn't have time at that moment all worked in my favor. In two salons, we were refused an interview[3] and were given the excuse of a lack of time. Three were closed when we wanted to administer the interview. In two cases, the owners were of other nationalities (African American, Asian). And two of the 19 shops had U.S.-citizen owners of Mexican descent. This made for a total of nine shops where we did not administer interviews for different reaons. We were, however, able to carry out 10 interviews.

It should be clarified that when we began our fieldwork, the population that was the focus of our study was Mexican owners of beauty salons in Arizona; however, we also interviewed stylists. We interviewed five women owners of salons, one man who owned a salon, three women employees, and one part-time woman employee who also had a salon in her house (see table 10.1).

The owners of the salons whom we interviewed were people of Mexican descent who were either legal residents or citizens (see table 10.1). The fact that we interviewed only salon owners who had had regularized their immigrant status is not an indicator that the undocumented individuals are not establishing beauty salons. One reason that we did not obtain interviews with undocumented Mexican salon owners could have been that they were fearful of giving information to someone they didn't know. Additionally, they may have feared being inspected and being charged fines due to the new law that demands legal residency papers of business owners.

Therefore, the way we were able to understand the strategies that undocumented immigrants use to start up and develop their businesses was by obtaining information indirectly, asking those with legal status about their business experience when they were undocumented. In such cases they were likely to feel more comfortable speaking on the subject retroactively without suffering any consequences for their past acts (of the 10 interviews carried out, 5 are of this type). Additionally, we interviewed an independent worker who had a salon in her house and worked part time in another salon. Two employees of the beauty salons who were willing to speak on the subject knew the history of the business and of the owners, who did not have legal status.

Some Findings of the Research

The beauty salon owners tend to be individuals over 30 years of age who have lived more than 19 years in the United States. Another characteristic of the business owners, as we mentioned earlier, is that they are likely to enjoy legal status, unlike their employees, who are less likely to possess it. Three of the owners processed their residency in 1986 with the Immigration Reform and Control Act (IRCA) and two through the family

Table 10.1. General Characteristics of the Interviewees

Name	Position	Owner's Hometown	Years as an Immigrant	Age	Marital Status	Education	Migratory Status
Mireya	Owner	Empalme, Sonora	19	39	Married	Secretarial certificate	Resident
Idalia	Owner	Mocorito, Sinaloa	31	63	Married	Accounting assistant, Nursing assistant, Cosmetology	Resident
Laura	Owner	Chihuahua	32	49	Separated	Business, Cosmetology	Citizen
Josefina	Owner	Zacatecas	33	54	Married	Cosmetology	Citizen
Anna	Owner	Chihuahua	20	45	Separated	Stylist	Citizen
Herman*	Owner	Hermosillo, Sonora	35	32	Married	Photographer	Citizen
Karen	Part-time, independent employee in salon	Chihuahua	19	20	Single	Cosmetology	Undocumented
Lolita	Employee	Guasave, Sinaloa	14	34	Divorced	Cosmetology, Secretarial	Undocumented
Martha	Employee	Culiacán, Sinaloa	10	34	Separated	Secretarial, Cosmetology	Undocumented
Patricia	Employee	Hermosillo, Sonora	3	35	Married	Dental technician, Cosmetology	Undocumented

Source: Author's findings based on interviews with owners and employees in beauty salons. Interviews carried out in February 2009 in Phoenix, Arizona.
*We interviewed one male beauty salon owner who agreed to participate.

reunification provisions of the act. We also interviewed a male beauty salon owner, who obtained legal status through this family reunification provision.

Characteristics of the Salons That Were Owned by Mexican Immigrants

The businesses that we visited were characterized by the diversity of services that they offered, from providing haircuts to making nutritional evaluations and renting videos. Two women who were interviewed said:

> I do everything, I manage, I'm in charge of services of haircuts and other services, but now I'm diversifying, because I'm also a personal fitness and nutrition trainer. I have plans to expand to another location; that's what I'm doing right now, because I'm running two businesses (beauty salon and nutrition and exercise business), and this is what I like to do, work related to health. (Laura, divorced, 49 years old)

> Right here I have a video store. I decided to connect it to the beauty salon to be able to manage both businesses. I also sell sports uniforms and we have a business to send money to Mexico called "Sígueme," and I even sell Herbalife. (Mireya, married, 39 years old)

The beauty salons that we visited work in the following way: The business owners supply all the tools needed to the employees as well as a place to work and the employees offer only their services, without investing anything. Haircuts cost between 10 and 15 dollars and the owner pays the employee between 50 and 65 percent. This percentage varies according to the experience that the stylist has and the documents he or she presents in order to work there (work licenses). The stylists need to have a license issued by the state and they must fulfill certain requirements in order to obtain it. It is necessary to have legal residency and Social Security documents, and to pass written and practical tests in order to obtain a work license:

> You finish your 1500 hours of practicum, then you have to pass an oral and another exam that consists of cutting hair—two haircuts—then you take a written exam and if you pass both, they give you a license that you have to renew every two years; and I just studied for 10 months.

I graduated in '97. In January of '97 we opened the first barber shop. (Hernán, married, 34 years old)

The clientele of the barber shops are essentially Latinos, as Hernán stated.

Yes, the majority are Mexican, I'd say 80 percent. The rest are American. (Laura, divorced, 49 years old)

The clientele is more Latino, only about 10 customers don't speak any Spanish. They like to come here. I think they like the treatment they get. I've had some customers for ten years. I saw them as children and now they're all grown up. (Mireya, married, 39 years old)

The customers are primarily Mexican, but some Americans come as well as Vietnamese, African, Arabic—people from all over the world. I have very international clientele, even Filipinos. (Hernán, married, 34 years old)

Strategies Followed by Undocumented Immigrants to Start Up and Run Their Businesses

The lack of immigration documents and the new legal residency application required to open a business has not limited the participation of women as business owners, but it has made it more difficult. Undocumented immigrants tend to be innovative in their strategies for opening businesses; they overcome this problem and assume the risk of investing in a political environment that attempts to isolate and exclude them from the workplace. In the next section, we describe some of the strategies we found.

DEVELOPING ACTIVITIES IN THEIR OWN HOMES AND OFFERING SERVICES IN THEIR CUSTOMERS' HOMES

Migratory status in other jobs, such as in the case of domestic employees analyzed by Hondagneu-Sotelo (2001), is a factor that can facilitate or limit the work participation of migrant women. In the case of the stylists, not having proper immigration documents has not limited migrant women from participating in the workforce as business owners, but their participation has not been without difficulty. As Light points out (2007:

52), undocumented immigrants have been innovative with their business strategies in order to overcome this problem and they assume the risk of investing in a regulatory environment that attempts to isolate and exclude them from the workplace. If caught, they may lose their material investment with harsh consequences. This is true in the case of Karen, who works informally (in a beauty salon in her house) because her undocumented status does not permit her to legally register her business:

> *I have a beauty salon in my house, and I can work. I think this is better for me because my customers are mine, the money I make is mine and it's better for me. I can't drive, so I prefer to be at home. I'm not taking a lot of risk, I don't place ads or anything. I don't have business cards. I don't have signs on my house or anything. My customers are all family and friends.* (Karen, single, 20 years old)

Other stylists who don't have licenses work in people's homes. Some don't run their businesses out of their own homes because they risk being deported as a result of someone reporting them:

> *I could put my business in my home, but there's a lot of envy. . . . You know, I only work on people I know, but news travels fast and it's dangerous, they can come and inspect your business and take away your work license. There is no other option than to give out business cards, how else can you do it? . . . That's why they're closing so many salons since there are so many stylists without licenses, they leave low-paying jobs and go to work in people's houses. Many go to people's houses, they charge like 70 percent. It's better to go to houses because then they don't know where I live, they simply give me their address.* (Lolita, divorced, 34 years old)

REGISTERING BUSINESS ACTIVITY IN THE NAME OF
SOMEONE WHO IS A RESIDENT OR CITIZEN

It was difficult to obtain an interview with an owner of a formally established beauty salon who did not have residency documents; all those who agreed to give interviews had documents. However, through the employees, we were able to learn of the strategies the owners employed in order to avoid being sanctioned by the new law that went into effect in 2008, which indicated that in order to have a business, it is necessary to have residency documents. The testimony that we cite here is from an employee of a salon:

Well, first of all, the owners of this business (where she works) have been working for quite a while without a license. They were very worried about the new law. The owner has invested more than $60,000 in the business, so she had a headache everyday since the new law went into effect. But she had the idea of going into business with someone who has residency documents, a relative of hers, and registering the business in his name. It's easier this way with family who have documents and with the money. (Lolita, divorced, 34 years old)

Additionally, we interviewed a beauty salon owner who is currently a citizen, but when she started her business, she was undocumented. She told us about her strategy for solving that problem:

We put the business in my sister's name because she was the one who had residency papers, but in 2000, my sister went to Mexico and I got my papers and now the business is in my name. I never thought I'd be able to have the business. (Mireya, married, 39 years old)

USING FALSIFIED DOCUMENTS TO OBTAIN WORK LICENSES COULD BE A STRATEGY THE STYLISTS EMPLOYED

According to our interviewees, the stylists who don't own businesses and who are formally employed in the established salons don't have the requirements to obtain their work licenses and thus practice their profession legally. Some stylists know of the law that went into effect in January 2008 and they applied for their renewal beforehand. Others, according to our informants, are thinking about presenting falsified documents:

We're now starting to see this problem. My license was going to expire on March 16 of 2008 when the law went into effect. They weren't going to give us licenses if we didn't have an ID. A friend called and asked me, "When does your license expire?" I told her and she said, "you have to go [renew the license], if you don't [go now], they won't give it to you" so I went in December, like the 28th and they didn't ask for anything because the law hadn't gone into effect. I paid 80 dollars and they gave me a license for two years. . . . A lot of girls, way too many, didn't get their licenses. (Lolita, divorced, 34 years old)

This is why they're falsifying licenses; they don't have any other choice. They have to work and they've closed a lot of their beauty salons and sell them for much less than they are worth, because they didn't know. And before, it was a lot easier to get a work license, a business license and all that and now they can't, they've made it hard for undocumented people, but we're still here. And they're going to keep doing more and what they ask for, people are going to falsify. And another thing, this happened to me, a lot of girls are sending a fake ID to get their license, they put a different name, they don't list a clear address and they still send them their license. But I think eventually, [the authorities] are going to realize it. (Martha, separated, 34)

TRAVELING TO OTHER STATES TO OBTAIN A LICENSE

This is my plan: if there's nothing I can do (legalization), in other states there are possibilities. Are we going to stand there with our arms crossed? Imagine that! Or looking for another job could be another option, but I don't think so. I've been thinking about going to another state like New Mexico to get a license. (Karen, single, 20)

Some Concluding Reflections

The strategies followed by undocumented immigrants to open businesses include opening informal businesses in their homes, registering business activity in the name of someone who is a resident or citizen, presenting falsified documents in order to obtain licenses to work in salons and to open a business, and traveling to other states to obtain a license. The use of a quantitative and representative methodology is a useful tool for identifying these trends and for illustrating the behind-the-scenes stories of human sacrifice and fear. The questions raised and the methodological issues presented in this exploratory research will strengthen future directions for this line of investigation.

We consider it important to point out that during the exploratory part of the larger study, the methodology may not need to be completely defined, nor its design rigidly adhered to during the fieldwork. We are convinced that methodologies reflect the context of upheaval and uncertainly that they are a part of, adapting to the possibilities and the interests of both the researcher and the participants. During the research we adapted our strategies to help us answer some of the questions that the original research posed, and this was possible with persistent qualitative research and a lot of sensitivity to the context in which we found ourselves immersed. For the qualitative portion of this research, we had to broaden the population that was the focus of the study. In other words, at first we just looked for women owners of beauty salons, but when this effort was frustrated, we decided to also interview female stylists employed in the salons who were willing to participate.

The decision to interview employees in the beauty salons gave us the opportunity to interview Karen, an undocumented worker who had a salon in her house. This interview opened up a new angle that was very different from our original intention at the start of the study, which was to find formal establishments owned by undocumented immigrants. This fortuitous discovery allowed us to contemplate how informal activities may be in fact a product of anti-immigration laws that limit the participation of undocumented immigrants in formal employment. This discovery supports arguments from other researchers who have consistently pointed out the false claims by proponents of such laws who claim that the laws are necessary for reducing unlawful practices, when in fact they create more unlawful activity (Malone 2002).

The analysis of this vulnerable group of immigrant entrepreneurs thus became difficult, and on occasion impossible to carry out. Key to our successes were our efforts to make interviewees feel safe and to offer as much transparency as possible, including sharing with them our identities and our ethical imperatives to keep information confidential.

Another strategy we used to obtain information indirectly about the population we wanted to learn more about was interviewing salon owners with legal residency about their experiences when they were undocumented. We believe this information to be very valuable because these individuals are able to speak freely and openly without the fear of sanctions from the new anti-immigrant laws. Of course, the vulnerability of these individuals diminished once they obtained immigration papers. However, this information and the way it was obtained is a viable alternative to the initial aims we intended to accomplish: to interview undocumented women business owners.

The research findings show us that chaos is imposed on immigrant families as they navigate the flurry of legislative measures designed to remedy the so-called problem of undocumented immigration. The measures have produced anti-immigration laws and policies that affect the life, work, health, and education of *all* immigrants, and not only those who are undocumented (O'Leary and Sanchez 2011).

The lack of immigration papers and the new procedure for applying for legal residency to open a business have not limited the participation of women as business owners, but these factors have made it more difficult. Undocumented immigrants are innovative in their strategies for opening businesses; they overcome these problems and assume the risk of investing in an environment that tries to alienate and exclude them from the workplace. In limiting the participation of immigrants in the formal workplace, these policies encourage them to seek new alternatives to earning a living, as with the establishment of informal businesses run out of homes. The impact that such laws will have on the state's economy in general continues to be the subject of heated debate.

Notes

1. Verified by the federal database found online called the E-Verify System (formerly called the Basic Pilot Program). Using the verification system is voluntary under federal law, but the new law in Arizona obligates employers to verify the system for new hires (O'Leary 2009: 26–27).

2. "License" refers to any permit, certificate, approval, registration, letter, or similar form of authorization that is required by law and is issued by any agency in order to maintain a business in this state.

3. The two interviews that were refused could have been due to the fact that the owners did not have immigration documents. In one of the cases, an employee confirmed this supposition.

References

Barros Nock, Magdalena. 2006. "Entrepreneurship and Gender Relations: The Case of Mexican Migrants in Rural California. Second International Colloquium on Immigration and Development: Immigration, Transnationalism and Social Transformation. Hotel Hacienda Cocoyoc Morelos, Mexico, October 25–28.

50th Arizona State Legislature. 2011. www.azleg.gov.

Hillmann, Felicitas. 1999. "A Look at the Hidden Side": Turkish Women in Berlin's Ethnic Labour Market. *International Journal of Urban and Regional Research* 23(2): 268–282.

Hondagneu-Sotelo, Pierrette. 2001. Working "Without Papers" in the United States: Toward the Integration of Immigration Status as It Relates to Race, Class and Gender. In Esperanza Tuñón Pablos, ed. *Women on the Borders: Work, Health and Migration.* Pp. 205–231. Mexico: El Colegio de la Frontera Norte, México.

Hwan Oh, Joong. 2007. "Economic Incentive, Embeddedness and Social Support: A Study of Korean-owner Nail Salon Workers' Rotating Credit Associations. *International Migration Review* 41(3): 623–655.

Light, Ivan. 2007. Ethnic Economics. In Fundación CIDOB, ed. *Ethnic Business in Spain.* Spain. Pp. 41–68.

Malone, Nolan J. 2002. Breakdown: Failure in the Post-1986 U.S. Immigration System. In Douglas S. Massey, Jorge Durand, and Nolan J. Malon, eds. *Beyond Smoke and Mirrors: Mexican Immigration in an Era of Economic Integration*. New York: Russell Sage Foundation.

O'Leary, Anna Ochoa. 2009. *Arizona's Legislative-Imposed Injunction: Implication for Immigrant Civic and Political Participation*. Research Paper Series on Latino Immigrant Civic and Political Participation, No. 2, Woodrow Wilson International Center for Scholars. www.wilsoncenter.org/new/docs/ochoatucson1.pdf.

O'Leary, Anna Ochoa, and Azucena Sanchez. 2011. Anti-immigrant Arizona: Ripple Effects and Mixed Immigration Status Households under Policies of Attrition Considered. *Journal of Borderland Studies* 26(1): 115–133.

Oso, Laura, and Natalia Rivas. 2007. Ethnic Business and Gender Relations: Dominican and Moroccan Women in Madrid and Barcelona. Latin American Women Immigrants and Ethnic Business: Dominican Women in Madrid. In Fundación CIDOB, ed. *Ethnic Business in Spain*. Spain, Pp. 211–228.

United Nations. 2005. Population Division of the Department of Economic and Social Affairs of the United Nations Secretariat. *Trends in Total Migrant Stock: The 2005 Revision*. http://esa.un.org/migration, accessed June 8, 2009.

U.S. Census Bureau. 2007. Demographic and Housing Estimates. http://www.census.gov.

Valenzuela Blas, and Erika Montoya, eds. 2012. *New Pathways, the Same Destination: The Migration Process and Economic Insertion of Mexican Citizens in Phoenix, Arizona*. Jorale Editores.

CHAPTER ELEVEN

Research on Oppressed Communities

Pat Rubio Goldsmith

In this essay, I will discuss the ethical issues I encountered in relation to two research projects on Mexican migration and border issues. In the first, I was the co-principal investigator of a project that surveyed a gathering of people that was known in advance to include many unauthorized migrants from Mexico now residing in the United States. This discussion describes the ethical issues we confronted in surveying these people. In the second research project, I served primarily as a data analyst. Here, I discuss ethical issues related to the ways researchers use data to construct political and ethical meaning.

Project One: No-Match Letters

The initial impetus for researching no-match letters came from a pro-migrant and pro-labor community organization. They were concerned about the federal government's attempts to use data on names and Social Security numbers as a method of migration control (or, as some might argue, as a method of Latino/a oppression). For many years, the Social Security Administration (SSA) has been monitoring names and the Social Security numbers assigned to them. They have routinely sent letters to individuals whose names and numbers were a "no-match," but the reason for sending these letters—at least until recently—has been for the benefit of the worker. The SSA sent these letters to make sure that it credited individual wage earners with their full lifetime earnings. In certain situations, such as when the address of the worker was not available, the SSA sent the letter to the employer, who would act as an intermediary and deliver the letter to the employee. By law, employers cannot take action against these workers until a 30-day grace period has passed during which the worker can fix the discrepancy.

However, under the Bush administration, no-match information was being used to identify unauthorized migrants. The ACLU has successfully blocked this federal action through the courts by arguing that many people besides unauthorized migrants have names that do not match their SSNs and that this policy would result in harm to many individuals who do not have fraudulent SSNs. The case is currently under appeal, as the Obama administration is also considering no-matches as a migrant control strategy. The community organization that contacted us wanted to know the consequences of these no-match letters for workers of Mexican origin.

The research project we conducted had a variety of strengths and weaknesses that should be made clear at the outset. The research team consisted of co–principal investigators (myself and Laura Koury), five seniors from a capstone class, and two students taking independent study classes. We needed to work very rapidly, however, because we only had a few weeks before the date the survey would be administered. The construction of the survey posed the greatest challenges, as the research team was not intimately acquainted with the issue. The community organization, in contrast, was much more knowledgeable about the political issues, but not well versed in survey construction. We designed what we believed to be a short, simple survey that could be self-administered—a necessity because the workshop would be attended by hundreds of individuals.

To help individuals complete the survey, we created English and Spanish instruments and we recruited 15 bilingual people who would be available to answer subjects' questions. In addition, we were lucky because the survey was done at a workshop being put on by the community organization, which the migrants steadfastly trusted. Unfortunately, we did not anticipate how many respondents would need a lot of help. Many of the people were illiterate; others didn't have the kinds of eyeglasses they would need to read the print. Other issues, like the ordering of questions and a lack of depth in particular areas (which were difficult to foresee), made the information obtained less than what it could have been. Nevertheless, we managed to get 150 well-completed surveys in 30 minutes.

Beyond the logistical difficulties of conducting this research so quickly, the project involved a number of very serious ethical considerations. The portion of the research project that made us confront these issues directly lay in the process of seeking approval from the institutional review board. As many are aware, IRB approval has become much more onerous in recent years, and while I detest filling out bureaucratic paperwork as much as anyone else, I do think the new, more rigorous requirements made us think through our project more thoroughly. We came to realize these things more clearly: We would be surveying large numbers of unauthorized migrants; we would be asking them about information that could be incriminating; and the project was being conducted at the behest of an organization that was and is protecting the rights of a highly stigmatized population. Furthermore, the research team and I were and are not politically neutral; we were and are committed to improving the lives of people of Mexican origin, whether or not they are authorized to live in the United States.

Despite not being a legally protected subgroup of human subjects, unauthorized migrants are an extremely vulnerable population, especially if you are asking them, as we did, whether or not they are actually authorized to live in the United States. Such information, if it could be linked to an individual, could result in their exile from the United States, separation from loved ones, or detention. I thought that confidentiality was priority A-1. Sometimes researchers collect information on surveys that can be linked to individuals so they can go back to them for further questions. Such techniques are allowed if the researcher takes further steps, like obtaining that information on the actual survey and keeping those surveys under lock and key. But I didn't think that was good enough. I felt information that could link individuals with surveys was so dangerous that it was absolutely necessary that no one should have access to it. I did not want to possess any data that could identify individuals *in any way*; I did not want anyone on our team or from the community organization to possess it either. In part, confidentiality was a priority because we wanted to be able to tell the respondents that their responses would be kept confidential and they could fill out the survey without risk. But my own feelings about this were also important. I disagree with the policies that lead to the deportation of unauthorized migrants; I am opposed to them on moral grounds, and I will not collect data that could possibly lead to someone's exile.

We designed the survey with these considerations in mind. We obviously decided not to include any questions about their names or identifying numbers. However, we were also concerned about including questions that in combination could be used to identify individuals. For example, we wanted to ask them about their ages and occupations, but we didn't want anyone to be able to identify the respondent who was—for example, a 55-year-old meatpacker. For this reason, we measured age (and other similar variables) using broad categories like "less than 25," "26 to 45," "45 to 65," and "over 65."

The results of the survey showed that a full 36 percent of the respondents had received a no-match letter. The way they received this letter varied: 64 percent from the SSA, 21 percent from an employer, 3 percent from another government agency, and 13 percent "have been told about it but have not actually seen it." Of those who received a letter, 17 percent were dismissed, 10 percent had their wages cut, and 8 percent lost benefits. In addition, 30 percent became afraid to speak up at work and 12 percent left their jobs. Almost none of the respondents were given the required 30 days to fix the discrepancy. Of course, these occupational disasters were especially bad when it was the employer who gave the respondent the letter. For example, 58 percent of the people who learned of their no-match letters from their employers were fired.

There was one question that the research team proposed for the survey that the community organization did not want to include. This question asked respondents whether or not they had a fraudulent Social Security number. I cannot say specifically why we wanted it beyond that it seemed to be an important piece of information. The community organization did not want it included because it could potentially be used against their political aims. This organization is steadfastly committed to improving the lives of laborers and immigrants, and they saw this question as gathering information that could jeopardize their struggle.

We researchers decided not to fight over this question. In truth, the only defense I could make for keeping it was that I was offended not to have my expertise trusted (and how petty is that?). But the organizers' request does let us see how researchers and activists might come into conflict. Social science researchers can pursue questions or discover facts that can be injurious to political causes, even the causes the researchers support. Should the researcher hide these facts or not pursue these questions? While I believe in the ethical principles of research (like disclosure and academic freedom), how much weight should I give them in light of the political ramifications of injurious findings? To the people in the community organization, this probably seems like a ridiculous question. They are making incredible sacrifices to themselves to fight against powerful and dangerous social forces for the benefit of the oppressed. Part of the solution to this dilemma is in the construction of research projects, as is discussed below.

Ethno-Racial Profiling and State Violence in a Southwest Barrio

In the second study, I was basically a statistician in the analyses of secondary data. I was to analyze data from two independent random samples of residents of South Tucson, Arizona. The aim of these analyses, which were eventually published (Goldsmith and Romero 2008; Goldsmith et al. 2009), was to learn about the mistreatment of residents by state officials. We asked questions like these: At what rate do state officials mistreat residents? To what extent is knowledge of mistreatment common? What types of mistreatment are most frequent? Where does mistreatment tend to occur? When someone is mistreated, which state officials tend to be responsible? Which residents tend to be mistreated relatively more often?

When analyzing secondary data, that is, data that were collected by others, the statistician's charge is to use the data to construct meaning. I suppose this is a relatively straightforward process in some cases. Researchers create variables and answer questions following a preconceived plan. But I've never been able to generate interesting findings so easily. In crunching data, one has to distill, play, sift, or massage them before they tell stories about the world. This is a very complex process and it is filled with wrong turns and dead ends. Variables that would seem to hold promising information often do not; suspicions about how to proceed are more often wrong than right. Don Grant, one of my professors from graduate school, used to tell me, "Torture the data until it confesses."

I do not mean to make the process sound completely haphazard. Prior literature helps tremendously because findings from prior research are usually replicable. Still, these were unique data and we were using them to answer questions that had not been asked very often using quantitative methods.

I have read postmodern critiques of the process of number crunching. These thinkers are fond of saying that a data set can be manipulated an infinite number of ways and that one way is not any more correct than any other. But I don't believe that at all. There are plenty of incorrect ways to analyze data, ways that lead one to tell stories that are probably false—false in the sense that they do not capture the realities that people live. In the end, analyses require public justification to other smart and intelligent people. The stories one tells need to be supported by the evidence—in this case, by what the people said on the surveys.

In addition, quantitative methods are an especially influential method in debates on ideas and policy. Quantitative methods are widely viewed as the most legitimate method of investigation in the social sciences. According to Mark Solovey (2001), social scientists were under attack following World War II and in the burgeoning Cold War. Unlike natural scientists, social scientists were accused of being unimportant for national interests—and even more than that, of being socialist- and communist-leaning disciplines. Federal government agencies at that time (and to this day) overseeing funding for science were heavily staffed by positivist scientists. This meant that social scientists needed to adopt a natural science model of investigation and pursue programs helpful to the state (especially the military) to receive federal funding. Across divisions of the social sciences, quantitative social scientists doing research useful to the state became prominent and influential, leading in the long run towards quantitative methods becoming the most respected methods in the social sciences. To give a more recent example, this very paper is part of a research project being funded by the Department of Homeland Security. In all, the DHS gave 15 million dollars to the University of Arizona to study border issues. Of this money, only a tiny fraction (less than 2 percent) went towards studying the "human angle" (this book and this chapter are part of that). The rest of the money funded research on ways to make the border more secure: how to tell if people are lying, the development of motion sensors that can distinguish a blowing bush from a Mexican migrant, and other "natural" science projects that serve narrowly defined state interests.

Hence, the natural science model in the social sciences has historically been used in the service of oppression, leading some activist scholars to reject it in favor of other methods (e.g., see Tufuku and Bonilla-Silva 2008). But this decision ignores what is even more important: the natural science model can be a powerful political tool, and because of that, it can be used as a tool of liberation, too.

In our case, we used quantitative analyses to identify injustices. One of the things I learned from Mary Romero, a coauthor of mine on these two studies, is that we were telling the story of state violence from the perspective of barrio residents. It was thus a very social (hi)story. But telling a story from the perspective of barrio residents builds into the study a point of view. We did not strive for neutrality. Every presentation of the social world necessarily must involve a process of including some information and deleting other information. It is impossible to include every single fact. In social research, we sift through material and present particular perspectives. If it is a political issue that is being presented, then the sorting and sifting of information—or in our case, a picture of state officials from the perspectives of barrio residents—inherently involves a political and ideological orientation.

How did our ideological and political orientation shape our method? We were going to tell the story about the relationships and social interactions between barrio residents and state officials. And our method was such that we wanted to tell this story by talking to the barrio residents. I think some people might see this as a bad move. Shouldn't we talk to state officials? After all, aren't they the people who think about this relationship the most? Or maybe we should have talked to people higher up in the state, like administrators in the Border Patrol, the police, or ICE. Howard Becker is helpful here:

> In any system of ranked groups, participants take it as given that members of the highest group have the right to define the way things really are. In any organization, no matter what the rest of the organization chart shows, the arrows indicating the flow of information point up, thus demonstrating (at least formally) that those at the top have access to a more complete picture of what is going on than anyone else. Members of lower groups will have incomplete information, and their view of reality will be partial and distorted in consequence. Therefore, from the point of view of a well socialized participant in the system, any tale told by those at the top intrinsically deserves to be regarded as the most credible account obtainable of the organization's workings. And since . . . matters of rank and status are contained in the mores, this belief has a moral quality. We are, if we are proper members of the group, morally bound to accept the definition imposed on reality by a superordinate in preference to the definitions espoused by subordinates. Thus, credibility and the right to be heard are differentially distributed through the ranks of the system. (1970: 126–7, as quoted in Becker 1998: 90)

Quite clearly, Becker is not telling us to believe the people at the top of the hierarchy. He is telling us the opposite. He adds, "The trick for dealing with the hierarchy of credibility is simple enough: *doubt anything anyone in power tells you*" (91). To exercise proper skepticism, look for "other opinions." By approaching our social problem from the perspective of barrio residents, we were learning about things that state officials would not address. We were learning about information that state officials didn't think was important, or perhaps more to the point, that they didn't want other people to know about.

But a focus on the perspectives of barrio residents goes further than just gathering different information. It is a privileging of their perspective. It is, as Ronald Takaki (1994) might say, seeing the perspectives of ordinary people as valuable perspectives. Howard Zinn, in *A People's History of the United States*, provides clues to why such perspectives are valuable:

> The history of any country, presented as the history of a family, conceals fierce conflicts of interest (sometimes exploding, most often repressed) between conquerors and conquered, masters and slaves, capitalists and workers, dominators and dominated in race and sex. And in such a world of conflict, a world of victims and executions, it is the job of thinking people, as Albert Camus suggested, not to be on the side of the executioners. Thus, in that inevitable taking of sides which comes from selection and emphasis in history, I prefer to try and tell the story of the discovery of America from the viewpoint of the Arawaks, of the Constitution from the standpoint of the slaves, of Andrew Jackson as seen by the Cherokees, . . . the postwar American empire as seen by peons in Latin America. And so on, to the limited extent that any one person, however he or she strains, can "see" history from the standpoint of others. (1995:10)

In this process of recentering knowledge, of turning the hierarchy of credibility on its head, power relations in the social construction of knowledge are shifted. The perspectives of the exploited people at the bottom of the social structure threaten the taken-for-granted ideologies of the powerful. But in exposing the perspectives of the exploited, it is also possible to unearth inconvenient facts. Recall, for example, the above discussion about whether or not we should have asked people if they had fraudulent Social Security numbers. Of course, that is just one example of a much broader issue of not being idealistic about the perspectives of exploited people. Zinn is helpful here as well:

> My point is not to grieve for the victims and denounce the executioners. Those tears, that anger, cast into the past, deplete our moral energy for the present. And the lines are not always clear. In the long run, the oppressor is also a victim. In the short run (and so far, human history has consisted only of short runs), the victims themselves desperate and tainted with the culture that oppresses them, turn on other victims. . . .
> I will try not to overlook the cruelties that victims inflict on one another

as they are jammed together in the boxcars of the system. I don't want to romanticize them. But I do remember (in rough paraphrase) a statement I once read: "The cry of the poor is not always just, but if you don't listen to it, you will never know what justice is." (1995:10)

Translated into the jargon of scientific methodology, I think Zinn is asking us to be objective in the following sense: to develop research questions and develop methods for asking them which privilege the perspectives of the oppressed, but do not mislead what you find out. But he is saying one thing more, which is very important. Telling the stories of the oppressed holds a promise of envisioning a different, more just reality. That kind of story, one that creates visions of a better world, is the one that becomes possible from the study of oppressed people. I would like to think that the research that came out of the South Tucson studies creates that kind of a story. It was a long and difficult process, and it would not have happened without many gifted scholars and community organizers working together. But I think that research produced a narrative that points us toward a better world.

References

Becker, Howard S. 1998. *Tricks of the Trade: How to Think About Your Research While You're Doing It*. Chicago: University of Chicago Press.

Goldsmith, Pat Rubio, Mary Romero, Raquel Rubio Goldsmith, Manuel Escobedo, and Laura Khoury. 2009. "Ethno-Racial Profiling and State Violence in a Southwest Barrio." *Aztlan: A Journal of Chicano Studies* 34(1): 93–123.

Goldsmith, Pat Rubio, and Mary Romero. 2008 "Aliens," "Illegals" and Other Types of "Mexicanness": Examination of Racial Profiling in Border Policing. In Angela Hattery, Davide Embrick, and Earl Smith, eds. *Globalization and America: Race, Human Rights, and Inequality*. Pp. 127–142. Lanham, MD: Rowan & Littlefield.

Solovey, Mark. 2001. Project Camelot and the 1960s Epistemological Revolution: Rethinking the Politics–Patronage–Social Science Nexus. *Social Studies of Science* 31(2): 171–206.

Takaki, Ronald. 1994. *A Different Mirror: A Multicultural History of the United States*. Boston: Back Bay Books.

Zinn, Howard. [1980] 1995. *A People's History of the United States: 1492 to Present*. New York: Harper Perennial.

Zuberi, Tufuku, and Eduardo Bonilla-Silva, eds. 2008. *White Logic, White Methods: Racism and Methodology*. Lanham, MD: Rowman & Littlefield.

PART FOUR

A Fence on Its Side
Is a Bridge

Methodological and Ethical Implications in the Design and Application of the Mexican Household Survey in Phoenix, Arizona (EHMPA 2007)

Blas Valenzuela Camacho

Introduction

Recent literature has argued the emergence of a "new profile" of the migratory phenomenon from Mexico to the United States. This post-IRCA and post-NAFTA migration has been characterized by a diversification of origins and destinations, a unidirectional movement that departs from previous patterns of circular migration, the urban characteristic of the origins, increased and different participation of women, and the growing incorporation of migrant children (Cornelius 2001; Woo 2004; Durand et al. 2005; Meneses 2005; Zúñiga and Hernández-León 2005, 2006; Anguiano and Trejo 2007).

The first of the processes mentioned, the diversification of origins and destinations (Cornelius 1992; Durand 1998; Canales 2003; Durand et al. 2005; Zúñiga and Hernández-León 2005, 2006; Light and von Scheven 2008), implies the convergence of two different but closely related phenomena. On one side, in Mexico, regions of the country that did not previously represent important participation in the migratory movement toward the United States, outside of the traditional migratory region, are beginning to incorporate themselves into markets in an increasingly important way (Zúñiga, Leite, and Nava 2004). In contrast, destinations in midsized and small populations have emerged in the Northeastern and Midwestern United States, for example in Iowa, Nebraska, Minnesota, Idaho, Utah, Arkansas, New York, Georgia, North Carolina, Kentucky, and Tennessee, which is a result of the implementation of IRCA in 1986 and reinforced by NAFTA (Zúñiga and Hernández-León 2005).

Between 1985 and 1990, 63 percent of Mexican citizens who arrived in the United States went to California, but between 1995–2000, this figure fell to 35 percent. At the same time, those who arrived in nontraditional states rose from 13 percent to 35 percent. Since 1970, new poles of attraction emerged in states such as Florida, Idaho, Nevada, New York, North Carolina, and others. Mexican migration to Arizona has risen from 4.4 percent in 2000 to 6.2 percent (Durand et al. 2005).

Until the growing dispersion of settlement destinations as the new century dawned, migrants of Mexican origin were concentrated in the gateway states of California, Texas, Illinois, and Arizona. In California there were 8,455,926 people of Mexican origin, who represented 25 percent of the total population of the state; the Mexican immigrant population in Texas was 5,071,963, which represented 24.3 percent of the total population of the state; Illinois had 1,144,390 people of Mexican origin, but they represented a minor percentage of the total population (9.2 percent); in Arizona, people of Mexican origin were fewer (1,065,578), but they represented 20.8 percent of the total population of the state (U.S. Census Bureau 2007).

As immigrants in the United States began settling in non-gateway regions in the mid-1980s, origin-destination systems that connected specific origins in Mexico with specific destinations in the United States became discernible. One of the origin-destination systems, documented by Harner (1995), is the migration pattern that emerged in the Mexican state of Sinaloa and was directed toward the Phoenix metropolitan area in Arizona. Out of this inquiry, research has emerged on the continuity and relevance of this migration pattern, as well as its patterns of residential settlements in the region, its sociodemographic profile, the economic/labor sectors in which it inserts itself, and the impacts associated within the origin as well as the destination. Responses to these inquiries will help us to better understand the recent changes in the migratory phenomenon between the two countries.

Locating and obtaining information from a population from a specific state such as Sinaloa in an environment that is hostile toward migration such as Phoenix, Arizona (*El Universal* 2005; *La Crónica* 2007; *La Jornada* 2007; *The New York Times* 2008), required the use of diverse sources of documented information, the collaboration of community organizations such as the Latino Health Council (Concilio Latino de Salud 2011), governmental institutions such as the Mexican Consulate in Phoenix, and finally, the application of an extensive survey of Mexican households in this metropolitan area.

The purpose of the present work is to document this process of seeking information, and the methodological and ethical challenges that a group of researchers from the Autonomous University of Sinaloa faced in seeking to analyze the migratory movements of Sinaloans toward Phoenix, Arizona.

Sinaloan International Migration

Until recently, there has been a scarcity of literature that discusses migration of Sinaloan origin. This is understandable if we acknowledge that Sinaloa is not considered to be a traditional part of Mexican migration and that, if one could document the historic migrations of Sinaloans to the United States, it wouldn't be quantitatively relevant until the second half of the 1980s. The qualitative and quantitative importance of Sinaloan migration has become evident through the level of migration from Sinaloa as well as in the locations in the United States that receive immigrants of Sinaloan origin. Ibarra (2005) calculates that immigrants born in Sinaloa who reside in the United States are around 3 percent of the total Mexican population in the U.S., with a total of 330,000 people. When including all immigrants of Sinaloan origin, this figure reaches 650,000 people. Additionally, Ibarra et. al. (2004), based on the Sinaloan Household Survey in Los Angeles in 2004, estimated that of the Sinaloans that migrated to the United States in 2003, 55 percent went to California and their total number oscillated between 80,000 and 87,000. Moreover, the municipal origins of Sinaloans who live Los Angeles are principally Culiacán (33 percent), Mazatlán (11.1 percent), Mocorito (8.5 percent), and Badiraguato (6.7 percent).

Lizárraga (2004) demonstrated that the migratory phenomenon in some highland Sinaloan municipalities is highly present and comparable to those municipalities with a strong migratory tradition. In Cosalá, he found that 45 percent of the families have at least one member who has been out of the country; in San Ignacio it was 29.4 percent; in El Verde, Concordia, 42 percent.

In agreement with Lizárraga, García (2007) found that California attracts the largest number of migrants from Agua Caliente, the location of the Sinaloan municipality of Choix (60.8 percent), who have mostly established themselves in the region of Victor Valley, where they recreate familial and social practices similar to those they maintained in their place of origin. Valenzuela Camacho (2007) also found the presence of a notable business community of Sinaloan origin in the cities of Huntington Park, South Gate, Lynwood, Bell, Bell Gardens, Paramount, and Compton in south-central Los Angeles. In his study he estimates the presence of 83,000 Sinaloan migrants in the Los Angeles region in 2003, which present high concentrations in the cities studied as well as participation in ethnic economies, especially in seafood restaurants. Additionally, he maintains that Sinaloan migration to this region shows evidence of being self-generated, with social networks, residential patterns, and established ethnic economies.

Montoya Zavala (2004) shows the economic impact of this migration in Gabriel Leyva Solano, a community in the Sinaloan valley. In the study she carried out in this region, Montoya Zavala showed how households used remittances and highlighted the importance of remittances in economically sustaining households and in installing local businesses. Moreover, she exposed the reality of Sinaloan migration to new U.S. states—not states that have traditionally received Mexican immigrants such as North Carolina, Louisiana, and Virginia.

Pintor and Sanchez (2012) found that social networks mature, Sinaloan migration becomes facilitated by transnational circuits marked historically by older social networks of migrants from Sinaloa to Mexicali, Tijuana, Los Angeles, and Tucson, as well as relatively new ones: the cities of Phoenix and Salt Lake City; the state of Utah more generally, as well as North Carolina, Nevada, and Washington. Sanchez (2012) also analyzed migration networks established by migrants from Culiacán, Sinaloa to California, finding that the migratory dynamics of the municipality of Culiacán necessarily rests not only in urban areas, but is also made up of networks consistent with those profiling migrants from rural and urban areas in Sinaloa.

Sinaloan migration to the United States has had as a consequence an increase in remittances appropriated by the state. In 1995, these remittances were 199 million dollars; for 2005, these resources rose to 370.6

million dollars, equivalent to 24 percent of the payroll of the formal sector in the state economy (Banco de México 2007). In 2004, remittances were equivalent to 53 percent of the export of manufactured products, 68 percent of new private investment, 48 percent of federal contributions to the state in this same year, and three times the value of fish export from the state (Department of Economic Development of the State of Sinaloa 2007).

Sinaloa–Phoenix Migratory System

The metropolitan area of Phoenix had, until 2007, one of the most accelerated urban growth rates in the United States. The population increased 39 percent from 1997, compared with a national average of only 12 percent. In the period between 2000 and 2005, Arizona was second only to Nevada in increase in relative population, with 13 percent compared with 16.4 percent in Nevada (Greater Phoenix Economic Council 2007).

At the time this was occurring, the state of Arizona became the main corridor for undocumented immigrants to enter the country from Mexico, due to increased border vigilance put into place in California and Texas (Cornelius 2001; Anguiano and Trejo 2007). Within Arizona, the metropolitan area of Phoenix is where Mexican immigrants as other Latin American immigrant groups are concentrated as well. In the period from 1990–2000, the percentage of Latino population grew from 8.3 percent to 14 percent. The main factor that contributed to the growth of the Latino population in this area was the militarization of the Mexican–U.S. border crossings. With "Operation Gatekeeper" in San Diego, California, and "Hold the Line Rio Grande" in El Paso, Texas, Arizona became the new gateway for immigrants. In this regard, Skop and Menjívar (2001) found in Phoenix, in addition to Mexican citizens, a mosaic of communities of new immigrants of Guatemalan, Salvadoran, Cuban, Honduran, and Colombian origin.

Harner (1995) used a random sample of files from the apprehension of undocumented immigrants (form I-213) available in the office of the Immigration and Naturalization Service in the Phoenix district during 1989, 1990, and 1991. With these data, Harner studied the geographical patterns of undocumented Mexican immigrants in Arizona, attributing the origin of the immigrants in Arizona to the states of Sonora, Sinaloa, and Chihuahua (24.5, 18.5, and 15.5 percent, respectively). Harner argued that the principal municipal origin of the immigrants in Arizona was Culiacán, Sinaloa, at 10.85 percent of the sample, surpassing Nogales (6.43 percent). Other Sinaloan municipalities that stand out in the sample are Guasave, Ahome, and Mazatlán, with a participation of 1.74, 1.61, and 1.14 percent, respectively. In this study, Harner highlights the high potential of Sinaloa in the subsequent movements to the United States. Additionally, he underlines the lack of participation in this movement of the numerous migrants that land in Sinaloa from other Mexican states (8.0 percent); he argues that those who were the main migrants between Sinaloa and the United States were from Culiacán, originating from the state capital. In contrast, in Nogales, the majority of the migrants found there were simply passing through; in this case, 35.4 percent of the total migrants were from Mexican states other than Sonora.

Additional evidence supports Harner's findings. In 2007, the Mexican Consulate in Phoenix was second of all Mexican consulates in the U.S. in expediting consular registries of Sinaloans with 4,020—representing 20.14 percent of the total, surpassed only by the Mexican Consulate in Los Angeles with 4,921 (24.65 percent). That same year in Phoenix, they issued a total of 35,872 consular registries to Mexican citizens, with Sinaloa being the state with the greatest number of applicants, representing 11.21 percent of the total (Instituto de los Mexicanos en el Exterior 2008). Assuming that these figures are representative of the total Mexican population in this location and from the figure of 1,124,219 Mexicans living in the metropolitan area of Phoenix (Phoenix-Mesa-Scottsdale, or MSA) in 2007 (American Community Survey 2007), we can estimate that 126,000 Sinaloans were living in the area, which represents 38 percent of the total Sinaloan population in the United States and 4.9 percent of the total Sinaloan population. Other sources support the above assertions; a study of urban day laborers by the University of California–Los Angeles, found that in Phoenix, close to 8 percent of those surveyed were of Sinaloan origin (Valenzuela, Jr. 2006).

As indicated, the search revealed that there is evidence that immigrants of Sinaloan origin represent a substantial portion of Mexican migration to this destination. A phenomenon of this nature demands to be studied. Understanding the dynamic of this migration to Phoenix can help in the design, promotion, and improvement of public policies that reflect the realities in Mexico and in the state of Sinaloa, where up until very recently these issues were ignored.

Methodological and Ethical Challenges in the Application of the Survey of Sinaloan Immigrant Households in Phoenix in 2007

The relevance of the study has been established in so many different sources, confirming the existence of an origin-destination migratory system between Sinaloa and Phoenix, Arizona. However, uncovering the possible causes of this migration, as well as its evolution and the impacts on the destination, requires obtaining more information. With this in mind, we considered applying a survey to representative Mexican households in the Phoenix metropolitan area, then collecting data, not just from Sinaloans, with the goal of establishing parameters of comparison, which has been scarce in the literature up until now. An antecedent to this effort was carried out in 2004 in the city of Los Angeles (Ibarra, et. al 2004). However, on that occasion, the questionnaire applied, though extensive, was not representative, since the subjects of study were located with the snowball method and it was directed only at Sinaloans. With this work, we attempt to surpass that effort.

The U.S. census offers information about the population by national origin and census tract, making it possible to calculate the size and location of the population of Mexican origin in the state of Arizona, in Maricopa County, and in the Phoenix metropolitan area; however, this instrument does not collect data about the state of origin of Mexican citizens who have settled there, which proves the hypothesis that the migratory system between Sinaloa and Phoenix needs methodological alternatives.

The census data allowed us to see that in 2007, the Phoenix metropolitan area contained a sizeable population of people of Mexican origin. It also allowed us to locate the population geographically based on the census tract. However, we needed to incorporate additional sources, which would confirm the residential settlement patterns and allow us to establish the application strategy of the survey. This made it possible to obtain the sociodemographic profile of this population, the population's state of origin, and many other things. This would allow us to predict an adequate strategy and the size and characteristics of the effort necessary to apply the survey. In fact, historical works on Mexican settlement in Phoenix have indicated a clear concentration in the southwest of the greater urban area (Rex 2000). If this were the case, would it be worth extending the effort beyond this area?

This unknown variable was resolved through various sources of information. The first reconciliation was obtained from the analysis of the concentration of the Latino population by census tract for the metropolitan area. Data to corroborate the results were obtained thanks to the collaboration of the Mexican Consulate in Phoenix, which was the link to establishing contact with the Concilio Latino de Salud, or National Alliance for Hispanic Health, a community organization established in Phoenix and dedicated to promoting healthy habits among the Hispanic/Latino community (Concilio Latino de Salud 2011).

Within their realm of work, in March 2007 the Concilio Latino de Salud had obtained authorization from the Mexican Consulate in Phoenix to carry out a very brief survey. At the time, the consulate was launching a project to deliver free textbooks to families of Mexican origin with school-aged children. The purpose of the survey was to detect the existence in the metropolitan area of Mexican native clubs, which the National Alliance for Hispanic Health was interested in contacting. Though it was not the objective of the survey, the questionnaire managed to get information regarding the state of birth (Mexican or U.S.) for the parents surveyed and their children, and the names of the schools the children attended in the Phoenix area. However, the National Alliance for Hispanic Health did not have the technical and logistical ability to process and systematize the information obtained and the questionnaires were archived for three months. Speaking with their directors, it was possible to come to an agreement through which a team of researchers from the Autonomous University of Sinaloa gained access to the questionnaires, which researchers systematized and analyzed in exchange for being able to share the resulting information.

The data obtained provided two valuable results: First, they provided a profile of the state origins of those surveyed whether they were born in Mexico or the United States; second, they provided information regarding the pattern of residential distribution of the population surveyed according to the geographical locations of the schools that the children attend. These results corroborated the state origins outlined in Harner's work (1995), and showed significant coincidence with the state origins registered in the consular registries for 2007, which were provided by the Mexican Consulate in Phoenix. They also indicated that the population of Mexican origin was dispersed across the urban area, with the exception of the northeast. This made the challenge greater than was expected as it obligated the research team to include the majority of the metropolitan area in the study.

Facing a challenge of this magnitude and with the objective of obtaining results that were representative of the whole metropolitan area, we chose to take a random, stratified sample to estimate the proportion of Mexican households in the Phoenix area that would form the sample. Employing geographical information methods, the first step was to delineate the area of study, a rectangle 96.5 kilometers wide by 74.9 kilometers in length, and covering an area of 7226.6 square kilometers located at 33.54402°N 112.10188°W. Said area contains 654 census tracts distributed in the cities of Phoenix, Mesa, Chandler, Peoria, Glendale, Scottsdale, Sun City, Avondale, Tempe, and Gilbert, which for the purposes of this study dominate the metropolitan area in Phoenix. Of these 654 census tracts, we made our first selection, choosing those that had a 25 percent or more Latino population with respect to the total population, according to population estimates for 2004; this was in order to focus the study on the most relevant areas, and to make the logistical effort more efficient during the survey period, which revealed 260 census tracts with this characteristic.

This procedure was determined after a pilot test carried out in the 10 census tracts chosen randomly. What we found was that as the concentration of Latinos in the census tracts lowered, they became more dispersed in the distant geographical areas that were difficult to manage during the survey. These conditions required great effort in the application and did not produce proportional benefits.

Previously, from the 260 census tracts that made up the new group, a representative sample was calculated, taking into consideration that the proportion of Mexican citizens with respect to Latinos for the metropolitan area is 90 percent, and with a margin of error of 5 percent. The result was 93 census tracts where the survey had to be applied, which were chosen randomly from the total of 260.

The number of questionnaires that had to be applied was determined in the second stage. At that point, we estimated the number of Latino households that there are in the 93 selected census tracts. We arrived at this number by dividing the total Latino population by 4, assuming a composition average of 4 members per household of Mexican citizens in the United States, equaling 54,999 households. Later, we estimated a representative sample, this time using the proportion of Sinaloans to the Mexican population that was considered to be 15 percent with a margin of error of 3 percent, equaling 561 questionnaires. The next step was to distribute the 561 questionnaires among the 93 census tracts selected. The distribution was proportional to the number of Latino households in each census tract. The minimum number of questionnaires for the census tract was 2 and the maximum was 15.

The selection of households was made by numbering the blocks in every census tract and randomly distributing the questionnaires. Every household had equal chances of being selected, and none were randomly eliminated if they had already been given a questionnaire; rather, they would continue in the process for the next survey. The orientation (north, south, east, or west) was also chosen randomly for each selected block. The result was a list of blocks selected randomly and a random direction where the surveyor would make the first visit. If there was at least one member of the household who was born in Mexico, we would complete the survey; if not, we would go clockwise around the block until we found a household with a member who was born in Mexico. If we still did not locate someone, we would go around the block immediately to the north. If we did not find anyone there, we would consider the survey unanswered.

However, the work done up to this point did not guarantee obtaining quality information, from our perspective. The main obstacle was the intimidating anti-immigrant climate that reigned in Phoenix in 2007 and that has not improved to date. There was a high risk of the population being studied simply refusing to answer the surveys out of mistrust and fear, or of them giving false answers in an attempt to protect their own privacy, especially in cases where they were undocumented. In order to confront this threat, we designed a questionnaire with security questions distributed throughout the survey and we avoided using words that could appear threatening to this population whenever possible. To provide an example: Upon asking about the migratory status of the household members, we gave the possible responses of "citizen," "resident," or "other." Obviously, the "other" category referred to undocumented. In the majority of the cases, the level of trust achieved by the interviewers was such that those interviewed answered, "I'm a mojado" (undocumented).

Once the application methodology was established, there were still pending ethical implications. On one side, the Autonomous University of Sinaloa does not establish the review process for research projects by the institutional review board, as is required in U.S. universities. However, consistent with these implications, we established contact with the Center for Population Dynamics at Arizona State University, whose researchers collaborated with us, providing technical support in the design and review of the questionnaire.

Of equal importance were the selection, training, and image of the interviewers. It was also important that the people who were in contact with the Mexican population be capable of projecting great trust and that they guaranteed the anonymity of the interviewees, taking into account the vulnerability of this population of which a large percentage, though it is unknown at this stage, could be undocumented. With this objective in mind, we trained young students from the Department of International Studies and Public Policy at the Autonomous University of Sinaloa (19 women, 5 men) to function as interviewers and we decided to use a uniform specially designed to make their identity and their origin and the name of the institution clear and in plain view. It was assumed that the elements of coethnicity as well as the identification of a well-known Mexican institution of higher learning and the projection of an unthreatening, trustworthy image would create the environment of trust necessary to complete the study. And this is indeed how it unfolded. The index of rejection was very low, less than 20 in the entire survey.

We organized five teams of interviewers that worked independently, with an equal number assigned to each team in the census tracts where they carried out interviews. The job required an uninterrupted 10-day period to be completed. The students did their work as unpaid volunteers. Because they were not working for wages, they traveled with tourist-type visas. That was not a problem with immigration officers, as we told them about our research at the border port of entry, and they agreed. Receiving proper authorization for students to participate freely in the research allowed them to rely on authorities for assistance if needed. Indeed, sometimes police officers gave them directions when they were trying to locate streets during the survey.

Results

The state origin reinforced Harner's statements (1995), as we found that for the individuals born in Mexico, Sonora participated with 15 percent, Sinaloa with 14.1 percent, and Chihuahua with 13.4 percent. Durango, Guerrero, Jalisco, and Michoacán were all far from these figures and represented values around 6 percent. It is significant that Sinaloa occupies the second place, only slightly below Sonora, when it is not in fact a border state. This apparent paradox invites further research.

Of the Sinaloan municipalities that sent migrants toward Phoenix, Culiacán occupies first place, with 28.8 percent. This figure is greater in part because the greatest population concentration is found here. The municipality of Guasave is next, with 14.4 percent, followed by Ahome and Sinaloa de Leyva, with 11.9 and 10.9 percent, respectively. It is interesting to note that Mazatlán, another municipality with high population density, does not figure among the main sources of migrants traveling toward Phoenix; participation from Mazatlán is limited to 2.9 percent and Choix, interestingly, has a participation of 5.9 percent despite its sparse population.

The year that Sinaloans arrived shows us that migration toward Phoenix is relatively recent in comparison to other cities like Los Angeles. This presents a considerable increase for the decade 1981–1990, which was up to 20.9 percent from 3.57 percent the previous decade. Since this increase took place, growth has been constant: 36.7 percent and 37.7 percent in the decades between 1991–2000 and 2001–2007, respectively. With respect to the migratory situation, of the 205 Sinaloans interviewed, 9 percent enjoyed the rights awarded to citizens of the country, 22 percent had residency, and the rest (69 percent) were undocumented.

Of the total Sinaloan population interviewed in the survey, the predominant occupation is construction, at 27 percent. Twelve percent work in services and 7 percent in gardening. Seven percent work in restaurants, and five percent work in cleaning. Forty-two percent are not salaried workers, which corresponds to the percentage of housewives (30 percent) and students (12 percent).

Conclusions

1. The state of Sinaloa, from the 1990s, became a significant contributor to the international migratory process. More than 10 percent of its population is found in the United States, the majority in the metropolitan areas of Los Angeles and Phoenix.
2. Migration exclusively from rural areas pales in comparison to the volume of migration from urban areas.
3. In the case of Phoenix, Sinaloan immigrants are predominantly undocumented (69 percent).
4. The type of migration can be characterized as family migration (30 percent housewives, 12 percent students).
5. Almost half of the economically active population claimed to be working in construction (46 percent), which appears to sustain the existence of a clear niche in the labor market for this occupation among Sinaloan immigrants in Phoenix.
6. The severe economic crisis that the United States and the world faced in 2008 seriously impacted this population. The fall in construction

activity and the severe anti-immigrant laws in Arizona are relevant factors. The magnitude of the effects is yet to be quantified.

7. The relevance of research on this phenomenon is impacted by the difficulty in implementing methodological protocols and ethical guidelines in the fieldwork in the absence of specific, simple, operative agreements that allow collaboration between universities on both sides of the border. There is a need for further study in this field.

8. Laws put into place in Arizona with the intention of halting undocumented immigration to the state also make it difficult to collect original information that contributes to understanding the phenomenon (see also the chapters in this volume by Montoya Zavala, Goldsmith, and O'Leary and colleagues). Any possible interaction with undocumented immigrants is penalized so severely that concerned researchers have to face the dilemma of not continuing or not deepening their research due to the risk of coming dangerously close to the margins of the law.

9. This situation winds up working against their own interests because how can one legislate justly something that one does not really understand? Complicating any scientific advancement of the study of the phenomenon, laws in Arizona defeat their own purpose. In addition to their humanitarian work towards justice for and the protection of immigrants, it is recommended that social organizations in the state as well as academics who are studying the issue request that laws be put into place to avoid getting in the way of such research.

Note

This work received support from the CONACYT–Government of Sinaloa Mixed Fund (FOMIX Sin-C2006-C01-42103) and from the Program for Promotion and Support of Research Projects from the Autonomous University of Sinaloa (PROFAPI 2007/130).

References

American Community Survey. 2007. One-year Estimates. S0201. Selected Population Profile in the United States. Population Group: Mexican. Phoenix-Mesa-Scottsdale, AZ, Metropolitan Statistical Area. U.S. Census Bureau: http://factfinder.census .gov, accessed March 25, 2011.

Anguiano Téllez María Eugenia, and Alma Paola Trejo Peña. 2007. Vigilancia y control en la frontera México–Estados Unidos: efectos en las rutas del flujo migratorio internacional [Vigilance and control on the Mexican–U.S. border: Effects in the routes of the international migratory flow]. *Papeles de población* 51: 45–75.

Banco de México. 2007. Balanza de pagos CE100—Ingresos por remesas familiares, distribución por entidad federativa. Período: Ene–Mar 2003—Abr–Jun 2012, Trimestral, Millones de Dólares, Flujos. http://www.banxico.gob.mx, accessed January and July 2007.

Canales, Alejandro I. 2003. Mexican Labour Migration to the United States in the Age of Globalization. *Journal of Ethnic and Migration Studies* 29(4): 741–761.

Concilio Latino de Salud. 2011. http://www.concilio.org/, accessed April 2011.

Cornelius, Wayne. 1992. From Soujourners to Settlers: The Changing Profile of Mexican Immigration to the United States. In Jorge Bustamante, Clark W. Reynolds, and Raúl Hinojosa, eds. *U.S.–Mexico Relations: Labor Market Interdependence.* Pp. 155–195. Stanford, CA: Stanford University Press.

———. 2001. Death at the Border: Efficacy and Unintended Consequences of U.S. Immigration Control Policy. *Population and Development Review* 27(4): 661–685.

Durand, Jorge. 1998. ¿Nuevas regiones migratorias? [New Migratory Regions?] In René M. Zenteno, ed. *Población, Desarrollo y Globalización.* Pp. 104–106. Mexico: Sociedad Mexicana de Demografía and El Colegio de la Frontera Norte.

Durand, Jorge, Douglas S. Massey, and Chiara Capoferro. 2005. The New Geography of Mexican Immigration. In Víctor Zúñiga and Rubén Hernández León, eds. *New Destinations: Mexican Immigration in the United States.* Pp. 1–19. New York: Russell Sage Foundation.

El Universal. 2005. Reitera SRE rechazo a ley antimigrantes de Arizona. January 12.

García Castro, Ismael. 2007. *Vidas Compartidas. Formación de una Red Migratoria Transnacional: Aguacaliente Grande, Sinaloa and Victor Valley, California.* Mexico: Plaza y Valdez.

Greater Phoenix Economic Council. 2007. http://www.gpec.org/index.asp, accessed March 21, 2007.

Harner, John P. 1995. Continuity amidst Change: Undocumented Mexican Migration to Arizona. *Professional Geographer* 47(4): 339–441.

Ibarra, Guillermo. 2005. *Migrantes en Mercados de Trabajo Globales. Mexicanos y Sinaloenses en Los Ángeles* [Migrants in global labor markets. Mexicans and Sinaloans in Los Angeles]. Culiacán, Sinaloa: DIFOCUR and UAS.

Ibarra, Guillermo, Blas Valenzuela, and Ismael García. 2004. Sinaloa en Los Ángeles: Encuesta a Hogares Sinaloenses en Los Ángeles 2004 [Sinaloa in Los Angeles: Survey of Sinaloan households in Los Angeles 2004]. Culiacán, Sinaloa: UAS.

Instituto de los Mexicanos en el Exterior. 2008. Matrículas consulares de alta seguridad expedidas en el consulado de México en Phoenix, AZ, 2007 [High-security consular registries expedited in the Mexican Consulate in Phoenix, AZ, 2007]. Secretaría de Relaciones Exteriores. http://www.ime.gob.mx/mapassite/consulados /phoenix.php, accessed April 18, 2011.

La Crónica. 2007. El alguacil Joe Arpaio es la única autoridad hasta el momento en Arizona en arrestar a indocumentados y encarcelarlos por violación a la ley "anticoyote" [Sheriff Joe Arpaio is the only authority to date in Arizona to arrest undocumented immigrants and jail them for violating the "anti-coyote" law]. July 29.

La Jornada. 2007. Inician migrantes "acciones colectivas" contra decomiso de remesas en Arizona [Migrants start "collective actions" against confiscating remittances in Arizona]. November 18.

Light, Ivan, and Elsa von Scheven. 2008. Mexican Migration Networks in the United States, 1980–2000. *International Migration Review* 42(3): 704–728.

Lizárraga Hernández, Arturo. 2004. *Nos Llevó la Ventolera: El Proceso de la Emigración Rural al Extranjero en Sinaloa. Los casos de Cosalá, San Ignacio y El Verde* [The Wind Carried Us: The Process of Rural Immigration Abroad in Sinaloa: The Cases of Cosalá, San Ignacio and El Verde]. Culiacán Sinaloa: Universidad Autónoma de Sinaloa.

Menesses, Guillermo Alonso. 2005. La dimensión femenina del cruce clandestino de la frontera México–Estados Unidos [The feminine dimension of clandestine border crossing between Mexico and the United States]. Paper presented at the Mobilités au Féminis International Colloquium, Tangier, Morocco, November 15–19.

Montoya Zavala, Erika. 2004. Exportando Trabajo, Importando Progreso: Migración a Estados Unidos y remesas en Gabriel Leyva Solano [Exporting Work, Importing Progress: Migration to the United States and Remittances in Gabriel Leyva Solano]. Culiacán Sinaloa: DIFOCUR-UAS.

Moran Taylor, Michelle, and Cecilia Menjívar. 2005. Unpacking Longings to Return: Guatemalans and Salvadorans in Phoenix, Arizona. *International Migration* 43(4): 91–121.

The New York Times. 2008. Arizona Law Takes a Toll on Nonresident Students. January 27.

Pintor, Renato, and Ernesto Sánchez. 2012. Repensar a Sinaloa como Estado emergente de migración mexicana [Rethink Sinaloa as emerging state of Mexican migration]. *Ánfora* 19(32): 137–156.

Rex, Tom. 2000. *Development of Metropolitan Phoenix: Historical, Current and Future Trends.* Tempe: Arizona State University, Morrison Institute for Public Policy.

Sánchez Sánchez, Ernesto. 2012. Migrantes culiacanenses en California: Diversidad en sus redes migratorias [Culiacan migrants in California: Diversity in migration networks]. *Migraciones Internacionales* 6(4): 243–272.

Secretaría de Desarrollo Económico del Estado de Sinaloa. 2007. http://www.sinaloa .gob.mx, accessed January 12, 2007.

Skop, Emily, and Cecilia Menjivar. 2001. Phoenix: The Newest Latino Immigrant Gateway? In Darrick Danta, ed. *Yearbook of the Association of Pacific Coast Geographers* 63. Pp. 63–77. Honolulu: University of Hawaii Press.

U.S. Census Bureau. 2007. American Community Survey One-Year Estimates. ACS Demographic and Housing Estimates, Arizona.

Valenzuela, Jr., Abel. 2006. Trabajar como jornalero urbano: ¿Última opción? O ¿Empleo alternativo? [Working as a day laborer: Last resort? Or alternative employment?] In Guillermo Ibarra and Ana Luz Ruelas, eds. *Inmigrantes y Economía Informal en Los Ángeles.* Pp. 25–66. Mexico: Casa Juan Pablos.

Valenzuela Camacho, Blas. 2007. Economías étnicas en metrópolis multiculturales: Empresarialidad sinaloense en el sur de California [Ethnic economics in multicultural metropolises: Sinaloan businesses in southern California]. Mexico: Plaza and Valdez.

Woo, Ofelia. 2004. La migración: Un asunto de seguridad nacional en Estados Unidos [Migration: A question of national security in the United States]. In José María Ramos García and Ofelia Woo, eds. *Seguridad Nacional y frontera, en la relación México-Estados Unidos.* Pp. 69–85. Guadalajara: Universidad de Guadalajara.

Zúñiga, Elena, Paula Leite, and Alma Rosa Nava. 2004. La nueva era de las migraciones: Características de la migración internacional en México [The new era of migration: Characteristics of international migration in Mexico]. Mexico: Consejo Nacional de Población. http://www.conapo.gob.mx/publicaciones/nuevaera/era.htm, accessed July 21, 2008.

Zúñiga, Víctor, and Rubén Hernández-León. 2005. *New Destinations: Mexican Immigration in the United States.* New York: Russell Sage Foundation.

———. 2006. El nuevo mapa de la migración mexicana en Estados Unidos: El paradigma de la escuela de Chicago y los dilemas contemporáneos en la sociedad estadounidense [The new map of Mexican migration to the United States: A paradigm of the Chicago school and the contemporaneous dilemma in U.S. society]. *Estudios Sociológicos* 24(1): 139–165.

CHAPTER THIRTEEN

Lessons for Border Research

The Border Contraceptive Access Study

Jon Amastae, Michele Shedlin, Kari White,
Kristine Hopkins, Daniel A. Grossman,
and Joseph E. Potter

Introduction

The U.S.–Mexico border has become increasingly a focus of and site for research. Interdependent economies, cultures, and natural environments on which a political border is overlaid contain both challenges and stimuli for inhabitants and investigators alike. Many of the topics and methods of our investigations require special sensitivity to the conduct of any project, including ethical and political issues. This paper describes some of these in a large study of access to and use of hormonal contraceptives among mostly Mexican-origin women in the border city of El Paso.[1]

Since their introduction nearly 50 years ago, oral contraceptive pills (OCs) have become one of the most effective and widely used family planning methods worldwide. New, lower-dose formulations also make OCs one of the safest options (Chaktoura et al. 2009; Khader et al. 2003; Vandebroucke et al. 2001; Farley and Collins 1999; Schwingl et al. 1999). The circumstances under which OCs are sold to women, however, vary considerably across countries. One of the main differences is whether a doctor's prescription is required before a woman can purchase OCs. In the United States, hormonal contraceptives require at least a health care provider's prescription if not a physical examination, which some public health experts consider unjustified (Stewart et al. 2001). In neighboring Mexico, while current law requires prescriptions for most medicines, in practice OCs have typically been readily available from pharmacies without a prescription. Policy debate about relaxing the U.S. prescription requirement for OCs has focused on whether over-the-counter (OTC) access is safe and how it might influence use (Trussell et al. 1993; Grossman 2008; Jarvis 2008).

The Border Contraceptive Access Study (BCAS) was designed to address a number of questions, previously unresolved empirically. Specifically, the primary aims of the study were:

1) to determine what motivates women to obtain OCs directly from a pharmacy in Mexico, as opposed to from a U.S. family planning clinic;

2) to measure and compare knowledge about OC use between Mexican pharmacy users and U.S. family planning clinic users;

3) to examine the effect of supplying women with a written informational leaflet on women's knowledge about OCs;

4) to assess whether women who obtain OCs over the counter from a Mexican pharmacy have poorer contraceptive satisfaction, compliance, continuation, and unintended pregnancy over the course of nine months; and

5) to assess the role of other factors that may lead to poor compliance, early discontinuation, or unintended pregnancy among OC users.

To assess these aims, we carried out a prospective survey of oral contraceptive users in El Paso, Texas—a unique setting along the U.S.–Mexico border where U.S. residents have the option of obtaining OCs at pharmacies in Ciudad Juárez, Chihuahua, Mexico, without a prescription at a cost of approximately US$5.00 per cycle. Previous studies have established that women in El Paso do indeed cross the border to Mexico to obtain hormonal contraception such as oral contraceptive pills and injectables (Potter et al. 2003; Grossman et al. 2008).

In the sections that follow, we describe some of the methodological issues we faced while implementing this prospective study, and their importance in conducting research in communities such as this one.

The combination of a personally and culturally sensitive topic; wide variation in several demographic characteristics of the sample; cross-border interaction, which fell by chance at a difficult time for the border region; changes in state funding for reproductive health services; and the organizational challenges of a large project required an agile and adaptive response on the part of the research team.

El Paso Context

The combined population of El Paso and Ciudad Juárez is approximately 2.4 million; the population of the El Paso metropolitan area is approximately 800,000 and is roughly 80 percent Hispanic, mostly of Mexican background. El Paso is among the poorest communities in the United States. According to the 2004 American Community Survey (Fronczek 2010), El Paso's median household income of $31,764 ranked 61 among the 70 cities with populations greater than 250,000. The border is quite porous; four bridges link the two cities, and thousands cross frequently in both directions for commerce, family visits, recreation, education, and health and other services. Previous studies (Bastida et al. 2008; Fernández and Amastae 2007; Amastae et al. 2009) have established that health services in Mexico are an important resource for many residents of El Paso and other Texas border cities for reasons such as lower cost, convenience, family networks, cultural comfort, and perceived quality of care.

Study Methods and Sample

Our goal was to recruit current pill users aged 18 to 44 stratified in two groups: 1) El Paso residents who use OCs obtained at family planning clinics in El Paso (target n = 500) and 2) El Paso residents who use OCs obtained over the counter at pharmacies in Ciudad Juárez (target n = 500). Most clinic users were recruited from the major family planning providers then functioning in El Paso, such as the Women's Health Center at University Medical Center (previously Thomason Hospital) and four Planned Parenthood clinics in El Paso, as well as local community health centers. In addition, publicity was distributed through the University of Texas–El Paso and El Paso Community College. However, the initial strategy of recruiting OTC users at pharmacies in Ciudad Juárez proved to be impractical. In the end, virtually the entire OTC sample was recruited using announcements, flyers, and presentations at El Paso community centers, as well as through referrals from other participants. The apparent paradox of recruiting patrons of Juárez pharmacies in El Paso is due to the selection criterion of El Paso residency as well as to the longstanding community practice of accessing health services selectively on both sides of the border (Fernández and Amastae 2007; Heyman et al. 2009; Byrd and Law 2009).

The participants resided in over 30 ZIP codes in the El Paso metropolitan area. The sample was not stratified by level of education or SES, but since it was limited to users of family planning clinics and users who obtained their pills OTC from pharmacies in Ciudad Juárez, it did not typically include women who used their health insurance or personal funds to obtain prescriptions from private sector doctors and then bought their OCs at pharmacies in the United States. In fact, the majority of study participants lived in sectors of the city where the average household income fell below the 2004 median income for the city.

After obtaining signed informed consent from participants who agreed to take part in the study, we administered an hour-long face-to-face baseline interview. Bilingual project staff conducted interviews in either Spanish or English in the respondent's home or a place of her choosing. Participants were offered a small compensation in the form of gift cards for completing the baseline and each of the following interviews. This study was approved by the institutional review boards (IRBs) at the University of Texas–Austin (UT–Austin) and University of Texas–El Paso (UTEP).

The baseline questionnaire contained a wide range of items related to the participant's background. Special emphasis was given to a series of items intended to gauge the participant's ability to take advantage of Mexican pharmacies as a contraceptive source, such as her contacts and relationships in Mexico, her ability to speak Spanish, and the frequency with which she crossed the border. We also asked about the participant's country of birth and level of education, and the country in which she completed her last year of schooling. The baseline questionnaire also collected detailed information on women's pill use history, focusing on their recent use. We asked for the month and year a participant had obtained her last pack(s), the number of packs acquired at that time, where she obtained her pill packs, and whether she had ever asked someone else to buy pill packs for her in Ciudad Juárez.

The second and third interviews took place approximately three and six months after the initial interview. These interviews were administered via telephone and lasted 15–20 minutes. In the telephone interviews, women were asked about changes in their health and their pill use practice during the prior three months, as well as follow-up questions on contraceptive knowledge. The final (time 4) interviews were scheduled approximately nine months after the baseline interview. They were conducted in person, either in the participant's home or other location of her choosing and took about one hour to complete. Recruiting for the study began in December 2006 and ended in February 2008, at which point we had successfully recruited over 1,000 participants. In total, we collected 1,046 baseline interviews (514 women who obtained OCs OTC from Mexican pharmacies and 532 women who obtained OCs from El Paso family planning clinics): 965 time 2 follow-up interviews; 936 time 3 follow-up interviews; and 941 time 4 final interviews. Retention was a high priority, and we implemented a variety of strategies to attain this goal, such as hiring interviewers with strong ties to the El Paso community, using an interview tracking system to identify when participants needed follow-up interviews, gathering extensive contact information, and providing modest incentives to women at the end of each interview. Overall retention for all rounds was 90 percent, with only 105 women lost to follow up. We believe the high retention rate indicates the success of recruitment strategies as well as the program of staff training to achieve trust and rapport with participants.

Sample Recruitment and Confidentiality Issues

In recruiting this sample and collecting data on a potentially sensitive subject, we faced a number of complex issues. Making first contact with potential subjects required a variety of strategies, as described above. Whether our first efforts to contact OTC users failed because of violations of cultural norms about dealing with such issues in a more or less public place is not known. Because pharmacies are typically a place to obtain information from pharmacists and pharmacy workers, more efforts at recruiting their assistance might have improved this strategy. It is clearly the case, however, that recruitment became much easier once we involved community health centers and personal networks.

Because many interviews were conducted in subjects' homes, the need to find times when children and others were not present determined the field interviewers' work schedules. Consistent attempts were made to maintain the privacy of the interview and to limit exposure of the interview to nonparticipants. Interviewers were trained to schedule interviews when privacy could be maximized, to react accordingly to unanticipated presence of others, to terminate an interview and reschedule gracefully if necessary, and to defuse a tense situation if one arose due to the presence of another person. Only in one or two situations did that occur. The telephone interviewers were also trained to listen for distracting activity and to reschedule at better times if they felt the integrity of the interview was compromised.

In all subsequent aspects of the investigation, standard ethical research practices were followed. These included obtaining consent to participate in written form on consent forms in either English or Spanish (and in a later part of the project, via audio recording); and obtaining authorization for re-contact in the event of continuing research. Few subjects requested that we not contact them again in the future, which was important feedback on satisfaction with our procedures and respondents' perception of scientific and ethical rigor in conducting the investigation.

Exacting procedures for the protection of confidentiality were followed during data management. Each participant was assigned a study ID, and the documents connecting the ID with any identifying information were stored securely (physically in locking cabinets, digitally in password-protected computers). The physical documents remain in one location only (UTEP). Digital copies were stored on secure drives and servers at both UTEP and UT–Austin. All project staff were trained in proper procedures for storing and handling such materials. The procedures were designed to ensure the objectives of maintaining privacy and preservation for later access by investigators.

Communication and Cultural Appropriateness

The effectiveness and appropriateness of communication was a salient concern for the project. In this study, the nature of the communication issues was complex, especially since the research was conducted among a largely bilingual population. All written materials (questionnaires, consent forms, flyers) were produced in both English and Spanish. Each one was reviewed extensively by the staff to ensure both substantive and communicative accuracy within each language *and* equivalence across languages. Moreover, the appropriateness of language style was analyzed consistently, particularly for medical terms, for which local usages were checked with a range of consultants. In every case the currency of both formal and informal terms was calibrated with medical personnel and community health workers. This was considered a matter of ensuring data accuracy and interactions that respected subjects' own knowledge.

A particularly challenging task was the development of consent forms and content. Many IRBs have adopted standard templates, and an accurate Spanish version of the standard template was not a problem. However, because consent forms are considered quasi-legal documents, they are characterized by a style and wording difficult to read in any language. In creating the Spanish-language version used by the majority of our participants, we had some flexibility in creating and testing one that maximized comprehensibility for our population.

Another way to address the complexities of communication was to ensure that all project staff were bilingual in varying degrees. Over the course of the project, approximately 12 interviewers and other staff participated, all experienced in working in Spanish-speaking communities. A few were highly dominant in Spanish, but since Spanish was the language predominantly used in the interviews, which numbered over 4,000, this was appropriate. Because the questionnaire responses were recorded on paper, all interviewers had to be literate in the language of the interview. In fact, all of the interviewers were members of the community and speakers of the Spanish used in the community, in both lexico/grammatical aspects and in appropriate sociocultural practice. Still, in our ongoing intensive monitoring of interviews and supervision of interviewers, we paid attention to practices of appropriate language usage within the sociocultural norms of the community.

In terms of the intersection of content and style, perhaps the most salient concern was how to approach sensitive subjects, especially sexual behavior. Not only did the interviews elicit information about general health, but the interviewers also measured height, weight, and blood pressure. All aspects of the interview therefore required extreme sensitivity to cultural and personal aspects of verbal and nonverbal communication, and the behavioral norms governing appropriate interactions between the women and the interviewers. These issues were addressed extensively in interviewer training and supervision.

In an investigation such as this, social networks are simultaneously an essential tool and a challenge. We have already mentioned the utility of networks in recruiting subjects. But they also served as effective channels of communication with subjects living in economically precarious circumstances with high mobility, which affected address changes, the disconnection of phone services, changing numbers, and the disappearance and reappearance of subjects. Anticipating this, the first interview included provisions for recording information for back-up contacts—relatives, friends, neighbors. While this proved useful in reaching subjects for subsequent interviews, it also created the possibility for leaks in information, at least about participation in the study. Thus, in dealing with secondary contacts, no information was given about the nature of the research, merely that it was a study by the university that the person had participated in previously.

Staff Selection and Training

All project staff completed human subjects compliance training, given through either the two universities or the National Institutes of Health (National Cancer Institute). PIs maintained current certification as a matter of course. However, all other staff, including interviewers, office workers, and student assistants, were also required to complete the training.

A primary criterion for interviewer selection was experience as a community health worker (*promotora*). Interviewers with this background provided many benefits for the project. They included knowledge of the city geography and population, knowledge of community health care centers and agencies, experience in outreach activities and informational dissemination, comfort with talking about health issues, and their own networks in the health fields.

Interviewers were trained extensively on interview techniques for research. The questionnaire included both closed and open sections requiring the interviewer's attention to detail and to the content and presentation of an answer, and skill in probing for clarification and/or additional information. This was accomplished through practice interviews followed by review/analysis with the investigators in which the interview record was examined item by item, and problems noted and improvements suggested. The process was continued throughout the interviews as new situations arose or variants of old ones reappeared. Some of these continually required skill in "interview management" in a broad sense, rather than interviewing skill in a narrow sense. Scheduling interviews when school was in session was a constant necessity, as many respondents were understandably reluctant to speak with children present. But interviewers also had to be trained in how to handle the presence of others, unanticipated interventions, etc., as already noted.

Interviewers are frequently in the position of receiving unsolicited information during the course of interviews. This may concern legal status, relationship issues, domestic violence, or other sensitive topics. Other than issues reportable by law, other topics not part of the study were not recorded. The interviewers were trained not to advise participants and to provide only basic information and referrals. This is particularly important when information emerges that would be harmful if known by others and thus referral rather than intervention is appropriate.

Despite all of the training and supervision, however, the interviewers were not professional researchers and the study team was cognizant of maintaining realistic expectations for their work. That fact, common to community-based research, had important implications for both training content and style to address crucial differences in knowledge, skills, experience, and abilities. Among the matters considered were:

- Confidentiality/Privacy: In many of the communities in which the research was carried out, a primacy exists on interpersonal relationships, including a personable, friendly manner. If recruitment is carried out within personal networks, the door may be open to inappropriate revealing of information about others, even if limited to the mere fact of having participated in the study.
- Quality control/Attention to detail: Appreciation of the need for constant vigilance in following the questionnaire/interview protocol exactly every time in order to ensure reliability and validity of the data can be difficult for people with nonresearch backgrounds. The potential conflict between the desire to have a comfortable, almost conversational interview and the objective of completeness, detail, and consistency of both data and process across subjects can be a problem for interviewers and those who supervise them.
- Schedules and production targets: A large project such as this cannot succeed without establishing and adhering to schedules and milestones. For those lacking this experience and perhaps having experience in activities with other requirements (such as maintaining interpersonal relationships, encouraging people to pursue a particular course of action, etc.), the exigencies of completing a certain number of interviews in a precise way by a particular date can seem excessively rigid.

These issues must be considered in light of the fact that the project was not designed or implemented as participatory research. A considerable literature is devoted to the advantages of employing community members in research (Poole et al. 2009), but little is written about the problematic implications, such as biases in what community interviewers are told in an interview by people from their own environment, biases in what they hear, how they present the questions, their comfort and discomfort with the topics and how that may be communicated to respondents, their per-ception of their roles and responsibilities, etc. (one exception is Buchanan et al., 2007). Although most of the interview questions had fixed response options (i.e., closed-ended questions), the last follow up contained a number of open-ended items. For these especially, where there is more person-intensive input, not only is training crucial, but monitoring of the data to detect biases and continuing training based on that monitoring are required.

Research Roles for Community Health Workers: Strengths and Limitations

A certain caution is required for involving community health workers as research aides in order to maximize their strengths without creating un-realistic expectations about what they are able to do or should do. Being knowledgeable about one's community does not automatically include either objectivity or research skills, and in fact, raises all the issues of bias previously mentioned. While the interviewers contributed significantly to the project, the objectives and design required standardization of process, something they found difficult to maintain. The very characteristics that enable their success in the field—knowledge of the community dynam-ics, personal acquaintances, a congruent verbal/interactive style—may also set up a mismatch with academically trained researchers who tend to be direct and directive in their attention to details of data collection and the management of the study. It is the responsibility of the professional researchers to recognize these differences in cultural behavior and com-munication norms and to make adjustments where possible to optimize cross-cultural communication and thus effectiveness.

Responsibility for Addressing Needs for Services in an Underserved Population

In addition to our learning process regarding the employment of com-munity interviewers (in a nonparticipatory action research model), our study raised the issue of researcher responsibilities to the community beyond scientifically accurate research and dissemination. Many of the respondents requested additional information about reproductive health issues and birth control of all types. To address this need, the interviewers distributed community resource guides that provided information and referral resources. In addition, because an objective of the original study was to determine the prevalence of contraindications to hormonal contraceptives among OTC users, we assessed contraindicated medical conditions via self-report as well as measured blood pressure. For those participants who reported medical conditions that were considered contraindications to the use of oral contraceptives, we provided an information sheet that suggested consulting a health provider and listed local providers.

In one of the supplementary studies linked to the main BCAS project (Amastae, Grossman, and Martínez 2009), a subsample of 34 women in the El Paso sample who had high blood pressure (i.e., readings ≥140/90 mmHg, which is usually considered to be the threshold for high blood pressure) were administered an additional questionnaire to examine their awareness of possible relationships between the use of oral contraceptives and hypertension. As part of the same supplemental study, an additional group of 12 hypertensive users of oral contraceptives in Ciudad Juárez was interviewed. Although this study was only exploratory, the data appeared to indicate that the women in Ciudad Juárez were more knowledgeable about a range of contraceptive options than the women in El Paso. This was further supported by the fact that past national campaigns in Mexico widely promoted family planning. Although small, the sample presents an unacceptable picture of lack of information among U.S. women and demonstrates the urgent need for additional resources to be allocated to family planning information and services.

Implications of Local and National Health Policy

Some of our findings illuminated the consequences of current health policies. In 2005 the 79th Texas legislature enacted changes in funding for family planning (Smith 2006). These changes took funding from the two major family planning providers in El Paso and redistributed them to federally qualified health centers (FQHCs) with little experience or expertise in providing family-planning services. University Medical Center and Planned Parenthood Center of El Paso were both forced to severely curtail their family planning services. Among the consequences of those cuts were additional restrictions on access to subsidized services, reductions in staff and hours of operation, fewer women served, closure of a training program for women's health-care nurse practitioners, and closure of clinic sites around the city. (As noted by Amastae et al. 2008, four Planned

Parenthood sites were closed; University Medical Center decreased patient numbers by 40 percent; and the local health department closed its only site in 2011. While some of these reductions occurred for other reasons, and the FQHCs increased capacity, the overall provision of services declined.)

Against this background we have seen it as our responsibility to work with UMC and other providers to publicize our findings, as well as the impact of such funding cuts especially on low income women. While most of our data were collected before the full impact of the cuts was felt, we suspect that were we to re-survey the 500 women who at that time obtained their pills through El Paso clinics, we might see increased interest in obtaining family-planning services in Mexico due to the reduction in services in El Paso.

The Implications of the Current Border Violence

Under normal circumstances we might also expect to see an increase in the utilization of health services in Mexico given the reduction in services provided in the United States. Since 2008, however, a series of events have created obstacles and reduced the incidence of border crossing. One obstacle is the implementation of the Western Hemispheric Travel Initiative, which now requires a passport for return entry to the United States. (Previously only a birth certificate was required, and even that requirement was frequently overlooked if the crosser had a driver's license or other identification.) Passports are expensive, and many border residents have simply suspended border crossing. There are reports of confiscation by border officials of passports and other documentation for undetermined reasons. Some Mexican pharmacies have begun requiring prescriptions, and U.S. Customs have been more stringent in requiring both U.S. and Mexican prescriptions for many medicines for personal use. But the major factor has been the well publicized and horrifying increase in violence in Ciudad Juárez. Explanations put forth by media and government include a turf war between drug trafficking cartels, common crime operating in the shadow of the drug trade, the lack of policing and security infrastructure, and governmental corruption. The result for residents of both Ciudad Juárez and El Paso who have always lived a binational life in what was considered to be a single metropolitan area has been a near collapse of public life in Ciudad Juárez and a sharp decline in the number of El Paso residents who cross to Ciudad Juárez for any reason. It is certain that reduction in crossing frequency results in reduced access to health services, not only for those who purchase hormonal contraceptives, but also for those who have traditionally accessed some or all health care in Ciudad Juárez (Fernández and Amastae 2007; Heyman et al. 2009; Byrd and Law 2009). It is all the more serious that this closing of a significant cross-border opportunity for health care should occur precisely when availability on the U.S. side has been reduced by policies of the state.

Responsibility for Addressing Unanticipated Findings

One of the unanticipated findings of the project was the identification of a large percentage (70 percent) of women in our sample of current OC users with at least one child who said they wanted no more children, and who also expressed a desire for surgical sterilization. This result was so striking that we felt obliged to follow it up, which we did through a supplement granted through ARRA funds, as well as a grant from the Society for Family Planning. A subsample of 120 women who expressed interest in surgical sterilization was reinterviewed to investigate the degree of their interest, the barriers to surgical sterilization, and the opportunities for surgical sterilization. In addition, focus groups were conducted with male partners of these women, as well as with local providers of sterilization services.

Discussion/Conclusion

A study of this breadth and depth, lasting five years or more in a community of striking complexity, cannot help but provide a wealth of lessons.

In the context of this research on border health, the ethical issues sort out into three types: 1) the issues inherent in conducting rigorous scientific research in the community and employing community health workers in recruitment and interviewing; 2) the need to assure that training and supervision of community research participants supports such critical issues as confidentiality, respect, and understanding of the research in the community, and an investment in community capacity building, even without a focus on participatory research; and 3) the ethical imperative for follow up, which includes the responsibility to provide information to the participants themselves, and the ultimate responsibility to inform public-health policy makers and program planners, as well as the research community.

The first type is in the contemporary world governed, at least initially, by a dense web of overt regulations and practices, such as requirements for IRB approval, informed consent, data management, privacy, and so on. Less overtly, there are professional standards that should permeate any sort of community-based research: responsibility for merging scientific rigor with community structures and practices in conceptualizing and structuring health practices.

The second type requires researchers to recognize the differences in backgrounds, experiences, and expectations between themselves as professional researchers and the community members they enlist in research projects, and to react appropriately. That includes both responsibility for training and creating a context that respects the community partners' experiences and skills.

The third type carries researchers into different territories. One of them requires feedback to participants on issues that concern their health. This may range from advice to seek immediate medical care to information on where to get information about services. Ultimately, though, there is a clear need and responsibility to carry the information into the public sphere, which brings new challenges for the project and team.

Therefore, in the BCAS study, after the conclusion of data collection but while still in the analysis phase of the project, the investigators organized two events to share some of the results with two important constituencies, which were the participants themselves and those in the region who work in the realms of providing reproductive health services or who have an advocacy role in the provision of services. While both events provided valuable information to the two groups, we emphasize here the feedback the investigators received.

More generally, a variety of lessons can be drawn from our experiences throughout the five years of the project. Because those who provide reproductive health services in the El Paso region were in some sense caught between what the state and federal governments allow and force them to do on the one hand, and what women need and are doing for themselves on the other, we thought it was particularly important both to share our results with them and to hear their perspectives on our findings. Both events were useful in bringing to light important perspectives on the issues under investigation.

Women had consistently mentioned problems with obtaining pills from clinics. The clinic staff were able to add their perspectives and experiences, detailing the regulations of insurers, governments, and pharmaceutical companies. On some issues the providers felt themselves to be in the middle between the women (consumers) and the insurers, the companies, or the government. Everyone in what we labeled the "Provider/Policy" session expressed particular concern at the prospect of substantial funding reductions in the near future, which would exacerbate all of the problems mentioned. On other issues, the women clearly perceived themselves to be caught in the web designed by and for others. Leaving the details of some of these problems for another occasion, we can say that the important lesson was that an adequate investigation must include all of these perspectives, and probably at multiple points in the investigative process.

The session with the participants was particularly enlightening for the suggestions that the women made. It began with a presentation of basic reproductive physiology by Dr. Grossman (in Spanish), and proceeded to a discussion of experiences with clinics, pharmacies, insurers, etc. Among the recommendations made was that a program of similar sessions for women in neighborhoods and *colonias* throughout the county, and one for men as well. (The women were not at all dismissive of the possibility that men would attend or learn from such sessions.) Follow up could be accomplished through a program of locating specially trained promotoras in each geographic area. Once again, the lesson here is not the details of the sessions, but the utility and necessity of their inclusion in such investigations.

Notes

This research was funded by grants R01 HD047816 and 5 R24 HD042849 from the Eunice Kennedy Shriver National Institute of Child Health and Human Development. The website for the entire project can be found at http://www.prc.utexas.edu /bcas/.

1. The authors thank Victor Talavera and Alma Hernández for their many contributions to the project described here.

References

Amastae, Jon, Carmen Díaz de León, Joseph E. Potter, Dan Grossman, Kristine Hopkins, and Michele G. Shedlin. 2008. Did the Texas Legislature Kill Family Planning? Paper presented at the Texas Society of Allied Health Professionals, El Paso, Texas.

Amastae, Jon, Dan Grossman, and Georgina Martínez. 2009. *Hypertension among Mexican-American and Mexican Users of Oral Contraceptives*. Final report to the Paso del Norte Health Foundation.

Bastida, E., H. S. Brown, and J. A. Pagan. 2008. Persistent Disparities in the Use of Health Care along the US–Mexico Border: An Ecological Perspective. *American Journal of Public Health* 98(11): 1987–1995.

Becker, D., S. G. Garcia, and C. Ellertson. 2004. Do Mexico City Pharmacy Workers Screen Women for Health Risks When They Sell Oral Contraceptive Pills Over-the-Counter? *Contraception* 69(4): 295–299.

Buchanan, David Ross, Franklin G. Miller, and Nina Wallerstein. 2007. Ethical Issues in Community-Based Participatory Research: Balancing Rigorous Research with Community Participation in Community Intervention Studies. *Progress in Community Health Partnerships: Research, Education, and Action* 1(2): 153–160.

Byrd, Teresa, and Jon Law. 2009. Cross Border Utilization of Healthcare Services by U.S. Residents Living Near the U.S.–Mexico Border. *Revista panamericana de salud pública* 26(2): 95–100.

Chakhtoura, Z., M. Canonico, A. Gompel, J. C. Thalabard, P. Y. Scarabin, and G. Plu-Bureau. 2009. Progestogen-only Contraceptives and the Risk of Stroke: A Meta-analysis. *Stroke* 40(4): 1059–1062.

Farley, T. M. M., O. Meirik, and J. Collins. 1999. Cardiovascular Disease and Combined Oral Contraceptives: Reviewing the Evidence and Balancing the Risks. *Human Reproduction Update* 5(6): 721–735.

Fernández, Leticia, and Jon Amastae. 2007. *Border Identities and the Accessing of Healthcare Services.* Final report to the Center for Border Health Research/Paso del Norte Health Foundation.

Peter Fronczek. 2005. *Income, Earnings, and Poverty from the 2004 American Community Survey, Table 1.* 2005. Washington, D.C.: U.S. Census Bureau. http://www.census.gov/prod/2005pubs/acs-01.pdf, accessed February 24, 2010.

Grossman, D. 2008. Should the Contraceptive Pill Be Available without Prescription? Yes. *British Medical Journal* 337: a3044.

Grossman, D., L. Fernández, K. Hopkins, J. Amastae, S. G. Garcia, and J. E. Potter. 2008. Accuracy of Self-screening for Contraindications to Combined Oral Contraceptive Use. *Obstetrics and Gynecology* 112(3): 572–578.

Heyman, Josiah, Guillermina Gina Núñez, and Victor Talavera. 2009. Healthcare Access and Barriers for Unauthorized Immigrants in El Paso County, Texas. *Family Community Health* 32(1): 4–21.

Jarvis, S. 2008. Should the Contraceptive Pill Be Available without Prescription? No. *British Medical Journal* 337: a3056.

Khader, Y. S., J. Rice, L. John, and O. Abueita. 2003. Oral Contraceptives Use and the Risk of Myocardial Infarction: A Meta-analysis. *Contraception* 68(1): 11–17.

Poole, G., J. P. Egan, and I. Iqbal. 2009. Innovation in Collaborative Health Research Training: The Role of Active Learning. *Journal of Interprofessional Care* 23(2): 148–55.

Potter, J. E., A. M. Moore, and T. L. Byrd. 2003. Cross-border Procurement of Contraception: Estimates from a Postpartum Survey in El Paso, Texas. *Contraception* 68(4): 281–287.

Smith, Jordan. 2006. The New Texas Family Planning. *The Austin Chronicle*, January 27.

Trussell, J., F. Stewart, M. Potts, F. Guest, and C. Ellertson. 1993. Should Oral Contraceptives Be Available without Prescription? *American Journal of Public Health* 83(8): 1094–1099.

Yeatman, S. E., J. E. Potter, and D. A. Grossman. 2006. Over-the-Counter Access, Changing WHO Guidelines, and Contraindicated Oral Contraceptive Use in Mexico. *Studies in Family Planning* 37(3): 197–204.

CHAPTER FOURTEEN

Social Research and Reflective Practice in Binational Contexts

Learning from Cross-Cultural Collaboration

Jack Corbett and Elsa Cruz Martínez

Many of the questions raised in the BREM discussions in effect conceive of the research process as a researcher or researchers acting in relation to subjects and populations. We assess vulnerability (of the population). We consider data access and ownership (vis-à-vis the population). We are concerned about ethical issues (in relation to the population). As we are the researchers and they are the researched, the logical frame would seem to be the ways in which the researchers manage the researcher-researched relationship from a perspective the former consider to be ethical, attentive to the canons of scholarship, and productive in terms of sets of goals or principles. Rarely do we turn the research lens on ourselves and review the ways in which the framing of interactions by researchers in their own context influences the research process and outcomes. The point of this chapter is to consider the research context in terms of how the researchers frame the individual and institutional dynamics that shape the significance of what we learn. Attention to these dynamics is particularly important when we construct binational teams to address sensitive issues in a binational context. After all, what leads us to assume the research process and outcomes are not affected by the baggage we bring to the project?

Two Cases

While our charge was to use a case-study approach in order to explore some of the nuances of deeply textured research designs and methodologies, this chapter will depart somewhat from that charge by reflecting on two cases. Each case consisted of a binational research team (different teams for each case), one working a case on the Mexican side of the border, one on the U.S. side. The single connective thread is that the senior author served as a co-principal investigator on both projects. Nevertheless, both projects confronted the reality that from conceptualization through execution to interpretation the process and product depended heavily on the understandings and perceptions actors on both sides of the border brought to the experience. The argument, therefore, is that in the end not only the outcomes of the research in terms of data and findings but also the nature of research dynamics has been contingent on the relationships among the researchers.

Project A was a study of the relationship between heavy out-migration from a rather isolated community in the Oaxaca Mixteca and observed patterns of significant mental depression among senior citizens (Corbett, Cruz Martínez, and Santillan Gonzales 2009; Corbett and Cruz Martínez 2010). The project emerged almost entirely by chance. A casual conversation between the senior author and the junior author, then a medical student staffing the clinic as part of a year of service and training, led to the realization that there was a surprisingly high volume of visits by seniors for reasons that seemingly had little to do with physical illness. Their complaints were not so much of aches and pains but of worry, of loneliness, of a sense that somehow their senior years—years they had envisioned as filled with the company and support of loved ones—were years spent in an increasingly barren social environment. Over 75 percent of the population had emigrated, most to Mexico City but some to cities such as Cordoba and Puebla, to the border, or to the United States.

Discussion suggested that perhaps traditional expectations of an old age enriched by extended family networks had been dashed by heavy emigration, and that this in turn produced depression among many. There is little research on mental health impacts of migration on those who stay behind, yet the topic has importance not only for the population immediately affected but also for the entire network of rural clinics in Oaxaca staffed by *pasantes*, more than 600 in total. Medical training in Oaxaca continues to emphasize mother-child health; the mental health of senior citizens is not a high priority. Yet Oaxaca, second only to the Distrito Federal in terms of the average age of the population, faces a growing burden of an aging population.

Here we enter the world of individual and institutional dynamics shaping research. Pasantes staff rural clinics for a year, then return to the city of Oaxaca to take examinations, finish a thesis, and prepare to seek employment or a residency. There is neither an expectation of field research nor financial support for such a project. Carrying out research meant working with the community at hand, one where the year spent tending medical concerns and building social relationships could be put to use to facilitate interviews. Data gathering took the form of semi-structured interviews carried out in conversational form, adjusted to the circumstances and temperaments of those interviewed. When necessary, interviews could be suspended or extended because everyone lives within walking distance of the clinic. Thus access, not science, determined what would happen as the research process moved forward.

Project B, in contrast, is a project constructed in a deliberate fashion to yield information that presumably will be used to evaluate public policy, although the policy itself was formed largely in the absence of information. The state government of Oregon, stung by a public outcry over manipulation of the process for issuing drivers' licenses to secure them for people who were not state residents, made a hasty change in state law to bar anyone considered to be an undocumented alien from obtaining a license. Afterwards, the Oregon Division of Motor Vehicles (ODMV) began to appreciate significant numbers of workers in agriculture and service industries could be left without transportation to their employment. While some of the proponents of the change saw the revised law as pressuring undocumented workers to leave the state, other interests grew concerned that either certain sectors of the state's economy would suffer as a consequence of the change or the state would see growing numbers of people driving without licenses and therefore without insurance (King et al. 2011).

ODMV approached researchers at Portland State University (PSU) with research experience related to immigration to conduct a study of the impacts of the change in the law on the immigrant population, with particular attention to undocumented workers from Mexico. The purpose was to anticipate potential problems as the law phases in over a seven-year period. Yet the undocumented status of the majority of the state's Mexican residents meant the likelihood they would freely discuss that status and the behavioral matters associated with it was low given the current hostility toward undocumented aliens; thus, the results of research by university faculty could be tainted as a vulnerable population pursued strategies of resistance.

To secure cooperation while reducing possible pressures on respondents and researchers, the ODMV agreed to support collaboration between PSU and a Mexican university with faculty who had already conducted immigration research in Oregon. To collect data among immigrants the research design contemplated a mix of survey-based data collection, in-depth interviewing, and focus groups. In July 2009, two faculty and four graduate students from Oaxaca experienced in survey research came to Oregon to begin fieldwork, with the PSU faculty playing a supporting role. Plans called for the Mexican researchers to take the lead in data collection from immigrants while a PSU team engaged in complementary research among employers and service providers. In accordance with research protocol, data-gathering instruments were reviewed and approved by the Portland State University Institutional Review Board.

Working with Vulnerable Populations

Both projects involve working with vulnerable populations, but the notion of "vulnerability" differs substantially from one case to the other. In Project A, vulnerability appears largely in terms of possible mental health impacts, and the management of the research process by a physician known to the population reduced the stress for respondents. As the community is small and tight-knit, few people showing signs of depression could or would keep it from others. Indeed, some of those interviewed suggested to the doctor that she should speak to someone else because that person was *muy triste*, or very sad, reflecting the degree to which the mental health status of any specific resident was common knowledge across the community. Thus vulnerability would be to a large degree an external notion, and the absence of any form of institutional review board at the university medical school reflects the extent to which vulnerability is seen as a foreign notion or as an expression of doubt about the professionalism and sensitivity of the researchers.

Most of the respondents in Project B, in contrast, faced a reality that their undocumented status put them in jeopardy of being deported, threatening economic and social disaster. In a formal sense, the PSU Institutional Review Board review of the data-collection instruments and procedures was intended to allay concerns, though in practice few undocumented workers would be impressed were they assured the project had IRB approval, even though such approval was necessary to go forward (Bosk and de Vries 2004; Hemmings 2006; Pritchard 2002). Bringing in the Mexican research team was far more meaningful because not only did it seem far less likely that the team would be acting on behalf of Immigration and Customs enforcement, it also maintained a physical separation between the American researchers and the participants. The PSU faculty understood the importance of this buffer although it had significant downsides as well. While such buffering created challenges in terms of data management, the responsibility for avoiding compromising the vulnerability of the undocumented drove the data gathering process.

Working with Research Counterparts

While both projects gave considerable attention to the challenges of working with vulnerable populations, in retrospect they devoted far less thought to the challenges of working with research counterparts. Both projects proceeded on the assumption that shared knowledge and experience, reinforced by prior contact, would produce the anticipated outcomes. Challenges would be logistical or technical in nature. That the interviews in Project A would be conducted by a known and trusted physician reduced apprehension among the research population. In Project B, carefully planned efforts to reduce vulnerability produced substantial buffering for respondents and informants. The relatively small size of both projects facilitated collaboration among the research team, meaning face-to-face contact could resolve any concerns or uncertainties. What could go wrong?

In practice, both projects experienced unanticipated drift from the original design as gaps appeared between Mexican and American conceptions of how the research process should advance. One of the ever-present realities of working in a binational framework is that behavioral patterns that are well established, even institutionalized, for one segment of the research team seem irrelevant, even bizarre, for their counterparts. The Mexican graduate students who formed part of the Project B field team were mystified by the near-sacred status the Americans attached to institutional review board (IRB) approval. When they altered question order and format in order to produce greater clarity or began to include additional questions to cover an unanticipated circumstance, they could not understand the nervousness of the Americans. They were especially puzzled by the apparent legitimacy of vesting significant control over data gathering in a panel without apparent investment in or concern for the accuracy of data. In the end the argument that proved most compelling had to do with the possibility that one might be compromising the scientific integrity of the project. Yet the Mexicans found it difficult to accept the notion that their American counterparts seemed willing to accept a reduction in the quality of the data generated in order to keep faith with the IRB.

Making the scientific integrity argument was complicated by the fact that the PSU research team had invested considerable effort in trying to convince their counterparts that the purpose of the study was not to produce a statistically significant database, something they had trained to do, but rather that a modest amount of funding needed to stretch across a variety of research strategies intended to produce a more diverse panorama of immigrant attitudes and perspectives. The Mexican researchers saw their mission as one of producing survey data, and many "frank and open" exchanges took place as they expressed surprise that the Americans would be so sloppy methodologically. Meanwhile the PSU faculty agonized over the creeping conversion of a multimethod project into a large survey research exercise and worried over potential deviations from the IRB-approved process. Unfortunately, while the project had anticipated an array of possible problems with technology and methodology, it had not given much thought to internal conflict resolution. Each party assumed the unassailable logic of its position would convince the other side.

As Project A was considerably simpler in structure and data gathering was clearly in the hands of the Mexican researchers, there were fewer complications, and the project appeared to move forward relatively painlessly. Yet once again drift developed as faculty at the Universidad Autónoma Benito Juárez de Oaxaca (UABJO) medical school, where the junior author was still a student, began to show interest. Although the research had been conceived as an exploration of potential linkages between out-migration and depression among elderly remaining in the community, faculty believed insufficient attention was devoted to measuring and characterizing depression. To accommodate more precise research on depression, including the application of clinical scaling, questions on migration and family relations were merged or dropped (Cruz Martínez et al. 2009). Here the absence of any institutional review or authority meant that drift intended to improve medical clarity unintentionally reduced some of the social science utility of the data collected. The small size of the community and researcher familiarity with the population minimized the loss, an outcome more fortunate than might otherwise have been the case.

Another set of researcher-researcher challenges emerged during the write-up and publication phase of the projects. Presumably all researchers share a common interest in the dissemination of their work, but once again presumptions of a shared interest obscured underlying complexities. As funding for Project B originated as a contract between PSU and Oregon's Division of Motor Vehicles, the latter retained the right to review and approve the final report. Completing that report required integrating the immigrant survey data with other data on the same population plus material from other stakeholders possibly affected by reduced worker mobility. After all the write-up was completed the bureaucratic review machinery began to grind slowly as Oregon's legislative session, then in progress, dominated agency priorities. Periodically the ODMV would request clarifications, revisions, and other adjustments to the text.

Meanwhile the Mexican team, back in Oaxaca, was eager to move forward with publication based on the data sets they had generated. There was more than a little unhappiness at the apparent American indifference to the implications publication could have for participation in the Sistema Nacional de Investigadores (SNI), a competitive system of income supplements paid to Mexico's most productive researchers, as well as on doctoral fellowships, institutional recognition, and other benefits. From Oaxaca it appeared that the Americans, having met the provisions of the contract with the state, were inclined to move on to other projects yet unwilling to share publication possibilities with their research partners. As of this writing, nothing beyond the report to the ODMV, finally released to the public, has been published from a two-year project, and beyond a few papers at scholarly conferences there has been no further dissemination (King et al. 2011). Given Mexican expectations for rapid turnaround from research to publication, the professional benefit from Project B continues to diminish.

A further complication lies in the respective institutional incentive structures. Correctly or not, Mexican scholars believe publication in English enhances their competitive position with the SNI. Publication in American journals in collaboration with U.S. scholars would therefore yield tangible benefits. And their home institution would also be pleased. In contrast, there is far less institutional incentive for scholars from PSU to publish in Spanish. While the university asserts a strong interest in "internationalization," middle-level managers with authority over promotion and tenure decisions explicitly state the language of the university and the American professional community is English, so to count for advancement publications must be in that language. Meanwhile the PSU scholars, mindful of assertions by their Latin American counterparts that publication only in English obstructs their potential to benefit from research collaboration, struggled to find opportunities to publish in Spanish. Desire to publish may be universal but idiosyncratic institutional policies, practices, and politics may create unanticipated frictions and/or challenges.

Project A also reflects diminished expectations. The sparse literature on mental health in rural Mexico and the link to migration fostered an early plan to produce at least one major journal article in addition to some conference papers or other documents. The gradual displacement of social science data from the field research rendered this unfeasible. The medical school at the UABJO lacks a strong research tradition and offers only basic training in mental health, so when the junior author moved on to a medical residency outside the state there was no one to see the medical data processed for publication. This underscores the fragility of opportunistic binational collaborations, as without an effective plan for association through the life of a project there is a high risk that centrifugal forces will pull the team apart before final work is complete.

Observations

What gets lost to a certain degree in this account is attention to the subjects or populations of study. Yet as the managerial details of research administration begin to intrude on the daily rhythms of work, the dynamics of researcher interaction, shaped by the institutional frameworks and individual predilections that are as much a part of the research scene as the target population itself, become critical elements in producing research outcomes. In one trivial but telling incident, the Project B team planned to interview undocumented immigrants at Portland's day labor center about drivers' licenses and access to employment. Officially, immigrants could not be compensated, and in any event there was no money in the budget for compensation, yet many would have had nothing to eat for a day or more. Why should hungry men respond to a research interview? The obvious solution was to go to the supermarket and purchase ingredients for sandwiches, then make sandwich packs for interviewees. At that point the Mexican graduate students balked, resisting the idea that having spent a long day interviewing they should now spend several hours making sandwiches. Their rebellion was a reminder that a single-minded focus on the research population at the expense of the researchers has its own risks.

In the end the sandwiches were made, laborers interviewed, and the students had a late start the following day. But the incident underscores the need to be sensitive to the way in which researchers interact with each other as well as with their target population. Had there been a more negative outcome the team might have appeared at the day labor center empty-handed, then tried to cage meaningful data out of hungry and disinterested respondents. Or they might have made the sandwich packs but approached their respondents with such a negative attitude that they would have influenced interview outcomes. Yet there would have been no direct evidence of the way in which the researcher had shaped the product of the event.

This suggests there is a "binational research paradox." Electronic communications and techniques for handling large-scale projects make it possible for teams to conduct significant research the length of the border and deep into the interior of both countries. Simultaneously, funding constraints, time pressures, and sometimes outright danger (Slack and Whiteford 2011) make personal contact and face-to-face interaction less common than it would have been in the past. Field research yields to secondary data analysis. Thus a paradox emerges where the enhanced capacity to mount large projects along the border parallels declining opportunities for sustained cross-border contact. Certainly there will be exceptions where adequate budgets or institutional stature underwrite direct engagement, but over time this will be difficult to sustain. In such circumstances the probability that binational research teams will make assumptions regarding shared perspectives and priorities increases. Yet as these reflections indicate, such assumptions all too readily pave the way toward research productivity proving to be less than funders hope, scholars could produce, or our two countries need.

References

Bosk, Charles L., and Raymond de Vries. 2004. Bureaucracies of Mass Deception: Institutional Review Boards and the Ethics of Ethnographic Research. *American Academy of Political and Social Science* 595: 249–263.

Corbett, Jack, and Elsa Cruz Martínez. 2010. Deceived by Time. Paper presented at the Annual Meeting of the Society for Applied Anthropology, Merida, Mexico. March 24.

Corbett, Jack, Elsa Cruz Martínez, and Roberto Santillan Gonzales. 2009. Mental Health and Migration in a Mexican Community. Paper presented at the Annual Meeting of the Western Social Science Association, Albuquerque, NM, April 25.

Cruz Martínez, Elsa, et al. 2009. *Prevalencia de Depresión en Adultos Mayores en la Comunidad de San Miguel Tequixtepec*. Universidad Autónoma Benito Juárez de Oaxaca, Facultad de Medicina y Cirugia, Oaxaca.

Hemmings, Annette. 2006. Great Ethical Divides: Bridging the Gap between Institutional Review Boards and Researchers. *Educational Researcher* 35(4): 12–18.

King, Mary, et al. 2011. *Assessment of the Socio-Economic Impacts of SB 1080 on Immigrant Groups*. Final report, SR 500-270. Salem, Oregon Department of Transportation.

Pritchard, Ivor A. 2002. Travelers and Trolls: Practitioner Research and Institutional Review Boards. *Educational Researcher* 31(3): 3–13.

Slack, Jeremy, and Scott Whiteford. 2011. Violence and Migration on the Arizona–Sonora Border. *Human Organization* 70(1): 11–21.

Conclusion

Scott Whiteford, Anna Ochoa O'Leary and Colin M. Deeds

The intent of this concluding chapter is not to summarize but to explore emerging border ethics issues, methodological directions, and policy challenges raised by the chapters of this book. Rapid political and socioeconomic change underlines the importance of how research and ethics are intimately interwoven regardless of discipline or research goals, especially in the context of international borders. For this reason, these parting summations also serve to introduce another important collaborative product of the Border Research Ethics and Methodology (BREM) workshops and conferences: The Code of Personal Ethics for Border Researchers (CEBR).

Globalization has changed the nature of all international borders, from the Middle East to Latin America, while creating new units with different boundaries. Consequently, states throughout the world continue to create new technologies for surveillance, controlling data on citizens and noncitizens alike, and reinforcing borders in the name of security, thus raising new images of nationhood and citizenship. At the same time, the processes generating change, including the expansion of digital technology, social media with instantaneous international communication, and new forms of capital flows, flow into and often collide with existing norms, resulting in a flourishing of new ways of creating new alliances based on religious, humanitarian, academic, familial, and political affiliations.

Within the short time period that has initiated the twenty-first century, we have witnessed remarkable transformations on the Mexico–U.S. border, including multidirectional changes in migration rates, and mobility patterns, increasing levels of federal investment in border security, outbreaks of violence, increased flows of commodities (including drugs), and binational collaborative efforts for combating illegal trafficking and for enhancing health and resource management. The transformations have fused with existent modes of social and economic organizations, the result of generations of community-building. The only thing certain about the pace of these synchronizing changes is that they will intensify, resulting in unanticipated directions and outcomes.

The border itself has increasingly become a focus of both the Mexican and the U.S. federal governments as they invest vast resources in the name of security, defined differently in the United States and Mexico, including the U.S. construction of a border fence. This trend, generated by uneven economic growth and power, will continue, at least until new bilateral strategies for addressing poverty are realized.

At the same time human ingenuity and determination to forge a better life will continue to create remarkable stories of individual and household risk-taking, calamity, and, in some cases, economic and social success. Understanding and documenting the structural causes of poverty and inequality as well as people's struggles to improve their lives will raise new methodological and ethical dilemmas and challenges for researchers, as the authors highlight in the chapters of this book.

Both the United States and Mexican governments have become increasingly responsible for funding science—including social science research. The power inherent in federal government funding raises a number of questions about potential research agendas and ethics. Many of the chapters in this volume focus on the heterogeneity of the people living in the borderlands, but give special emphasis to the most vulnerable, particularly the migrants moving both ways across the border. With a growing allocation of resources focused on national security on both sides of the border, and the private capital investment over the last 50 years especially on the Mexican side of border that drives migration northward, it is important to underline the point that vulnerable populations are part of vast economic and political power networks driven by interests outside the borderlands themselves. The low-income families of the region or those passing through it have limited voices, but their remarkable stories document agency and determination.

Despite the struggles of the diverse, vulnerable populations primarily impacted by these global trends—there continue to be stories that are rich with perseverance and triumphs—many researchers feel the ethical obligation to help give them voice and search for ways that governments and NGOs can help them improve their lives. Sharing the results of good research with the public is an ongoing challenge. Inherent for many researchers is the assumption that research will impact public opinion and policy, which of course is not always the case. How social justice, economic opportunity, and human rights can be enhanced will be the subject of debate and mobilization over the next decades for researchers, writers, planners, NGOs, and politicians.

A key question emerged in many of the chapters. What role does the international border play in terms of ethics and research, and in particular a border as long and varied as that between Mexico and the United States? Few borders in the world divide such vastly different economies as those of these two countries. In addition, the border divides two different legal and political systems, suddenly changing the meaning of citizenship and accompanying rights. At the same time, the speed of the integration of the two economies, cultures, and populations through migration, mass media, and economic investment is rapidly transforming the borderlands. The border regions of both countries are located thousands of miles away from the national capitals and in some ways share more with their neighbors than with populations in their respective capitals.

Good research and ethical protocols stand on their own wherever the research is carried out, as chapters in the volume demonstrate. However, the border still makes a difference. The participants in the BREM workshops and conference seminar put together a Code of Personal Ethics for Border Research to highlight guiding principles that we hope will enhance our working through potential ethical dilemmas that we and other researchers wrestle with when doing border research—especially as we work with vulnerable communities who live in the borderlands, or are just passing through in their hopeful quest for new opportunities and human dignity.

The complex binational structure of power and control that transcends the border is made up of a matrix of subregions. Future research will refine the work on "the border" into comparative frames that will lead us to better understand it and appreciate its complexity. As part of that research, new scholarship and journalistic analysis is needed to critically focus on the powerful borderland actors including U.S. Homeland Security officials, cartels, arms dealers, investors, and a range of others who play a critical role in managing and controlling the borderlands. To do this will require methods beyond the scope of this book. For example, GIS (Geographic Information Systems) instruments are already used by many scholars working on the border as a critical research tool. Good historical archival research is a key to understanding the interlocking bases of power. Excellent work by economists on trade, migration, environmental regulation, and resource management will continue to add to our understanding of the borderlands and the structure of power and growth.

Many of the contributors to this volume (Mexican and U.S.) began doing research based on their desire to address issues of vulnerability, social injustice, and human rights abuses. Yet changing federal policies or agencies is a challenging, complex, and slow process. Policies are a product of political power, but in democracies information and access to information can impact the political process—and rightfully so. During the early part of the twenty-first century, public concern in the United States has been focused on security and closing the border to undocumented migrants, drugs, and terrorists. Now, the root causes of migration have become inextricably intertwined with this phenomenon: Violence on the border is now inseparable from border security intended in part to keep illicit drugs from entering into the United States, yet the demand for drugs in the United States and the high cost that comes from intensified border enforcement is a narrative that is largely ignored politically by U.S. federal policy agendas. At the same time, increased poverty south of the U.S.–Mexican border incentivizes commercial engagement in this increasingly lucrative industry. These are emerging research topics ripe for exploration, and all raise questions about research methods and ethics.

How can research be used to change federal, state, or city policies and laws? How can research propose alternative approaches or legislation? In many cases researchers must address problems in their own country, but binational research is critical because many problems are multinational or bilateral in origin. In a functioning democracy there is always the hope that information from good research can be presented to an informed citizenry who will vote for a more just society. Of course, that is too simple, but it is an underlying hope that knowledge will empower and improve the human condition. Can research lead to profound federal policy change? Can research show the way to a new understanding of shared security, the tearing down of border walls and free movement of labor in the same way that capital moves across the border? Can research inform the public about the conditions for migrant children in U.S. detention centers, separated from their families, or Central American children suffering on the long trips through Mexico and the United States in the search of their parents, and bring change? Can research help the people of Arizona address the problems of their own legislation, like SB1070? Can research lead to improved human rights and quality of life? Can scholars and activists play a role in converting the border from a fence that divides families and dreams into a bridge that reflects social and economic connections?

There are valid reasons to be cynical, but there is evidence that political debates and decisions are often based on sound data from well-designed and well-executed research.

The very nature of border or borderlands research creates a unique opportunity for binational collaborative research. Many of the chapters in this book are written by authors trained in diverse disciplines who draw on different research methods. We expect this will become increasingly common for research on border issues where biologists, hydrologists, and geographers, for example, have long collaborated on environmental issues, and researchers in public health have worked with sociologists and anthropologists.

Binational research is emerging as a critical new direction. Research collaboration between Mexican and U.S. colleagues was carried out as far back as the 1970s, but often institutional and cultural factors provided challenges to collaboration. A number of chapters in this volume are products of binational efforts. From an ethics perspective, binational collaboration is critical for border research, and we expect as border researchers become increasingly bilingual, binational, and bicultural, it will flourish. Yet there are a number of barriers that today make it challenging.

Collaborative research increasingly will require all parties to engage in the discussion of the ethical issues. If the funding is managed through U.S. universities, it has to pass through a formal review process managed by institutional review boards (IRBs). Whether Mexico will move in the direction of implementing federal ethical requirements and review processes depends upon Mexican scholars and policy-makers, but some institutions include institutional reviews. Colleagues continue to work together, sharing their understanding of their ethical responsibilities to the human beings who will be included in their studies.

In the future we expect to see a much higher level of shared scholarship between Mexican and U.S. scholars. Binational research has been slow to development despite being critical for borderland scholarship. There continues, despite notable exceptions, to be a shortage of binational publications, shared conferences, and publications being released in both English and Spanish, regardless of the origins of the authors.

Language and cultural differences still pose a barrier to binational cooperation. Too frequently U.S. scholars publish and draw on scholarship published in English, and Mexican scholars draw on books and articles published in Spanish. Scholars working on the border have made progress in this area, but this progress needs to be enhanced. Scholars from both countries need to participate in teaching exchanges ranging from short courses or seminars to semester-long teaching and writing while in residence in other countries.

Increasingly, the new generations of scholars are bilingual and bicultural, but there is still a great need for graduate students in both countries to take a semester or a year of coursework in the other country. Offering greater benefits than a study abroad program, such an approach would be a critical step in building friendships and collaboration, exposing students to new scholarship and a deeper understanding of the academic culture.

As in the United States, Mexico has developed a sophisticated social science research community with its own internal audience and reward system. Often scholars of one country do not understand the deadlines and institutional pressures faced by coauthors of the other country. It is imperative, for example, that U.S. researchers collaborating with Mexican colleagues understand the importance of the Mexican Sistema Nacional de Investigadores (SNI), with its specific deadlines, rewards, and requirements that are important for many Mexican colleagues. The SNI can reward binational publication and conferences, but Mexican colleagues must educate their U.S. counterparts about the requirements they face. Binational collaboration is challenging, but very critical.

Social media offer a special resource for binational collaboration. In the new digital era significant changes are rapidly emerging. In some cases binational research teams are incorporating social media including Facebook, Twitter, blogs, and Skype into the binational team coordination. This offers an exciting new direction for collaborative research.

In addition to university-affiliated investigators, a plethora of other actors carry out research in the borderlands: official government agencies, community and religious action committees, non-governmental organizations (NGOs), and international organizations. This is crucial. At the same time, it is imperative that the results of all research be shared in a timely fashion. Research results should be open to critical examination and, whenever possible, scrutiny at open forums with borderlands citizens.

Because funding for research is scarce and competition between different research actors for money is intense, there is an opportunity for great cooperation. This raises the importance of funding programs (via government or foundations) to support collaboration between grantees by providing support for conferences and workshops, especially along the border where travel from one sector to another is expensive.

The growing array of action-focused NGOs has emerged as a powerful political force on both sides of the border, but generally these organizations do not have the staff to do the long-term research projects characteristic of many university-based projects. Nor do they have to go through the IRB reviews that often hold up university proposals. In all instances the work calls for rigorous research and careful negotiation through the maze of ethical dilemmas. The continued rise of NGOs carrying out research and their growing political importance underline the importance of sharing data and the assumptions under which they were gathered. Transparency about research methods, data, and ethical assumptions has never been more important.

As part of the workshops that led to this volume, participants explored the idea of developing a Code of Personal Ethics for Border Researchers; recognizing that a code is not a sacred document, colleagues aimed to grapple with contentious issues in order to build toward a shared understanding of them. The discussion led to agreed-upon principles that chapter authors and the manuscript reviewers thought merited inclusion in this volume. In developing the Code of Personal Ethics for Border Researchers, the contributors assumed most U.S. academics will have had an experience with, if not deep knowledge of, the protocols required by their IRBs for the protection of human subjects, and the ethical requirements contained within them. Border research by U.S. journalists, filmmakers, business researchers, and historians generally does not have to go through an IRB review, but not because their work does not raise ethical dilemmas or issues. We hope the CEBR can be used to enhance the discussion of ethical questions in those fields, as well as within the NGO community and social sciences.

In crafting the CEBR it was assumed that all researchers would be sensitive to the IRB guidelines, including the need for research designs based on sound scientific principles that will lead to defensible conclusions; the selection of volunteer participants for the research to be carried out with the use of informed consent where appropriate; the ability of participants to withdraw from the study with no consequences; standards of confidentiality that will protect participants from exposure to risk of harm, psychological or physical.

The CEBR is intended to generate discussion among colleagues about our obligations as researchers. We consider it a living document, a work in progress that, while imperfect, will be read and considered, serve to stimulate discussions, and provide points to be weighed and questioned. We are entering a challenging new era as we grapple with improving people's lives and protecting their rights. As scholars, students, citizens, and researchers we have a responsibility to be educated and engaged in helping address the social and economic problems of those who are less privileged. The challenge is ongoing and increasingly complex in an era of competing pressures to secure our borders while providing communities the spaces where economic growth and peace might be shared with others.

A Code of Personal Ethics for Border Researchers

I. Personal Integrity
    A. Clarity and Disclosure
        I will act with clarity, transparency, honesty, integrity, and consistency, and with full disclosure of the goals and intentions of our work with all involved.
    B. Access to Findings
        I will share research findings with stakeholder communities and make the necessary adjustments so that they are truly accessible.
    C. Commitment
        I will abide by the principle of continuous reexamination of all the components of our research to make sure that we recognize our commitments, and be clear and honest with ourselves and others (process over product).
    D. Privilege
        I will be conscious of our privilege and role as researchers and understand that our careers are partly being built on a vulnerable population.
    E. Respect
        I will respect and demonstrate receptiveness for the dignity and humanity of our subjects.

II. To Value Research Participants
    A. I will be respectful and vigilant of the rights and needs of my subjects, even at the expense of my research.
    B. I will represent subjects objectively, and capture their voices as objectively as possible.
    C. I will protect data from being misused.
    D. I will recognize risks, interests, vulnerabilities, and benefits, and consider them throughout my entire research process.

III. To Respect the Norms/Principles of Research
   A. I will defend the ideals of human rights and social justice without losing the rigor of science.
   B. I will promote the flexibility of the research process while considering research norms.
   C. I will be conscious of the limitations of theory, hypotheses, and methodology, and be as transparent as possible during the whole process of the research.
   D. I will maintain integrity in all research components, being conscious of the differences between research participant, investigator, third party, and funders.

IV. Maintaining Excellence in Research
   A. I will maintain the rigor and thoroughness of the research.
   B. I will work to ensure binational collaborations through the following:
       • Binational literature reviews
       • Multilingual publications
       • Binational peer-review processes
   C. I will maintain a research process that is flexible and remain mindful that the process is continuous and reflective.
   D. I will collaborate with research communities during all phases of the research project, including sharing findings with subjects and with those outside of the academic community.
   E. I will challenge myself to include a heterogeneous sample of voices.
   F. I will make research relevant to the issue of human rights.

Editors

ANNA OCHOA O'LEARY is an assistant professor in Mexican American studies at the University of Arizona in Tucson. Her doctorate is in cultural anthropology, with training in applied anthropology. Currently she codirects the Binational Migration Institute at the University of Arizona, an interdisciplinary association of scholars who focus on how immigration and border enforcement impact communities. She is a 2006–2007 Garcia Robles Fulbright scholar for research that examined the interaction between border enforcement officials and repatriated and deported migrant women on the U.S.–Mexico border. Her publications have focused this topic as well as on other issues that pertain to immigrant and Mexican origin women, such as education and reproductive health. Her interest in immigration politics has also led to research that examines how these laws impact immigrant families. She has developed a textbook, *Chicano Studies: The Discipline and the Journey* (Kendall-Hunt, 2007), and is also editor of a two-volume encyclopedia, *Undocumented Immigrants in the United States Today: An Encyclopedia of Their Experience* (ABC-CLIO/Greenwood Press).

COLIN DEEDS is the assistant director at the University of Arizona Center for Latin American studies, where he is the director of graduate studies and co-PI on a U.S. Department of Education Title VI National Resource Center grant. He received an MA in Latin American studies and a BA in anthropology, both from the University of Arizona. He teaches courses on U.S.–Mexico border issues and comparative Latin American politics. He has lived in Mexico and Argentina and has traveled extensively throughout Latin America. His research interests are Mexican politics, U.S. immigration and border policy, and community-based research and development models. Deeds has organized numerous workshops, conferences, and public events related to border issues.

Scott Whiteford is professor of Latin American studies at the University of Arizona. He has been the director of Latin American studies and professor of anthropology at Michigan State University (1974–2005) and director of the Center for Latin American Studies at the University of Arizona (2005–2010). His research interests include issues of migration, violence, unequal power, research methods, and the political ecology of water. Twice a Garcia Robles Fulbright Scholar at COLEF-Mexicali, he was researcher at CIESAS-Mexico and in Argentina. His publications include *The Impacts of NAFTA on Small Farmers in Mexico*, coedited with Juan Rivera and Manuel Chávez Márquez (New York: Scranton University Press); *Seguridad, Agua y Desarrollo: El Futuro de La Frontera México-Estados Unidos*, coedited with Alfonso Andrés Cortez Lara and Manuel Chávez Márquez (Tijuana: Colegio de la Frontera Norte); *Globalization, Water and Health: Resource Management in Times of Scarcity*, coedited with Linda Whiteford (Santa Fe, NM: School of American Research); *Managing a Sacred Gift: Changing Water Management Strategies in Mexico*, coedited with Roberto Melville (La Jolla, CA: Center for United States Mexico Studies, University of California, San Diego); *Nueva Economía Política de la Globalización y Bloques Regionales*, coedited with Manuel Gomez Cruz, Rita Schwentesius, and Manuel Chávez Márquez (Mexico: Universidad Autónoma de Chapingo); *The Keepers of Water and Earth: Mexican Rural Social Organization and Irrigation*, with Kjell Enge; and *Workers from the North: Plantations, Bolivian Labor and the City in Northwest Argentina* (Austin: University of Texas Press). He was awarded the Teacher/Scholar honor at Michigan State University and has been awarded funding from the Ford Foundation, the William and Flora Hewlett Foundation, the Tinker Foundation, the National Endowment for Humanities, the U.S. Department of Education, and the National Science Foundation. His present collaborative research focuses on border violence, migration, and (in)security, and is funded by the Ford Foundation.

Contributors

Jon Amastae teaches at the University of Texas–El Paso. He received his bachelor of arts at the University of New Mexico and his doctor of philosophy from the University of Oregon. Recently Jon has worked on issues of demography and health in the U.S.–Mexico borderlands. He has also served as department chair of languages and linguistics (1986–1993) and director for the Center for InterAmerican and Border Studies (1999–2007) at UTEP.

Blas Valenzuela Camacho received his doctor of philosophy in social sciences from the Autonomous University of Sinaloa. He is currently teaching at the Autonomous University of Sinaloa on the faculty of the School of International Studies and Public Policy. His most recent publication addressed Mexican migration and immigrant labor markets in Arizona.

Katherine Careaga received her PhD in sociocultural epidemiology from El Colegio de Sonora. She has extensive experience in international health and education, with a focus on Mexico and the U.S.–Mexico border. Currently, she teaches public health at Fort Lewis College. She has also worked as program officer for EducationUSA Outreach Adviser in Chiapas and Tabasco, Mexico, at the Institute of International Education and as traveling faculty in the International Honors Program, Health and Community.

Dr. Manuel Chavez teaches international and Latin American journalism at the School of Journalism at Michigan State University's College of Communication Arts and Sciences, where he is also the director of graduate studies. He is the author of several books and articles on international relations, border studies, and the news media. He also works on community participation in editorial decision making and on the role of the media in international and border policies.

JACK CORBETT is an associate professor in the Hatfield School of Government at Portland State University and executive director of the Welte Institute of Oaxaca Studies, a research center and library in Oaxaca, Mexico. His principal interest is local-level social dynamics, especially in the fields of community resource management, migration impacts, and governance. Corbett has held Fulbrights in Canada and Mexico and helped found the doctoral program in planning and regional development at the Instituto Tecnologico de Oaxaca.

DR. ELSA CRUZ MARTÍNEZ is a graduate of the Facultad de Medicina y Cirugia, Universidad Atonoma Benito Juarez de Oaxaca. Currently she is in an advanced residency in the Division de Neonatologia, Hospital de Gineo-obstetricia, Centro Medico Nacional de Occidente, Guadalajara, Mexico.

CELESTINO FERNÁNDEZ has served since 1976 as professor of sociology at the University of Arizona, where he also has served in several administrative positions, including as the university's first vice president for undergraduate education and vice president for academic outreach and international affairs. Currently, Professor Fernández serves as a university-wide faculty fellow, and as director of undergraduate studies in the Department of Sociology. He teaches courses and conducts research on various topics and issues pertaining culture, immigration, ethnic diversity, and education.

JESSIE K. FINCH is a PhD candidate at the School of Sociology at the University of Arizona. She specializes in immigration and race as well as culture, specifically popular culture and media. She has an MA in sociology from the University of Arizona (2011) and a BA in sociology and music from the University of Tulsa (2007). Finch also has won and is currently support by the National Science Foundation's Graduate Research Fellowship.

JUDITH GANS received her master's degree in public administration from Harvard University's John F. Kennedy School of Government with a concentration in immigration and economic development. Currently, she is program manager for immigration policy at the Udall Center for Studies in Public Policy at the University of Arizona. Her areas of expertise include U.S. immigration policy, economics, and Latin American development policy.

PAT RUBIO GOLDSMITH is an associate professor of sociology and associate director of the Census Research Data Center at Texas A&M University. He received his doctor of philosophy from the University of Arizona in sociology (1999). His research focuses primarily on education, race and ethnicity, sociology of sport, quantitative methods, and the U.S.–Mexico border.

DANIEL A. GROSSMAN received his bachelors in molecular biophysics and biochemistry from Yale University and an MD from Stanford University. He completed his residency in obstetrics and gynecology at the University of California–San Francisco. His research focuses on improving access to contraception and safe abortion in the United States, Latin America, and sub-Saharan Africa.

SANTIAGO IVAN GUERRA is an assistant professor of Southwest studies at Colorado College. He completed a PhD in social anthropology with a thematic concentration in the Mexican American Borderlands Program and a doctoral portfolio in Mexican American studies at the University of Texas at Austin, and he has also been trained in the field of drug-related research by leading researchers from the National Hispanic Science Network on Drug Abuse. His research centers on the social construction of illegality and criminality along the South Texas–Mexico border through an analysis of the intersection of the war on drugs, border policing, and drug trafficking.

KRISTINE HOPKINS received her doctor of philosophy in sociology with a specialization in demography from the University of Texas at Austin. She is currently a research assistant professor of sociology at the University of Texas at Austin. Her research focuses on reproductive health issues in Texas and Latin America and on the U.S.–Mexico border.

ROCÍO MAGAÑA is assistant professor in the Department of Anthropology at Rutgers, the state university of New Jersey. Her research on the Arizona–Sonora region of U.S.–Mexico border examines the complex social, economic, moral, and political space that emerges from the tension between securing the border, procuring the safety of those who try to cross it illegally, and managing the bodies of those who die or become injured in the attempt. She received her PhD from the University of Chicago in 2008, and has been a visiting scholar at the American Academy of Arts and Sciences and a visiting researcher at the University of Michigan's National Center for Institutional Diversity.

Daniel E. Martínez is an assistant professor in the Department of Sociology at The George Washington University and an affiliate of the Binational Migration Institute. He has conducted extensive research on migrant deaths in southern Arizona and is one of the co-principal investigators of the *Migrant Border Crossing Study* (MBCS), a multi-institution binational project that explores the crossing experiences of undocumented migrants along the U.S.–Mexico border. His research interests include migration, criminology, drug trafficking organizations, and the sociology of race and ethnicity. Martínez holds an MS in Mexican American studies, and an MA and PhD in sociology from the University of Arizona.

Erika Cecilia Montoya Zavala received her doctor of philosophy in social sciences at the University of Guadalajara. Currently, she is a faculty member of in the Department of International Studies at the Autonomous University of Sinaloa where she also directs its doctoral program. She recently was a visiting scholar at the University of Arizona in Tucson, where she collaborated with various scholars on research projects and conducted her own CONACYT-funded research on the entrepreneurship of immigrant women in the context of global migration.

Silvia Nuñez Garcia is the director of the Center for Research on North America at the National Autonomous University of Mexico (CISAN-UNAM), where she has also held the position of researcher of U.S.–Mexico relations since 1989. She teaches U.S. and Canadian studies at the School of Social and Political Sciences at UNAM, and is a distinguished member of the U.S.–Mexico Fulbright Commission. In June 2011 she was been appointed as member of the advisory board of the Woodrow Wilson Center Mexico Institute, and she lectures at prestigious academic institutions in North America, Europe, and Asia.

Joseph E. Potter received his doctor of philosophy in economics from Princeton University. He is currently a professor in the Department of Sociology at the University of Texas at Austin. His interests lie in the areas of reproductive health, population and development, and demographic estimation. Since fall 2011, he has been leading a project to evaluate the impact of legislation affecting reproductive health enacted during the 2011 Texas legislative session.

Azucena Sanchez is a doctoral student at Sherman College of Chiropractic in South Carolina.

Michele Shedlin is a professor in the NYU College of Nursing and a professor (adjutant) in the Department of Epidemiology & Health Promotion at NYU College of Dentistry. She also holds the title of university professor at University of Szeged (Hungary). She is a medical anthropologist with extensive experience in reproductive health, substance abuse, and HIV/AIDS research in Latin America and the United States. Dr. Shedlin has designed and implemented behavioral studies and qualitative research training nationally and internationally to inform and evaluate prevention and care.

Jeremy Slack is a doctoral candidate in the School of Geography and Development and a co-principal investigator of the MBCS. His research interests include migration, the U.S.–Mexico border, violence, drug trafficking, and state practices. He has published in *Human Organization, Norte América: La Revista de CISAN/UNAM, Practicing Anthropology* and *Social and Legal Studies,* among others. He also received the Richard Morrill Award for Public Outreach from the Political Geography Specialty Group of the Association of the American Geographers in 2013 for his contributions to the report, *In the Shadow of the Wall: Family Separation, Immigration Enforcement and Security.*

Kathleen (Kathy) Staudt, PhD (University of Wisconsin 1976), is professor of political science at the University of Texas at El Paso. Kathy teaches courses in public policy, democracy, leadership, border politics, and women and politics. She has published 17 books, the last nine of which focus on the U.S.–Mexican borderlands. Her latest volume, with Tony Payan as lead co-editor, is *A War that Can't Be Won: Binational Perspectives on the War on Drugs* (University of Arizona Press 2013), and her forthcoming book, co-authored with Zulma Méndez, is *Courage and Resistance: Civil Society Activism in Ciudad Juárez* (University of Texas Press). Kathy is active in community organizations and nonprofit boards.

Gloria Ciria Valdez-Gardea received her PhD from the Department of Anthropology at the University of Arizona and is currently a professor-researcher at El Colegio de Sonora. She has been a member of the National System of Researchers since 2007 and is PROMEP profile. She has conducted several binational immigration research projects and is general coordinator of the Seminario Permanente Niñez Migrante and the Del Encuentro Internacional Migración y Niñez Migrante at El Colegio de Sonora.

PRESCOTT VANDERVOET lives in Nogales, Arizona, and works as an importer/distributor of Mexican fresh fruits and vegetables to the United States and Canada. He completed an MA in Latin American studies at the University of Arizona in May 2008, focusing on issues related to undocumented migration across the southern Arizona borderlands. Vandervoet also played an important role in the creation and translation of the survey instrument and data collection process of the first wave of the MBCS. His interests include borderland history and culture, as well as binational commerce and trade between Arizona and Sonora.

KARI WHITE received her PhD from the University of Texas at Austin with a concentration in demography. She is currently an assistant professor in the Department of Health Care Organization and Policy at the University of Alabama–Birmingham. Her primary area of interest is contraceptive use and access among low-income, immigrant, and racial/ethnic minority women.

Index

abuse, 31–32; of research participants, 25, 26–27; of migrants, 106, 107
advocacy, 45–46
agencies: border policing, 83–84
agency, 169, 193
agenda setting, 159
agents: change, 179
Ahome (Sin.), 238, 243
Altar (Son.), 15, 85, 186; border crossers in, 112–13, 114; public health in, 168, 169, 174–81, 185, 187, 188–89, 190–91, 192–93; as transit location, 170–71
anthropology/anthropologists, 13, 92, 96, 168; goals of, 121–23; and informants, 123–25, 138–39, 177–80; native, 126–27
anti-immigrant actions, 8, 87; in Arizona, 194–95, 206, 207–8, 211, 242, 245
Arizona, 84, 191; anti-immigrant laws, 8, 33, 160, 245; border enforcement, 102–3, 143; Border Patrol in, 85–87; business participation in, 208–18; health services, 186, 194–96; Mexican migrants in, 234, 237–38; migrant routes, 103–4; undocumented persons in, 207–8; women-owned businesses in, 206–7
Arizona SB 1070, 8, 33, 160
Arizona–Sonora border, 85, 93; unauthorized migrants on, 101–3, 110–18
Arizona State University Center for Population Dynamics, 242–43
auto/ethnography, 128–29; methodology, 126–27

bandits, 10, 106, 108
beauty salons, 210, 211-18, 219
Belmont Report, 28
birth control, 261. *See also* contraceptives
Border Contraceptive Access Study (BCAS), 250, 259, 262; methodologies, 251–58
border crossers, 11, 35; conditions, 12–13; in migrant shelters, 110–18; tragedy, 91–92; women, 108, 169, 170, 193
border enforcement, 3–4, 143, 237; Arizona and Sonora, 101–4
Border Forum, 92–93
Border Fulbright program, 67
borderlands, 55, 279
border life, 57–58
borders, 2, 3, 55, 66, 277; fear and protection of, 87–88; security of, 4, 152, 237, 276
Border Security Industrial Complex (BSIC), 60–61
border walls, 4, 16, 276
boundaries. *See* borders
Bush administration, 223
businesses: immigration status and, 219–20; Mexican-owned, 208–10, 236; women-owned, 206–7, 210–18
business licenses, 220n2; beauty salons, 214–15, 216–17; immigration status and, 208, 217–18
Bustamante, Jorge, 107, 145, 151–52

California, 4, 106, 146, 234, 237; immigrant as threat in, 33–34; Sinaloans in, 235–36

health workers, 17. *See also promotores de salud*
households: origin-destination survey, 241–42
Human Development Index (HDI), 105
Humane Borders, 95
humanitarian parole, 91–92
human rights, 10, 42, 50n1, 71, 161
human smuggling, 9, 13, 103
human subjects. *See* subjects

identity, 8; borderlands, 53, 55; national, 2, 71
illegal immigrants. *See* undocumented/unauthorized persons
illnesses, 87, 186
immersion: ethnographic, 89–90
immigrants, 4, 14, 83, 87, 101, 143, 152; counter-stories, 40–41; economics and, 72–75; education and, 35–36; exclusion of, 36–37; fiscal impacts on, 75–78; legal status and, 32–33; marginalization of, 105–7; mental health of, 37–38; and policy making, 46–48; stigmatization of, 33–34; vulnerability of, 11, 25, 107–9
Immigration and Customs Enforcement (ICE): apprehensions by, 106–7
Immigration and Naturalization Service, 237
immigration debates: framing, 69–70
immigration policy, 70–71, 76, 77, 78, 144
Immigration Reform and Control Act (IRCA), 35, 152, 234
immigration status, 8, 10, 194, 208; and business ownership, 210, 212, 214; and health care, 196–98
incarceration: of drug smugglers, 134–35
incentives, 48, 116–17
income levels, 32, 73–74
individuals: border policing and rescue, 83–84
Industrial Areas Foundation (IAF), 58
informants, 122; building rapport, 123–24; relationships with, 124–25, 138
Information Society Technologies (IST) Programme, 30

informed consent, 27, 192, 254
injured: representation of, 95–96
insiders: ethical dilemmas, 13–14
institutional review boards (IRBs), 5, 28, 60, 61, 62, 64, 224, 268, 279, 281; consent forms, 254–55; contraceptive access study, 252, 262; data gathering and, 269–70; research protocols, 92, 192, 201
institutional shrouds, 58–59
Instituto Nacional de Migración, 114
interdisciplinary research, 7, 56
International Conference of Harmonization (ICH), 29
interviewees, 242; choices of, 179–80; fear of, 198–99; locating and accessing, 199–201; perceptions of, 177–79; recruitment of, 190–92
interviewers: contraceptive study, 256–58, 261; origin-destination study, 242–43
interviews: of business owners, 211–12; contraceptive study, 252, 253; location of, 113–14; public health, 176–80, 189
isolation: of researchers, 14–15; social and cultural, 36–37

Jalisco: migrants from, 145, 243
Jornada, La (newspaper), 147, 148, 151, 159; content analysis, 154, 156, 157
journalism; journalists, 14, 84; ethics, 150, 161; Mexican, 141, 147, 148–49, 151–52, 155–59

labor market: U.S., 244–45
language: and vulnerability, 35–36
Latino Health Council, 16, 235
law enforcement, 32, 85, 86, 101–2, 130–31
lawlessness, 4, 83, 171
Legal Arizona Worker Act, 208
legal status, 12, 16, 194; business ownership and, 208, 212, 214, 217–18, 219–20; and immigrants, 32–33
liberation anthropology, 41–43
licenses, 220n2; beauty salon, 214–15
life history: reflexivity and, 126–27
Lopez, Xavier (El Armadillo), 130–32